Macs

for
dummies®
A Wiley Brand

14th edition

by Edward C. Baig

P9-CRT-956

for
dummies®
A Wiley Brand

Macs For Dummies®, 14th edition

Published by: **John Wiley & Sons, Inc.,** 111 River Street, Hoboken, NJ 07030-5774, www.wiley.com

Copyright © 2016 by John Wiley & Sons, Inc., Hoboken, New Jersey

Published simultaneously in Canada

For general information on our other products and services, please contact our Customer Care Department within the U.S. at 877-762-2974, outside the U.S. at 317-572-3993, or fax 317-572-4002. For technical support, please visit www.wiley.com/techsupport.

Wiley publishes in a variety of print and electronic formats and by print-on-demand. Some material included with standard print versions of this book may not be included in e-books or in print-on-demand. If this book refers to media such as a CD or DVD that is not included in the version you purchased, you may download this material at http://booksupport.wiley.com. For more information about Wiley products, visit www.wiley.com.

Library of Congress Control Number: 2016938698

ISBN 978-1-119-23961-1 (pbk); ISBN 978-1-119-23963-5 (ebk); ISBN 978-1-119-23962-8 (ebk)

Manufactured in the United States of America

10 9 8 7 6 5 4 3 2 1

Contents at a Glance

Table of Contents

Introduction

Wwhat an amazing time to get to know the Mac. For years, these elegantly designed computers have been models of simplicity and virus-free stability. But that's never stopped Apple from making these machines even harder to resist by applying stunning changes.

You can benefit from what remains the best marriage in personal computing — the blessed union between Mac hardware and Mac software. You also don't have to ditch the Microsoft Windows–based software you currently use out of habit, due to business obligations, or because you don't know any better.

Indeed, this book partially targets Windows vets who are at least thinking about defecting to the Mac. It's also squarely aimed at people who are new to computers — and the Internet — period. And though this book is primarily for beginners, I trust that people who have already dabbled in computers in general and Macs in particular will find it useful.

About This Book

A word about the *For Dummies* franchise, of which I'm proud to be a part: These books are built around the idea that all of us feel like dopes whenever we tackle something new, especially when the subject at hand (technology) reeks with a jargon-y stench.

I happen to know that you don't have a dummy bone in your body, and the publishers at Wiley know it too. *Au contraire.* (How dumb can you be if you speak French?) If anything, you've already demonstrated smarts by purchasing this book. You're ready to plunge into the best computing environment I know.

Because you're so intelligent, you're probably wondering, "Who is this guy asking me for 400 pages or so of my time?" Go ahead and read my bio, which appears in the back of the book.

What you won't find in the bio is this: I'm a relative latecomer to the Mac. I grew up on MS-DOS computing and then migrated to Windows, like most of the rest of the world. I still use Windows machines every day.

But I've long since become a devoted Mac convert, and I use my various Apples every day, too. (No snide remarks, please; I find time for other pursuits.)

Foolish Assumptions

The most foolish assumption that I can make as a writer of a book like this is to assume I should reach out to one specific type of reader. Not the way to go, friends. My assumption — not foolish at all, actually — is that all of you are coming at this from different levels of computing knowledge, from tyro to more seasoned user, if not quite a full-fledged computer engineer or programmer. Maybe this entire computing world is foreign to you. Maybe you're the only one on your block who hasn't spent any time on the Internet, or at least it seems that way. Or maybe you're just new to Apple's way of doing things. Heck, you can just rely on this book as a reference when you need an assist at troubleshooting.

My takeaway: You need not apologize for what you do or don't know. As I laid out the groundwork for your Mac education, I've tried explaining the stuff that needs explaining without talking down to those of you who've already mastered this or that topic. Back when I started as a journalist, one of my editors occasionally added the acronym "DARK" to my raw copy. It stood for "Don't Assume Reader Knows." It's a piece of advice that has served me well through the years.

Icons Used in This Book

Sprinkled in the margins of these pages are little pictures, or icons. I use the following four throughout this book.

REMEMBER

A Remember icon means that a point of *emphasis* is here. So along with remembering your spouse's birthday and where you put the house keys, you may want to retain some of this stuff.

TIP

I present the Tip icon when a shortcut or recommendation may make the task at hand faster or simpler.

TECHNICAL STUFF

Some percentage of *For Dummies* readers get so hooked on computing that they become the geeks of tomorrow. These people will welcome the presence of these pointy-faced little icons. Others among you would rather swallow turpentine than read an overly technical passage. You can safely ignore this material. (Still, won't you be the least bit curious about what you may be missing?)

WARNING

This icon is my way of saying, "Pay heed to this passage and proceed gingerly, lest you wreak the kind of havoc that can cause real and possibly permanent damage to your computer and (by extension) your wallet."

Beyond the Book

At the time I wrote this book, I covered every Mac model available and the latest versions of Mac OS X and other Mac software. Apple occasionally slips in a new Mac model or a new version of OS X between book editions. For details about significant updates or changes that occur between editions of this book, go to www. dummies.com, search for *Macs For Dummies,* and open the Download tab on this book's dedicated page.

In addition, the cheat sheet for this book has handy Mac shortcuts, comparisons to Windows terminology, and tips on other cool features worth checking out. To get to the cheat sheet, go to www.dummies.com, and type *Macs For Dummies* in the Search box.

Where to Go from Here

I've made every effort to get things right and present them in a coherent manner. But if I've erred in any way, confused you, made you mad, whatever, drop me an email at baigdummies@gmail.com. I truly welcome your comments and suggestions, and I'll do my best to respond to reasonable queries in a timely fashion. I encourage you to follow me on Twitter, too; @edbaig is my Twitter handle. (If you're unfamiliar with how Twitter works, you can find out more about it in this book, too.)

One thing is for sure: Mac people aren't shy about voicing their opinions. Oh, and because all writers have fragile egos, feel free to send *complimentary* comments my way too.

Above all, I hope you have fun reading the book, and more important, I hope you have a grand old time with your Mac. Thanks for buying the book.

1

Getting Started with Macs

IN THIS PART . . .

Get to know the lay of the Mac landscape by familiarizing yourself with the tools of the Mac trade.

Find out how to do Mac basics — such as turning on your Mac, working with the mouse and keyboard, and running applications

See how to get around the Mac desktop and how to navigate the folder structure on your storage drive.

Check out the many Macs to choose from when looking to fulfill your computing needs.

Chapter 1

Adventuring into the Mac World

Forgive me for getting too personal right off the bat, but next to your spouse or significant other, is there anyone or anything you touch more often than a computer keyboard? Or gaze at more intensely than a monitor?

If this is your initial dalliance with a Macintosh, you're probably already smitten — and quite possibly at the start of a lifelong affair.

Despite its good looks, the Mac (whichever model you choose) is much more than a trophy computer. You can admire the machine for flaunting intelligent design, versatility, and toughness. A Mac can take care of itself. As of this writing, the Mac has avoided the scourge of viruses that from time to time have plagued PCs based on Microsoft Windows. Apple's darlings are a lot more stable, too, so they crash and burn less often.

Mac-Spectacular Computing

You shouldn't be alarmed that far fewer people own Macs compared with PCs. That's like saying fewer people drive Ferraris than drive Chevys. Strength in numbers is overrated — and even at that, the trend toward Apple's computers is in plus territory. Besides, as a new member of the Mac community, consider the company you are about to keep. Mac owners tend to belong to the cool crowd: artists, designers, performers, and (can't resist this one) writers.

Sure, these same people can be smug at times. I've had Mac mavens go ballistic on me for penning *positive* reviews that weren't flattering enough, or for even daring to suggest that Macs aren't always perfect. The machines come pretty darn close, though, so you're in for a treat if you're new to the Mac. It's been suggested that most Windows users go to their computers to complete the task at hand and be done with it. The Mac owner also gets things done, of course. The difference is that using machines branded with the Apple logo tends to be a labor of love. Moreover, with Intel chips inside Macs, Apple's computer can double as a pretty darn effective Windows machine.

Checking out shapes and sizes

Apple has a tremendous advantage over the companies promoting Windows PCs because it's the single entity responsible for producing not only the computer itself, but also the important software that choreographs the way the system behaves. Everything is simpatico.

This situation is in stark contrast to the traditional ways of the PC world. Companies such as Dell, Hewlett-Packard, and Lenovo manufacture hardware. Microsoft produces the Windows software that fuels the machines. Sure, these companies maintain close ties, but they just don't share Apple's blood relationships.

You'll find a variety of Macintoshes meant to sit on top of your desk — thus the term *desktop computer.* These Macs are discussed in greater detail in Chapter 4. Just know for now that the main examples of the breed are the iMac, the Mac mini, and the Mac Pro.

Mac *laptops,* so named because they rest on your lap and are portable, are the MacBook Pro, the Twiggy-thin MacBook Air, and the even–Twiggyer MacBook. (You remember the svelte 1960s supermodel Twiggy, right?) They're often referred to as *notebook computers* or just plain *notebooks.* Like spiral-bound paper notebooks, they can fit into a briefcase or backpack. These days, MacBook Pros are also anorexic.

Matching a Mac to your needs

Haven't settled on which Mac to buy? This book provides assistance. Cheap advice: If you can eyeball the computers in person, by all means do so. Apple operates more than 460 retail stores worldwide, mostly in North America. You also find retail outlets in the United Kingdom, Italy, China, France, Spain, Germany, Japan, and elsewhere. Trolling through these high-tech candy stores is a delight. Of course, you can also buy Macs on the Internet or in traditional bricks-and-mortar computer and electronics stores.

Just be prepared to part with some loot. Although the gap between the cost of PCs and Macs is narrowing, you typically pay more for a Mac than for a comparable unit on the PC side.

(Uh-oh! The Mac diehards are boiling at that remark. I can practically see their heads exploding as they rant, "There's no such thing as a *comparable* Windows machine.")

Selecting handy peripherals

As you might imagine, a full range of peripherals complement the Mac. Although much of what you create in *bits* and *bytes,* to put it in computer-speak, stays in that electronic form, at some point, you're probably going to want to print your work — on old-fashioned paper, no less. Fortunately, a number of excellent printers work with Macs. I provide details in Chapter 8.

You may also choose a *scanner,* which in some respects is the opposite of a printer. That's because you start with an image already in paper form and then scan it — translate it into a form that your computer can understand and display. Okay, so you can also scan from slides or microfiche, but you get my point.

Many machines combine printing and scanning functions, often with copier and fax capabilities too. These are *multifunction,* or *all-in-one,* devices.

Communicating with Your Mac

The Mac isn't at all standoffish, like some human objects of affection. It's friendly and approachable. In the following sections, I tell you how.

It's a GUI

Every mainstream computer in operation today employs what's called a *graphical user interface,* or GUI. The Mac's GUI is arguably the most inviting of all. It consists of colorful objects or pictures on your screen, plus windows and menus (for more, see Chapter 3). You interact with these by using a computer *mouse* or other *pointing device* to tell your machine and its various programs how to behave. The latest Macs also incorporate *multitouch gestures* that control actions on the screen; your fingers glide across a touchpad (on Mac laptops) or the Magic Trackpad 2 accessory that you can purchase to use with a desktop. You can also use gestures on the surface of the Magic Mouse. Either approach sure beats typing instructions as arcane commands or taking a crash course in programming. For that matter, OS X El Capitan, the operating system that you'll get cozy with throughout this book, lets you use voice commands and dictation as well.

With great tools for you

Given the Mac's versatility, I've often thought it would make a terrific product to peddle on one of those late-night infomercials. "It slices, it dices. Why it even does more than a Ginsu Knife or Popeil Pocket Fisherman!"

Indeed, have you ever paused to consider what a computer is, anyhow? Consider a few of a computer's most primitive (albeit handy) functions. A Mac can tell time, display family portraits, solve arithmetic problems, play movies, and let you chat with friends. I daresay that you didn't surrender a grand or two or more for a simple clock, photo album, calculator, media player, or telephone, but it's sure nice having all those capabilities in one place. And as that announcer on TV might bark, "That's not all, folks."

I can't possibly rattle off all the nifty things a Mac can do in one section, and new uses are being found every day. (Many software programs preloaded on new Macs get their own sections later in this chapter, and I encourage you to read the rest of the book.) But whether you bought or intend to buy a Mac for work, play, or more likely some combination of the two, some little birdie tells me that the contents of the Mac's tool chest will surpass your expectations.

And output, too

I'm confident that you'll spend many pleasurable hours in front of your computer. At the end of the day, though, you're going to want to show other people how productive and clever you've been. So whether you produce legal briefs, spiffy newsletters for the PTA, or music CDs for your summer house's beach bash, the Mac will make you proud.

Living the Essentials Life

All the latest Macs are loaded with a terrific suite of software programs. These were collectively called *iLife* to help you master the digital lifestyle you're about to become accustomed to and are now lumped together as *essentials* in the App Store. Here's a sneak preview:

- » **iTunes:** Apple's popular program for buying, streaming and listening to music, and buying or renting movies and TV shows. It's available free on all Macs. iTunes is also found nowadays on Windows computers.

- » **Photos:** The great photographer Ansel Adams would have had a field day with Photos. This software lets you organize and share your best pictures in myriad ways, including placing them in calendars or in coffee-table books. You can even find pictures by where you took them and who's in them. For all intents and purposes, Photos replaced the old Mac photographic app known as iPhoto.

- » **iMovie:** Can an Academy Award be far behind? iMovie is all about applying cinematic effects to turn your video into a piece of high-minded art that would make Martin Scorsese proud. Who knows? Maybe Apple will find work for you at Disney or Pixar.

- » **GarageBand:** Did somebody mention groupies? GarageBand lets you make music by using virtual software instruments. The latest version also helps you create online radio shows, or *podcasts.*

Working with Work Stuff

Macs of recent vintage also come with productivity software, an application suite that helps you . . . well, get work done. That's why these were grouped together as iWork apps, Apple's answer to Microsoft's Office productivity suite (versions of which, by the way, also work on the Mac). The iWork name no longer formally applies either, but the reasons to use these programs surely does. The Mac iterations of these apps are similar to versions on Apple's iOS 9 devices, most notably the iPad, as well as web-browser based versions for Macs and Windows. Apple's productive trio includes

- » **Pages:** Are you writing your thesis or the great American novel? Using Apple's polished word processor is a great way to accomplish this gigantic task. You can even save your finished documents as Word files to share with all the folks who still rely on Office.

- » **Numbers:** Who says a spreadsheet has to be dry, boring, or even just about the numbers? The Numbers spreadsheet program helps you visualize those numbers and make them come alive with predesigned templates and interactive charts.

- » **Keynote:** Cinematic animations, Apple-designed themes, and engaging charts — such are the tools Apple provides in Keynote to help you create the kind of spiffy and professional presentations that are sure to get your point across.

Reaching Outside the Box

The modern computing experience extends well beyond the inner workings of the physical contraption on your desk. Computing is more about what occurs in the magical kingdom of cyberspace, better known as the Internet.

Getting online

In Chapter 9, you discover all there is to know about finding your way to the Internet and the many paths you can take when you get there. The Mac comes with the software you need to get started (and the circuitry required) to connect online through fast broadband methods. And throughout this book you'll hang out in iCloud, Apple's place to manage photos, music, documents, contacts, calendars, and a lot more, across all the Macs you own and other devices too.

Networking with or without wires

Ask a few people to explain what networking is all about, and they'll probably utter something about trying to meet and cozy up to influential people who might help them advance their careers or social lives.

A Mac can help with such things, too, but that's not the kind of networking I have in mind. Computer networks are about having two or more machines communicate with one another. Getting online to connect with various online outposts is a kind of networking (your computer connects with a web host, which is another type of computer, to put it simply). You can also set up a network that enables your Mac to share files, pictures, music, a printer, and more with other Macs or Windows computers in your home.

This second type of networking can get kind of geeky, though Apple does as good a job as anyone of helping to simplify the process. You can network by connecting certain cords and cables. The preferred method is to do so without wires by using Wi-Fi. Networking is explained in Chapter 17.

Staying Safe and Trouble-Free

No matter how much care went into producing these beautiful computers, when all is said and done, we're talking about physical contraptions filled with circuits and silicon. Machines break or at the very least get cranky. So drop by Chapter 19, where I outline common troubleshooting steps to ensure that you and your computer develop your relationship gracefully. It's the high-tech alternative to couples counseling.

Chapter 2

The Nuts and Bolts of Your Mac

Have you taken the plunge and purchased a Mac? If so, you've made a fabulous decision.

I bet you're dying to get started. Maybe you began without even reading these initial instructions. Fine with me. No offense taken. The Mac is intuitive, after all, and the title on this cover notwithstanding, you're no dummy. I know, because you had the good sense to buy a Macintosh — and this book. Besides, what would it say about Apple's product designers if they couldn't make you understand how to turn on the computer?

If you didn't jump the gun, that's cool too. That's why your humble servant . . . um, author is here.

Turning On and Tuning In Your Mac

To borrow a line from a famous musical, "Let's start at the very beginning, a very good place to start . . ." In the "Do-Re-Mi" of Macintosh computing, plugging the computer into the wall is a very good place to start. If you bought a Mac laptop, you won't even have to do that (though I still recommend you do so) because Apple has partially charged the machine. In either case, it doesn't get a whole lot more complicated from there.

Finding the On button

Take a second to locate the On, or power, button. Where it resides depends on the Mac model you purchased, but finding it shouldn't be too taxing. I'll even give away the secret on recently issued models. On the latest iMacs, the On button is on the bottom-left back panel of the monitor (when you're facing the monitor). On Mac laptops, the button is at the top-right corner of the keyboard.

Go ahead and press the On button now. To let you know that all is peachy (or should I say Apple-y?), you hear a musical chime while the Apple logo briefly shows up on the screen in front of a gray or black background. A spinning gear appears just below the Apple logo.

Getting credentials

Powering up a new Mac for the first time may make you feel like you're entering the United Nations. After the Apple logo disappears, a lengthy interrogation process commences. I've broken it down into a (more or less) step-by-step process for you:

1. **Choose your language.**

You're kindly instructed to pledge allegiance to a particular language. In fact, Apple welcomes you in more than 30 languages, with greetings like *Welkom, Tevetuloa, Vitejte, Bem-vindos, Deutsch als Standardsprache verwenden,* and *Gebruik Nederlands als hoofdtaal.* If you don't know what languages these phrases represent, you probably should make another choice. As you move up or down the list, you may hear an audible voice explaining how to set up your Mac. "To use English as the main language, press the Return key" is what most people will hear initially, because English is the top choice in the list. But as you highlight alternative options, you'll hear instructions in other languages.

TIP

In fact, you have the option throughout the process to take advantage of VoiceOver, the Mac's built-in screen reader. Press ⌘+F5 to turn it on here (or later on to turn it on). Make your selection by scrolling with the keyboard or by clicking with the mouse or trackpad (see details later in this chapter). After making the selection, press Return on the keyboard or click Continue.

2. **Tell your nosy computer your country or region.**

Because I chose English, the countries shown include the United States, Canada, United Kingdom, Australia, New Zealand, Ireland, Singapore, Malaysia, and even Hong Kong SAR China. You can select the Show All check box to display dozens of other countries. You don't need to whip out a passport. But you need to click Continue to move on. Select the Show All check box to see all the possible country options — nearly 240 at my last count.

I clicked the United States and then clicked the onscreen Continue button (a right-pointing arrow inside a circle), but you can obviously select whichever language and/or nation is appropriate for your living situation.

3. **Select a keyboard layout.**

U.S. and Canadian English are the main choices if you stuck with English. Again, you can choose Show All for additional choices.

4. **As the cross-examination goes on select any available *Wi-Fi*, or wireless Internet, service to use.**

You may have to enter a network password. If you don't connect to the Internet wirelessly or for the moment lack an Internet connection, click the Other Network Options button (a circle with right- and left-pointing arrows). That's where you can choose a wired Ethernet connection, assuming that your Mac is so equipped and that you have an available Ethernet cable. Or you can indicate that you don't have an available Internet connection. (For more on networking, I direct you to Chapter 17.)

5. **Transfer your user settings or data to your new Mac. If you don't have such data or don't want to transfer it right now, skip to Step 6.**

You're presented the option to transfer network settings, user accounts, documents, applications, files, email, and various preferences from another computer to this one. The process once typically involved connecting a *FireWire* cable, which you discover more about later in this chapter. But you have other options, including the speedy *Thunderbolt* connector that's now standard on new Macs.

With the introduction a few years ago of the MacBook Air notebook, Apple upgraded its software so that you could migrate from another Mac wirelessly over a computer network. The reason: Air models and most Macs introduced since then lack the FireWire option. But as I just mentioned, the computers have a variety of other ports that I also discuss later in this chapter.

TECHNICAL STUFF

You may also be presented the option to transfer information from another Mac, a startup disk, or even a Windows PC. On older systems, you saw the option to transfer info from another partition on this Mac. *Partition* is a geeky term I'll skip for now. Okay, a hint: Think of it as another *volume* though that's kind of a geeky term too. An external hard drive would be a typical example.

Also, you can migrate from another Mac *volume* by using OS X's Time Machine feature. Read Chapter 12 to find out how to go back in time. Oh, and you can also transfer information from a Windows PC.

6. **If this is your maiden voyage on the *SS Macintosh*, the previous choices are unimportant. Instead, select the Not Now option and click Continue.**

    Don't worry; you can always transfer settings later by using the Mac's Migration Assistant.

7. **Provide your Apple ID.**

    Your Apple ID is the credential that lets you buy songs, books, and videos in the iTunes Store, download apps in the Mac App Store, use iCloud, and more. You can use different Apple IDs for each of these features. Chances are that you already have an Apple ID if you own an iPhone or iPad.

    If you don't have an Apple ID yet, creating one is free and easy. Apple does ask for your birthday and the year that you were born, which it says it will use to determine appropriate services as well as to retrieve your password if you ever forget it (though that process hardly seems all that secure). Type your first and last name, and choose the email address that you want to use for your Apple ID — either a current address or a new free iCloud address. In choosing a new Apple ID, enter a password and choose a security question to help you retrieve that password later — perhaps the first record album you ever owned or the first celebrity you ever met. And no, Apple won't ask for your Social Security number or driver's-license information.

8. **As the interrogation drill continues, decide whether to allow iCloud to use the location of your Mac.**

    Through the wonders of technology, the Mac can determine your approximate location, which can help you find nearby places to eat or shop, or assist you in getting from one place to another.

    Cluing the Mac in on your location permits you to exploit an iCloud feature called Find My Mac, which (as its name suggests) is a way for you to find a computer that you may have inadvertently left behind in a taxi or that was — heaven forbid — stolen. (You have to turn on Location Services for Find My Mac to function.) Read more about this potential life, um, Mac-saver in Chapter 12.

    Location Services also work with a variety of *apps,* or programs, including Twitter, Reminders, and Safari. There are lots of reasons why enabling this feature can be a good thing. Heck, Apple can even choose your time zone based on the current location of your machine. If knowing your location wigs you out from a privacy perspective, Apple understands and gives you the chance to opt out. But if you're okay with the concept (as your humble author is), select the Enable Location Services on This Mac check box and click Continue.

9. **Read through the legalese, and click Agree if you agree.**

   Before your setup is complete, you can read the terms and conditions required to use your Mac and all matters of legalese pertaining to OS X, iCloud, Game Center, Privacy, and more. You just knew the attorneys had to get their two cents in somewhere, right?

Read the next section to find out about creating your computer account.

Creating an identity

You're almost ready to begin touring the computer, but not quite. An important step remains. You must choose an identity, or a *computer account,* to tell the Mac that you're the Grand Poobah of this particular computer. As this almighty administrator, you and you alone can subsequently add accounts for other members of your family or workplace, each with a password that keeps him or her from snooping into another user's computing workspace (see Chapter 5).

Choose the name carefully because this name will be used on your home folder.

After doing so, you get to choose whether to take advantage of *iCloud Keychain,* a method of storing your passwords. I have more to say on this feature later.

Another security option follows: You get to consider FileVault Disk Encryption, which secures and locks up your data behind a password. Among the options presented here is one that allows you to unlock your disk with your iCloud account.

Sharing diagnostics data

In the next section, you can choose to share Diagnostics & Usage data on your Mac with Apple and with third-party app developers. In theory, this can help Apple and its partners improve their products and services. You can also select a box to share crash data with app developers. Apple says that all this information is collected anonymously. Choose the options you feel comfortable with. For what it is worth, I'm okay with sharing such data.

Making acquaintances

Depending on how you set things up, you may see a *welcome screen* listing all the people who have user accounts on the computer, each with a personal mug shot or other graphical thumbnail next to his or her name. Click the name or picture next to your thumbnail. You're asked to enter your password (assuming that you have one). Type it properly, and you're transported to the main working area, or *desktop.*

REMEMBER

The desktop I'm referring to here is the *interface* that you see on the computer display, not to be confused with a desktop–type machine.

Shutting down

I begin this chapter with a noble discussion of how to turn on the Mac. (Humor me if you don't think the discussion is even remotely noble.) So even though you barely have your feet wet, I'm going to tell you how to turn off the dang thing. Don't you just hate people who not only give away the ending (it's the butler), but also tell you to do something and then tell you why you shouldn't have done it?

Okay. Ready? Sayonara time:

1. Choose Shut Down.

Using the arrow-shaped *cursor,* which you control with your mouse or trackpad, stab the small logo in the top-left corner of the screen. Click once, and a drop-down Apple menu appears. Move the cursor down until the Shut Down entry is highlighted. You know when a command or an entry is high-lighted because a blue strip appears over its name.

Pressing Enter on the keyboard or clicking Shut Down brings up what's called a *dialog* (see Figure 2-1). I'm no shrink, but it's obvious, based on the question the computer asks inside this dialog, that it suffers from separation anxiety ("Are you sure you want to shut down your computer now?").

FIGURE 2-1:
Are you sure you want to shut down?

2. When the dialog box appears, you can

- *Do nothing,* and the machine will indeed turn itself off. On the comput-ers running more recent versions of OS X — such as Lion, Mountain Lion, Mavericks, Yosemite, and El Capitan, (the current iteration) — you have up to a minute.

- *Click the Shut Down button* if you want to say "So long" immediately.

- *Click Cancel.* Having second thoughts? Click Cancel to return to the desktop interface.

TIP

If you hold down the Option key when choosing Shut Down, this dialog is bypassed. If you want the computer to reopen the same windows that are open when you shut the machine down, check the box that presents this option.

Giving your Mac a nap

Apart from guilt, why not shut down? The main reason is that you can let the computer catch a few Zs without turning it off. A sleeping Mac consumes far less energy than one that's in a conscious state. Macs don't snore, but you know they're alive because a dim light keeps blinking. As it turns out, your machine is a light sleeper. You can wake it up quickly by pressing any key on the keyboard. Best of all, whatever you happened to be working on is just where you left it. That's also the case when you restart a Mac running Lion, Mountain Lion, Mavericks, Yosemite, or El Capitan that you've completely shut down, as all your open apps and documents get restored on restart by default.

TIP

If you're going to leave the Mac on for an extended period of time, make sure that it's plugged into a surge protector that can protect the machine from lightning. More-expensive surge protectors have backup batteries and are often referred to as UPSs, short for Uninterruptible Power Supplies.

REMEMBER

You can make a Mac laptop go to sleep immediately by shutting its cover. Lift the cover to wake it up. To make a desktop machine go to sleep, click the Sleep command on the menu — you know, that menu at the top-left corner of the screen bearing the logo.

As part of Mountain Lion, Mavericks, Yosemite, or El Capitan, some Mac notebooks (those with built-in flash storage) can exploit a feature known as Power Nap. Though you may think your Mac is in dreamland, it still periodically updates Mail, Contacts, Calendar, Reminders, Notes, Photo Stream, Find My Mac, and an iCloud feature known as Documents in the Cloud. Don't worry if you don't know what all these features are; I get to them throughout the book. Just take comfort in the fact that your Mac may be sleeping, but it's not sleeping on the job.

With Mavericks, Apple introduced a new power-saving feature called App Nap. If an open app isn't otherwise engaged by, say, playing music or fetching a file on your behalf, your Mac can automatically put it into a drowsy state, at least until you must summon said app back to work.

Mousing Around the Interface

By now, you're catching on to the idea that this computing business requires a lot more clicking than Dorothy had to do to get back to Kansas. She used ruby slippers. You get to use a mouse or (increasingly) a trackpad.

A computer mouse is generally less frightening than that other kind of critter. In keeping with this *Wizard of Oz* comparison, not even the Cowardly Lion would be scared of it. And though your high-tech rodent can get finicky at times, you're unlikely to set traps to bring about its demise.

Your model of mouse (or trackpad) determines how to do the basic mousing actions. So, first I introduce you to the most popular models. Then, I walk you through the basic moves so that you can navigate around your Mac desktop and programs. You'll be as fast as a real mouse scurrying under the stove, but not nearly as startling.

Knowing your mouse type

Older mice connect to the computer through cords. The mice included with Macs sold in the past several years are wireless. (These connect with a technology called Bluetooth, which I explain in Chapter 17.) Not every Mac is sold with a mouse, however. Laptops come with trackpads. On a Mac mini, you have to supply your own mouse (and monitor and keyboard, for that matter).

That's the cut-and-dry version, but there's a little more to the mouse story. . . .

>> The latest iMac desktops come with a Magic Mouse 2 as the default choice, though you can also go with the Magic Trackpad 2, which I'll have more to say about shortly. Magic Mouse 2 is a multitouch mouse without any visible buttons. Unlike its predecessor, which relied on standard AA batteries, Magic Mouse 2 employs rechargeable (nonremovable) batteries. It also relies on a Lightning connector, the same connector found on iPhones and iPads. (You find out what multitouch means in an upcoming section.)

>> A vintage Mac mouse is either a one-button mouse or Mighty Mouse. The one-button mouse has a single button at the top. The Mighty Mouse, which Apple retired in favor of the Magic Mouse and eventually Magic Mouse 2, was a programmable critter that behaved like a multibutton mouse. If you're coming to a Mac from the Windows or Linux operating system, you may be used to a two- or multi-button mouse.

>> If your Mac is a laptop, your Mac doesn't include a mouse but has a *trackpad* — a smooth area just below the keyboard. You glide your finger on the trackpad to choreograph the movement of the cursor.

>> You can attach a regular mouse to any Mac laptop, or a trackpad to your desktop. For $79, you can buy the Magic Mouse 2. For $129, you can get the Magic Trackpad 2. (Of course, you'd only want whichever one didn't come with your Mac.)

You can also use what are called *trackballs*, though Apple doesn't ship them. They're available from companies such as Kensington and Logitech and they have relatively small but devoted followers. There is also a market for pen devices or styluses, made by companies such as Wacom.

Learning the basic mouse (or trackpad) moves

If you're new to mousing — or just Mac's *multitouch* gestures, which respond to your fingers — I'll explain:

>> **Moving the pointer or insertion point:** You move the cursor or insertion point because you want to point at something on screen. Simply roll the mouse across a flat surface (typically, your desk or perhaps a specialized mouse pad). As you do so, a cursor or insertion point on the screen miraculously apes the movement of your hand gliding the mouse. (Note to self: The mixed-metaphor police, aka my editor, must love the mention of a mouse and a monkey in the same breath.) If the mouse loses touch with the surface of your desk, the cursor will no longer move.

   On a trackpad, set a single finger on the trackpad and move your finger around as you would a mouse.

>> **Clicking:** Clicking usually serves the purpose of selecting things on screen. When you place the cursor precisely where you want it, you're ready for the clicking part. Place your index finger on the top portion of the mouse, press down quickly, and let go. You hear a click, and in some cases, your entire body tingles with satisfaction. You've mastered the fine art of clicking.

   On a trackpad, you can mimic a click by tapping the surface of the trackpad itself. Or, on older Mac notebooks, the button just below the trackpad handles clicking chores.

>> **Double-clicking:** Don't get too cocky. Now try *double-clicking,* an action often required to get something accomplished. You're pretty much repeating the preceding exercise, only now you're clicking twice in rapid succession while keeping the cursor in the same location. It may take a little practice, but you'll get it.

   On a trackpad, tap twice in rapid succession.

>> **Right-clicking:** *Right-clicking* refers to clicking with the right mouse button. You right-click to open a contextual menu, so called because the commands you see on the menu vary depending on what you click. (Apple also calls right-clicking *secondary* clicking.)

Although your mouse or trackpad may not have a right button, right-clicking is still no big deal:

- *On a Magic Mouse, Magic Mouse 2, or a one-button mouse,* press Control on the keyboard while you click.

- *On a trackpad,* you can also press Control on the keyboard while clicking anywhere on the trackpad. But you have a few other options. You can click using two fingers simultaneously. You can click with your thumb while pressing two fingers against the surface of the trackpad. Or you can click in the bottom-left or bottom-right corner of the trackpad. To handle this last chore, visit System Preferences ⇨ Trackpad and make sure the Point & Click tab has been selected. Next, click to place a check mark in the Secondary check box (if not already selected). From the drop-down menu, you can choose either the option to click in bottom-right corner or the option to click in bottom-left corner. The default setting is to click with two fingers.

» **Dragging:** Dragging moves things around onscreen. To drag, position the cursor on top of the symbol or icon you want to drag. Then hold down the mouse button and roll the mouse across your desk. As you do so, the icon moves to a new location on the screen.

On a trackpad, press and drag the cursor across whatever it is you want to drag to select it. Drag the cursor until it's on top of the area you've selected. Press and hold the surface of the trackpad with a single finger and, without letting go of that finger, use a second finger to glide against the surface of the trackpad to move your selection elsewhere on the screen.

» **Scrolling:** While gently touching the surface of the trackpad or Magic Mouse with two fingers, move those fingers in the direction in which you want the scrolling to take place, keeping in mind that you may be able to move right or left as well as up or down.

» **Force Touch:** The latest MacBook and MacBook Pro (as of this writing) as well as the Magic Trackpad 2 let you take advantage of a pressure-sensitivity technology called *Force Touch*. Basically, how hard you press down on the trackpad or click changes an outcome on the screen. For example, pressing hard on a word on a web page may let you quickly summon a definition or synonym for that word. Pressing down hard on an address may open a map. You'll come across other ways to apply Force Touch throughout this book.

TIP

Here's one more nifty trick that arrived with El Capitan. If you rapidly wiggle your mouse or quickly run your finger against a trackpad, your mouse pointer will momentarily swell in size so that you can more easily locate it on the screen.

You find more details about using the trackpad in Chapter 4.

TIP

If you use any of the Mac's distant cousins — the iPad, iPhone, or iPod touch — you already know how cool it is to spread your fingers and then pinch them together to zoom in and out of photos and web pages, among other gestures. Macs of recent vintage are touchy, too, but only in a good way. You can employ various gestures on MacBook Pro, MacBook Air, and MacBook laptops with silky-smooth glass trackpads. You can swipe your fingers to flip through pictures and do such tricks as rotate images, for example.

Knowing What's Handy about the Keyboard

As with any computer — or an old-fashioned typewriter, for that matter — the Mac keyboard is laid out in *QWERTY* style (at least in the U.S.), meaning that the top row of letters starts with Q, W, E, R, T, and Y. But a computer keyboard also contains a bunch of specialized keys that the inventors of the typewriter wouldn't have dreamed of.

Finding the major functions

The top row of the Mac keyboard carries a bunch of keys with the letter *F* followed by a number. From left to right, you go from F1, F2, F3, all the way (in some cases) to F16. These keys are your loyal *function keys*, and their particular marching orders vary among Mac models. Depending on your setup, pressing certain F keys has no effect at all.

Table 2-1 explains what you can do with these keys on newer keyboards and laptops, and with the most recent operating system.

TABLE 2-1   **Function Keys**

Key	What's It For	For Details
F3	Using Mission Control	Chapter 5
F4	Using Dashboard or Launchpad	Chapter 5
F7, F8, F9	Rewinding, playing, pausing, and fast-forwarding music, movies, and slideshows	Part 4
F10, F11, F12	Muting the sound, and lowering and raising the volume	Part 4

TECHNICAL STUFF

On older Macs (in this case, those running a pre–Lion version of the Mac OS), the F9, F10, F11, and F12 keys relate to a feature called *Exposé*, since folded into the *Mission Control* feature, which I explain in Chapter 5. And F8 used to launch a feature called *Spaces*, also now part of Mission Control.

On Mac laptops, the F1 and F2 keys can raise or lower the brightness of your screen and F5 and F6 can raise or lower the brightness (where applicable) of backlit keys. The screen-brightening functions are performed by the F14 and F15 keys on other types of Apple keyboards. And just to keep your fingers on their . . . um, toes, be aware that some exceptions exist.

REMEMBER

Those various F keys may be difficult to spot at first on a laptop. They have teeny-tiny labels and share keys. It's a good thing that some function keys also have little pictures that help explain their purpose. In System Preferences, you can choose whether you'll have to press the fn key at the same time you press a function key to make it . . . well, function as a function key.

Pressing the keys to success

You'll find these other keys extremely useful, but remember, not all keyboards look the same or have each and every key mentioned here:

- » **esc:** The great Escape key is the equivalent of clicking Cancel in a dialog.

- » ◄› ◄)) ◄: These keys raise, lower, or mute the volume of the computer's speakers, though in laptops, certain function keys perform these duties.

- » ▲: No doubt this key is James Bond's favorite. Press it, and one of two things is supposed to happen. On Macs with a CD/DVD drive (also known as an optical drive), a CD or DVD loaded inside the guts of the computer spits out of a hidden slot. On a Mac Pro with an optical drive, the tray holding the disc slides out. But you won't find this key on all models, because the optical drive is no longer standard issue on Macs.

>> **Delete and Delete:** You're not reading double. Some Mac keyboards have two Delete keys, each with a different assignment. Regular Delete is your Backspace key. Press it, and it erases the character directly to the left of the cursor. The second Delete key (which sometimes appears as Del and sometimes as *delete* accompanied by an *x* inside a small pentagon) is the forward Delete key. You won't see it on newer Mac keyboards. It wipes out the character to the right of the cursor. Confusingly, on some laptops as well as on Apple's aluminum keyboard, you can purge the letter to the right of the cursor by pressing fn+Delete at the same time.

>> **Home and End:** These keys are the jumpiest keys you'll come across. Press Home, and you may be instantly vaulted to the top of the document or web-page window in which you're working. Press End, and you often plunge to the bottom, depending on the application. You won't see Home or End on all Mac keyboards either.

>> **Page Up and Page Down:** These keys are keyboard alternatives for moving up or down one huge gulp or screenful at a time. Again, you won't see these keys on all keyboards. If you don't see them, press the fn key with the up- or down-arrow key.

>> **Option:** Pressing Option (labeled Alt Option on some keyboards) while you press another key generates a symbol or accent such as an umlaut. You can't possibly recall them all, though over time, you'll learn the key combinations for symbols you regularly call upon. Press Option+2 for ™, Option+V for √, and Option+R for ®, for example. Feel free to play around with other combinations.

>> **Control:** The Control key and the mouse click make a powerful combination. Control-clicking yields pop-up *contextual menus* that make sense only in the moment. See the earlier section, "Mousing Around the Interface" for more details.

>> **⌘:** Pressing the cloverleaf key while you press another keyboard character creates keyboard shortcuts, a subject worthy of its own topic (see the next section).

Taking a shortcut

If you hold the mouse in high regard, you may want to give the little fellow time off now and then. That's the beauty of keyboard shortcuts. When you simultaneously press ⌘ and a given key, stuff happens. You just have to remember which combination of keys to use under which circumstances.

To understand how such shortcuts work, consider the popular act of copying material from one program and reproducing it in another. You're about to practice *copy-and-paste* surgery.

I present two ways to do this. One method leaves pretty much everything up to your mouse. The other, while still using the mouse a little, mainly exploits keyboard shortcuts.

The first option follows:

1. **Use the mouse to highlight, or select, the passage you want to copy.**

2. **From the menu bar at the top of the screen, choose Edit ⇨ Copy.**

3. **Move the mouse and click to place your cursor where you want to paste the text.**

4. **Choose Edit ⇨ Paste.**

   The copied material magically appears at its new destination.

Here's the keyboard-shortcut method:

1. **Highlight the text you want to copy.**

2. **Hold down the ⌘ key while you press the C key (an action often abbreviated as ⌘+C).**

   The result is the same as the result of choosing Edit ⇨ Copy.

3. **Move the mouse and click to place the cursor where you want to paste.**

4. **Press ⌘ and the V key (or ⌘+V).**

   You've just pasted the text.

Many clickable menu items have keyboard-shortcut equivalents. These shortcuts are displayed in the various menus to the right of their associated commands, as shown in Figure 2-2. Note that some keyboard shortcuts shown in the menu appear dimmed. That's because the commands can't be used at this particular point. Also, some shortcuts require both the ⌘ key and one or more additional modifier keys, as in Shift+⌘+N to select New Folder.

FIGURE 2-2:
To use a keyboard shortcut or not to? That is the question.

TIP

You can modify keyboard shortcuts in System Preferences. Choose System Preferences ⇨ Keyboard ⇨ Shortcuts. Select the shortcut you want to change, click the key combination, and type the new keys.

Storing Stuff on the Hard Drive or SSD

You keep lots of things on a computer. Software you've added. Photos, songs, movies. Your graduate thesis comparing Lady Gaga's appeal with Madonna's popularity. Apple left a lot of stuff behind, too, mainly the files and programs that make your Mac special.

The bottom line: Computers are a lot like houses. The longer you stick around, the more clutter you accumulate. And despite your best rainy-day intentions, you almost never seem to get rid of the junk.

Besides, you have plenty of treasures worth holding on to, and you need a place to store them. The great storage closet on your computer is called the *hard drive,* and just as with a physical closet, the bigger it is, the better. You may even choose to add a second or third hard drive. You can almost always take advantage of the extra storage. What's more, you can use an additional hard drive to *back up,* or keep a copy of, your most precious digital keepsakes. For that matter, an additional hard drive is required for Time Machine — a feature well worth exploring, as you discover later.

REMEMBER

Indeed, I can't ram into your heads hard enough the following point: However you choose to do so, back up, back up, back up.

TIP

A hard drive isn't the only form of storage on the Mac. On some models, you can substitute or add a *solid-state drive,* or *SSD.* Advantages: SSDs have no moving parts, making them more durable than hard drives in laptops you cart around, and such drives are faster than their hard-drive counterparts, so they're useful on desktops as well. Chief down side: SSDs don't yet offer nearly the storage capacities of most hard drives and they're way more expensive. Apple refers to SSD drives built into the motherboard as *flash storage.*

When you order a Mac that has both a hard drive *and* an SSD, Apple preloads applications and Mac OS X itself on the SSD. The hard drive is best reserved for your documents, pictures, and other files.

On recent iMacs, Apple offers an option called a Fusion Drive, which combines the benefits of both: greater storage through a traditional hard drive and the speed of an SSD. Apple loads the operating system in flash, plus all the apps, pictures, and other data you call upon most frequently. Everything is managed in the background automatically; to you, the system appears to have only one drive. Apple claims that the Fusion Drive has up to 3½ times faster performance compared with a regular hard drive, but be aware that a 1TB Fusion Drive, at this writing, added $100 to the price of the computer, and a 3TB Fusion drive added $400. Such drives aren't cheap.

Memory Essentials, or RAM On

I'm not sure whether you caught my not-so-subtle use of the word *ram* in the preceding section. That's to get you thinking about the other kind of *RAM*, which stands for *random access memory* or (mercifully) *memory* for short. (I can't help but think that accessing my own memory is random, which may explain why I can recall things from the third grade but not from yesterday.)

REMEMBER

Just as you want to have as capacious a hard drive or SSD as possible, you want to load as much RAM into your system as you can possibly afford.

Here's why. The hard drive is the place for your long-term storage requirements. RAM is *temporary storage,* and having lots of RAM on hand helps when you open several programs at once and work with large documents. You may be editing videos, listening to music, and crunching numbers, all while pausing your work to defend the planet by deep-sixing evil aliens in some computer game. Dude, you're doing some serious high-tech juggling, otherwise known as *multitasking.* Multitaskers guzzle up RAM.

TECHNICAL STUFF

Geeks refer to the amount of memory and hard drive space you have in terms of *bits* and *bytes.* The itsy-bitsy *bit* (short for *binary digit)* is the tiniest unit of information handled by a computer. Eight bits make up a *byte,* and a byte typically represents a letter, a punctuation mark, or a digit on your screen. I know. That's an awful lot to chew . . . um, byte on.

When you're checking out how much RAM you want (or have), you'll see measurements in the following units of memory:

- >> *Kilobytes,* or KB (actually, 1,024 bytes)
- >> *Megabytes,* or MB (1,048,576 bytes)
- >> *Gigabytes,* or GB (1,073,741,824 bytes)
- >> *Terabytes,* or TB (1 trillion bytes)

Perspective:

- >> At this writing, the least expensive iMac comes with a 1-*terabyte* (TB) hard drive and 8GB of RAM. The least expensive laptop is the MacBook Air, with 128GB of flash storage and 4GB of RAM.
- >> At the other extreme, the souped-up tubular Mac Pro computer can handle up to 1TB of internal flash storage and up to 64GB of RAM.

The minimum specs are typically enough to surf the web, create documents, and use the basic apps preloaded on your system. The same is true for streaming a movie via iTunes or Netflix — although not all at once. Eventually, you may need to supplement the included storage with a USB drive or cloud storage for your photos or music. The highest level of memory and storage is overkill for most people, but if you work with high-end graphics or professional video, you'll need the storage for those huge files and finally love the speed of your machine.

Locating the Common Ports and Connectors

Industry-standard jacks, holes, and connectors on the back or side of your Mac (depending on whether you have a desktop or laptop and which model) may look funky. You may think you can't live without most of them — until you discover otherwise, because over the years, Apple has had a way of changing the standard ports and connectors. Either way, think of these connectors as your bridge to the gaggle of devices and peripherals that want to have a relationship with your computer. Figure 2-3 shows the connectors on an iMac.

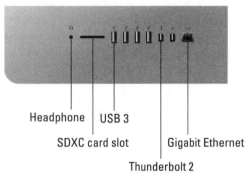

Headphone | USB 3

SDXC card slot | Gigabit Ethernet

Thunderbolt 2

FIGURE 2-3:
Hook me up, Scotty.

Adding everyday peripherals with USB

Ralph Kramden never drove a *Universal Serial Bus*, or *USB*, but you'll take the USB route quite often. That's because USB (pronounced "you-S-bee") connects printers, scanners, digital cameras, webcams, iPods, joysticks, speakers, keychain disk drives, piano keyboards, and even your mouse and computer keyboard to your desktop or laptop.

The state of the art for USB ports on modern Macs is USB 3.0 (or 3.1 Gen 1). Older Macs have slower USB 1.1 or USB 2.0 ports.

Plugging in a USB device is as simple as . . . well, plugging it in (though in rare instances, you have to load software first). You can often remove USB devices from the computer without causing harm merely by pulling the cable or device out of the jack.

Sometimes, however, the Mac prefers that you let it know before pulling out the cable or device. To remove an iPod connected by USB — also referred to as *unmounting* the device — your Mac typically wants you to click a tiny icon in the iTunes software's Source list, next to the name you've assigned to the portable music player. Failure to click the icon can cause unpleasant consequences. (For complete details on iTunes, see Chapter 13.)

TIP

USB generally works like a charm, but like most things in life, it occasionally has drawbacks. For one thing, given all the devices that love USB, you may run out of available ports. In that case, you can buy a USB *expansion hub.* If you do so, I recommend buying a hub that you can plug into an electrical outlet.

TIP

Many USB devices don't require any kind of electrical outlet because they draw power from the Mac itself. You can recharge an iPhone, for example, by plugging it into a Mac's USB port. But some USB ports — typically, those that reside on the keyboard — are relative weaklings. They work fine with low-power devices such as your mouse but may not work with, say, a power-thirsty digital camera. If you plug a USB device into a port in the keyboard, and the device doesn't work, try plugging it into a USB port on the back or side of the computer.

Meeting USB-C

The modern MacBook (not to be confused with an older computer that carried the same name) is the first Mac to include an emerging industry standard known as *USB-C* or *USB Type-C.* It's certainly among the most versatile connectors out there. For starters, USB-C cables are reversible, which means the plug can be inserted in either direction. The port itself is small, about one-third the size of regular USB port.

USB-C is also starting to appear on other computers, including versions of the Chromebook from Google. It fits into some phones too. So you might use your Mac adapter to charge those devices or use chargers from them to juice up your Mac.

Meantime, this fast connector can also be used to hook up external monitors, TVs, and projectors, sometimes via adapters. And it is backwards compatible with USB 2.0 and 3.0.

FireWire: Pumping data through a bigger hose

FireWire is the friendly name coined by Apple for a connector that Sony calls iLink and that is also known by the unfortunate descriptor IEEE 1394. (I won't bore you with an explanation except to say that it's the reason why engineers are engineers and not marketers.) FireWire is a speedy connector that's often used with digital camcorders, but it also connects external hard drives and older iPods.

TWO OF A KIND: THE PHONE JACK AND ETHERNET

Now that we've entered the speedy broadband era, dialup modems are yesterday's news, which is why Apple long ago ditched them as standard issue on newer Macs. If you get a hand-me-down Mac, it may have a phone jack that's identical to the wall outlet where you plug in a regular phone. You connect a phone line to this jack to take advantage of a dialup modem to connect to the Internet (see Chapter 9). Well, *take advantage* may not be the best way to put it anymore. For extreme situations in which dialup is your only option, you can purchase a USB dialup modem online.

The end of the cable that plugs into an *Ethernet* jack looks just like a phone jack on steroids. Ethernet's main purpose in life is to provide a fast outlet to the Internet or your office computer network. The latest Macs that have any type of Ethernet have Gigabit Ethernet ports because of their zippy speeds.

FireWire comes in two flavors: the older *FireWire 400* specification and its faster cousin, *FireWire 800.* Only certain Macs can handle the speedier guy, and if you have an older FireWire cable, you'll need an adapter to plug it into a FireWire 800 port. As I mention earlier in this chapter, the MacBook Air doesn't have a FireWire port. Neither do the latest MacBook Pro laptops. And neither does the latest iMac. How come? Read on.

Introducing Thunderbolt

I just told you that Apple has a way of changing the ports and connectors on its computers, along the way completely doing away with some. Apple sometimes does this to popularize a new standard, even before too many devices that can connect to this particular new port are available.

Such is the deal with Thunderbolt. This versatile port is Apple's zippiest ever, letting you shovel data to and from peripherals up to 20 times faster than USB 2.0, up to 12 times faster than FireWire 800, and twice as fast as USB 3.0. If your Mac is so equipped, you can connect a Thunderbolt-capable high-resolution display or certain storage devices.

A more modern version of Thunderbolt, known as Thunderbolt 2, was built into the newest, iMac, Mac Pro and MacBook Pro with Retina display models at this writing. Lest you fret, Thunderbolt 2 is compatible with devices that can connect to the original Thunderbolt. Thunderbolt 2 can push data at 20 GB per second through a single channel, useful for streaming 4K video, whereas the original

Thunderbolt uses two channels of 10 GB per second each. Meanwhile, if you still need FireWire, Thunderbolt to FireWire converter cables are available as an accessory.

Jacks of all trades

The appearance of the following connectors varies by machine:

>> **MagSafe power port:** This clever connector is used to plug in and power up your Mac, with a magnet ensuring that the power cord stays connected. A variation of this connector, called MagSafe 2, appears on newer machines. Alas, it's incompatible with the original, at least without an optional adapter.

>> **Mini DisplayPort (or Video Out):** This port (currently on the Mac Pro), connects a Mac to an external monitor or projector for, say, giving classroom presentations. You can buy adapters for connecting to systems that use DVI or VGA connectors. On other current Mac models, the capability is via the Thunderbolt port through an adapter.

>> **Audio In and Audio Out:** These two separate ports are for connecting microphones and external speakers or headphones. You can use headphones, of course, to play games or take in tunes without bothering your next-door neighbor or cubbymate.

>> **Lock:** Appearing on laptops and the Mac mini, this tiny hole is where you fit in a Kensington Security lock cable. With one end securely attached to the computer, you loop a Kensington cable around the leg of a heavy desk or other immovable object. The hope is that you'll prevent a thief from walking off with your notebook. The laptop cable is similar to a bicycle lock and cable that you wrap around the bicycle wheel and a pole to help stymie a thief.

>> **SD card slot:** Secure Digital (SD) memory cards are used with many popular digital cameras. When you have pictures or videos stored on such cards, you can easily transfer them to a recent Mac that has an SD card slot. These slots are sometimes referred to as *SDXC,* with *XC* signifying *extended capacity.*

>> **HDMI:** With a cable connected to HDMI (shorthand for *High-Definition Multimedia Interface),* you can hook up certain models to a high-definition television.

>> **ExpressCard slot:** The ExpressCard slot (for adding memory-card readers or TV tuners) started to replace the PC Card slot on older Mac notebooks, but then Apple ended up nixing this slot as well. You'll still see it on some older models, which is why I list it here.

Making the right connections on your Mac, as in life, can take you a long way.

Chapter 3

Getting to the Core of the Apple

Although I'm sure he never used a personal computer a day in his life, the wise Chinese philosopher Confucius could have had the Mac in mind when he said, "If you enjoy what you do, you'll never work another day in your life." People surely enjoy their Macs, even when they *are* doing work on the machine. Before you can totally whoop it up, however, it's helpful to know a few basics about getting around the interface. That way, you'll better appreciate why this particular Apple is so yummy.

Navigating the Mac Desktop

All roads lead to and depart from the Mac's *desktop,* a confusing name if ever there was one. In this context, I don't mean the physical hardware that might sit on top of, say, a mahogany desktop. Rather, the Mac desktop is the desktop that takes over the whole of your computer screen. On a PC, this element is known as the Windows desktop. On a Macintosh, it's the Mac desktop or (as an homage to the machine's operating system) the OS X desktop. Think of it as your primary workspace.

Here's a top-to-bottom overview your Mac desktop, as shown in Figure 3-1:

» **Menu bar:** The menu bar is so-named for the menus that live on the left-hand side, each of which hold related commands so you can ask your Mac for whatever you need. You can't order tapas (it's not that kind of menu), but the computer tasks are pretty impressive. You learn more about the apple menu and how menus work in general in the next section.

Although the icons near the top-right corner of the screen were left out of the menu bar's moniker, this space provides useful status information and — most handily — displays the time. You learn about these icons at the relevant points in this book.

FIGURE 3-1:
A typical Mac desktop.

» **Desktop background:** Figure 3-1 shows the default background for El Capitan, an imposing rock formation inside Yosemite National Park. But if you're not wedded to the desktop that Apple has chosen on your behalf, the cosmetics are entirely up to you, as you discover in Chapter 5.

» **Dock:** This strip of icons at the bottom of your screen enables you to open, frequently used programs. The face-like icon in the lower left opens Finder, which is a place to organize and sometimes search through the files and folders of your Mac. Time and time again, you'll return to the Finder, which can serve as a launchpad for all that you do on your computer. On the other end of the dock, you see a trash can. Look around, and you'll see other funky-looking graphical icons on the screen. You discover the ins and outs of the Finder — and the dock as a whole — later in this chapter.

Let me try this comparison. A Major League Baseball ballpark always has foul lines; bases 90 feet apart; and a pitcher's rubber 60 feet, 6 inches from home plate. These are standard rules to be followed. But outfield dimensions and seating capacities vary dramatically. So do dugouts, bullpens, and stadium architecture.

Certain conventions apply to the Mac desktop too; then you can deviate from those conventions. So in the end, everyone's Mac desktop will look different. For now, I address some of the main conventions (the way menus, icons, folders, and windows work) while also leading you a little deeper into key features of the Mac OS (namely, the apple menu and Finder).

Biting into the Apple menu

REMEMBER

On the menu bar at the top, you can click the apple, and a menu drops down, listing some important functions. Readers of Chapter 2 are already familiar with the Sleep and Shut Down commands. You also find About This Mac, System Preferences, App Store, Recent Items, Force Quit, and the Log Out command. Suffice it to say, the menu is so relevant that it's available from any open application.

Now click the top item below the menu, About This Mac. The *window* that appears lets you know the version of the OS X operating system software you're running (see Chapter 6), the type of computer you have (MacBook Retina, iMac Retina 4K, and so on), when that computer was manufactured, the kind of *processor,* or main chip, that the system is operating on, and the amount of on-board memory.

You also see the type of graphics capabilities that the machine has and the computer's serial number, which is darn useful information if you're ever captured by the enemy. I trust that you already know your name and rank. (According to the Geneva Conventions, that's all you need to reveal to Microsoft.)

This is just the information available at your fingertips. You can also click the System Report button to summon the *System Information utility* (previously known as System Profiler). Some of the stuff in System Information, frankly, is a lot of technical mumbo-jumbo presented in list form. However, there's plenty of stuff that's worth knowing, including your system power settings and the connected printers.

In the Mac App Store, you'll be notified of any programs acquired through the App Store on your computer that have pending updates, along with a list of programs that have been recently updated. The Mac App Store is also where you'll find any updates to OS X, which Apple now updates every year or so.

Finding icons and folders

You've already been introduced to *icons*, the cutesy pictures that miraculously cause things to happen when you click or double-click them. The beauty of graphical computing is that you just need to click an icon; you need not give a moment's thought to the heavy machinations taking place under the hood after you click an icon.

Try clicking the Finder icon near the bottom-left corner of the dock. The icon you've just clicked summons Finder, and a window containing more icons appears. These icons represent the various software applications loaded on your hard drive or solid-state drive (SSD), plus *folders* stuffed with files and documents.

In Finder, is something called the *home folder*, except the name that this folder carries is your own name or the user name you chose when you set up the Mac. Each user on the Mac gets a home folder, with a picture of a house. In the Mac OS, your home folder and the home folder created for each user on the Mac hold documents, preference settings, and more.

If you don't see the home folder in the sidebar of the Finder window, you can locate it by clicking the Go menu on the top of the screen. Click the home folder, and examine the subfolders in the Finder window, ones for the documents you've created plus movies, music, pictures, and more. And you can always add home folders and other folders to the sidebar by selecting them and then choosing File⇨Add to Sidebar.

Unlocking the Finder window

The mere mention of windows may make some of you skittish. The windows under discussion here start with a lowercase "dubya."

There's nothing small about these windows' capabilities. Just as opening windows in your house can let in fresh air, opening and closing Mac windows can do so too, at least metaphorically.

Of course, the windows on the Mac can do a heck of a lot more than your typical windows at home, unless you live with Willy Wonka. After you unlock any window in the Mac OS, you can do the following:

> **»** **Change a window's size:** To make your entire window grow and take over the full screen, click the green gumdrop icon in the upper left. Click it a second time to bring the window back to its original size. To hide the window, click the

yellow gumdrop, also known as the Minimize button. To close a window, click the red gumdrop (the Close button). If you're closing certain types of windows, such as a document window, clicking the red gumdrop gives you a chance to save the file.

>> **Drag a window to a new locale on the desktop:** When you want to move a window, click and drag it by its title bar at the top.

>> **Lay one window one on top of another:** If you have more than one window open, you can drag one window over another.

The Finder window has all these features, too. You see where each one is in Figure 3-2:

>> **Back and Forth:** Click the respective arrow to move to the previous or next window.

>> **View buttons:** Click a button to change the view. You learn more about the different views later in this section.

>> **Sort:** Sort the icons shown in your Finder by name, kind, application, date, size, label, or tags.

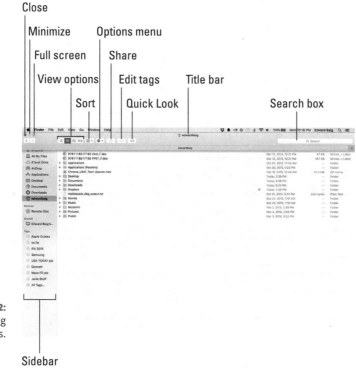

FIGURE 3-2:
Doing windows.

>> **Quick Look Slideshow:** Click here to take a quick peek at your files. See the upcoming sections for more detail.

>> **Options menu:** Open this gear-shaped menu to move the selected file to the trash, create a new folder, and other choices.

>> **Share:** You can share a selected file through numerous methods, including by email, message, and social media accounts.

>> **Tags:** Assign tags to more easily find files. You can edit tags here, too.

>> **Search box:** Type search terms here, and Finder displays relevant items.

>> **Sidebar:** This area holds a list of frequently used folders, tags, programs, and more.

Getting a stunning view

The Mac graciously lets you peek at information from four main perspectives. Open the View menu in the menu bar and choose to view the contents as icons, in a list, in columns, or with Cover Flow.

Alternatively, click the appropriate View button on the toolbar at the top of the Finder window, as shown in Figure 3-3, and choose Icons, List, Columns, or Cover Flow. Can't . . . um, view those View buttons? I'll zoom in for a close-up of these views.

List

Column

Icon   Cover Flow

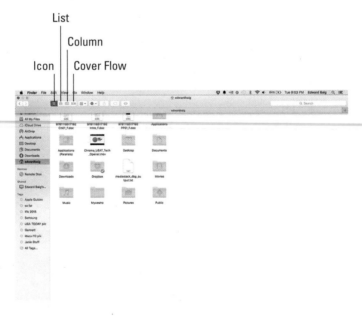

FIGURE 3-3:
An icon view
of the home
folder.

By icon

In the example shown in Figure 3-3, I explore the home folder window through what's known as the *Icon view* because the windows are populated by those pretty little pictures. You know the Music subfolder by its icon of a musical note. And you know the Movies subfolder by the small picture of a strip of film.

Here are a few special things you can do in Icon view:

TIP

>> **Resize the icons:** If you're in a playful mood, when you're back in the desktop or Finder (or have nothing better to do), you can change the size of the icons by choosing View⇨Show View Options and dragging the Icon size slider from left to right. Okay, so a more practical reason for changing the size of the icons is that they may be too small for you to see. Or maybe it's just the opposite, and you have such keen vision that you don't want to take up computing real estate with icons that are too large.

>> **Change the icon spacing:** Drag the Grid spacing slider to change the distance between icons.

>> **Position labels:** By accessing View Options on the View menu, you can also alter the position of an icon label (by clicking the Bottom or Right option).

>> **Customize the background:** You can change the color of the window background or use one of your own images as the background.

>> **Arrange the icons:** Organize the icons by the date they were added, modified, created, or last opened, or by their size, kind, or tag.

>> **See folder data:** Select the Show Item Info check box to display how many items are in the various folders.

>> **Set Icon view as your default:** You can also select check boxes to make sure that you always open Finder in the Icon view or are always able to browse in this view.

>> **Tidy up:** Choose Clean Up Selections to make icons obediently align themselves in rows and columns. You can also click Clean Up By to do this by Name, Kind, Date Modified or Date Created, Size or Tags. Choose Arrange By to arrange icons by these and other criteria.

By list

Look on the View menu, and note the check mark next to the As Icons item. Now click the As List item, and the check mark moves there. The icons shrink dramatically, and the subfolders appear . . . well, as a list. Alternatively, click the List icon. Now you're living in *List view* land, as shown in Figure 3-4. A lot more info is displayed in this view, including the date and time a file was modified, its size, and the type of file (such as application or folder).

FIGURE 3-4:
The List view.

REMEMBER

By clicking a column heading in List view, you can sort the list any way you see fit. Suppose that you're looking for a file in your Documents folder. You can't remember the name of the file, but you can remember the month and day you last worked on it. Click the Date Modified heading, and subfolders and files are now listed chronologically, oldest or newest first, depending on the direction of the tiny triangle next to the heading. Click the Date Modified heading again to change the order from most recent to oldest, or vice versa.

If size matters (and doesn't it always?), click the Size heading to display the list from the biggest file size to the smallest or smallest to biggest. Again, clicking the little triangle changes the order.

If you'd rather organize the list by type of file (such as JPEG image, Microsoft Word document, or folder), click the Kind column heading to clump together like-minded entries.

By columns

Next, choose View ⇨ As Columns. Again, the check mark moves, altering your perspective. (Of course, you can click the Columns icon as well.) Several vertical panes appear inside one large window. These smaller windows within windows show a progression.

At the far left is a pane called the *sidebar*, a regular hangout for your network, storage drive, home folder, applications, documents, movies, tags, and more.

Now suppose that the home folder is highlighted in the sidebar. The pane to its immediate right displays its contents. Highlight an item in that pane, and the column to its immediate right reveals its contents. Each time you highlight an entry in a particular pane, a new pane appears to its right.

You can resize a column pane by positioning the mouse pointer on the line between columns. The arrow becomes a cross. Then drag the line in either direction, as shown in Figure 3-5. To resize all the columns simultaneously, press the Option key while dragging. You can expand the entire window by dragging it from either edge or the bottom.

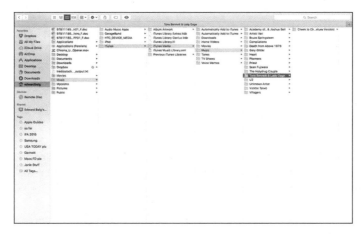

FIGURE 3-5:
When in Rome, try the Column view.

By Cover Flow

If you're old enough to have owned a record collection, you likely remember rummaging through album covers to find one you wanted to play. Heck, some of you did the same with CD jewel cases (are you old enough to remember those too?). That's the principle behind Cover Flow, the three-dimensional album art feature that Apple introduced a while back in iTunes.

Cover Flow is pretty nifty. To access Cover Flow, click the Cover Flow icon on the Finder toolbar or choose View ⇨ As Cover Flow.

You can scroll to flip through high-resolution previews of documents, images, Adobe PDF files, and more, just as you can flip through those album covers in iTunes.

What's more, you can skip past the first page in multipage PDF documents or slides in a presentation created with Apple's own Keynote program. To do so, move the mouse over the Cover Flow image and click the arrows that appear.

TIP

Try playing a movie from Cover Flow by clicking the arrow that appears. Here's how. Click Movies in the sidebar and then drag the slider until the movie you want to watch shows up. Click the still image from the movie in question so that a circle with an arrow appears, as shown in Figure 3-6. Click the circle to start playing. The inside arrow turns into two horizontal lines when you mouse over the movie that's playing; click the circle again to pause the movie. Without knowing it, you've just had your first quick look at Quick Look, as the next section elaborates.

FIGURE 3-6:
Watching a
movie inside
the Cover
Flow view.

Having a Quick Look

Apple gives the Mac faithful a clever way to peek at the contents of files on the computer without having to launch the applications that created or can otherwise open those files.

More than living up to its moniker, Quick Look lets you look at a file as a pretty decent-size thumbnail or even full-screen. Quick Look might also be called Quick Listen because you can even play music. Indeed, the feature works with all sorts of files — PDFs, spreadsheets, Word documents, movies, and more — because Quick Look plug-ins for many other formats are available on the Internet.

Here's how to invoke Quick Look:

1. **Highlight a file in Finder.**

2. **Click the Quick Look button (labeled in Figure 3-2) on the toolbar or press the spacebar on the keyboard.**

   The file jumps out at you in a window, as shown in Figure 3-7. To display the file full-screen, click the button that resembles a + in a small circle. To exit full-screen, click the two diagonal arrows pointing in opposite directions. If you don't see the Quick Look icon in the toolbar, click View⇨Customize Toolbar and drag the icon directly onto the toolbar. While here, you might drag other icons onto the toolbar too.

3. **If you're looking at a picture and want to add it to your Photos image library, click the Share button in the top-right corner of the Quick Look window and then click the Add to Photos button on the menu that appears.**

FIGURE 3-7:
Quick, take
a look at my
picture.

4. **If you decide to open the file you're previewing inside its associated program, click the Open With button just to the left of the Share button.**

   The Mac suggests the program with which to open it: Preview, Microsoft Word, and so on.

5. **To exit Quick Look, click the *x* in the circle or press the spacebar again.**

TIP

You can preview multiple images in Quick Look. Just highlight more than one file and click the Quick Look toolbar button or press the spacebar. You can then use the Forward or Back arrow to navigate through the files manually or click Play to preview the files in a slideshow. Finally, you can click the Index Sheet button — visible only if you've selected more than one file at a time — to peek at documents in a grid. The button resembles a rectangle with four small squares in it. A good way to find all your photos in one place is to click All My Files in Finder, sort them by Kind, and start sifting through all those that are picture-type files (typically, but not always, JPEG images).

TIP

Throughout OS X El Capitan, you'll see the aforementioned Share button and the associated Share menu that make it simpler to share digital files with other folks. So it goes in Quick Look. If you click the Share button, you can whisk the file off in an email, share it in an instant message (through Messages), or share it with another nearby Mac through AirDrop. You can add it to the Notes app. And you can also post it to Twitter, Facebook, Flickr, or Vimeo.

What's Up, Dock?

Your eyes can't help but be drawn to the colorful bar at the bottom of the screen, shown in Figure 3-8. This is your *dock*, and it may comfort those familiar with Microsoft's way of designing a computer interface to think of the dock as a rough cross between the old Windows taskbar and the Windows Start menu. Drag a window near the bottom of the screen, and you'll sort of see the window's reflection illuminate that part of the dock.

FIGURE 3-8:
Docking your
icons.

Try single-clicking a nonrunning icon on the dock. The little picture bobs up and down like a school kid desperate to get the teacher's attention so that he can make it to the bathroom safely.

What you'll find on the dock

The dock is divided into two parts by a faint vertical line:

>> To the left of the line is where most of the action is, with programs and other tools.

>> To the right are any open files and folders, plus a collection of expandable folders or icons called *Stacks,* of which I have more to say later in this chapter. You also find the Trash.

Keep in mind that the mere act of single-clicking a dock icon launches a program or another activity. When you mouse over a dock icon, the title of the appropriate application, document, or folder appears.

Through the years, Apple has made several refinements to the dock. On newer Macs with OS X El Capitan, most of the following icons appear by default on the left side of the dock (the order in which they appear is, for the most part, up to you):

>> **Finder:** With a goofy face on top of a square, the Finder icon looks like it belongs in a *SpongeBob SquarePants* cartoon. Single-clicking here brings up the main Finder window, which I discuss earlier in this chapter.

>> **Launchpad:** As its name suggests, the Launchpad is a launching pad for all the apps on your system, each represented by a colorful icon. It bears a striking resemblance to the home screens on iOS devices such as the iPad and iPhone. Use the trackpad, if your computer has one, to swipe from one Launchpad screenful of icons to another.

>> **Safari:** This icon represents Apple's fine web browser (see Chapter 9).

>> **Mail:** Yes, Apple has a built-in email program, and a good one (see Chapter 10).

>> **Contacts:** Formerly named Address Book, this application is the place for phone numbers, email addresses, and other contact information (more later in this chapter).

- >> **Calendar:** Once known as iCal, this is your Mac's excellent built-in calendar (more later in this chapter).

- >> **Notes:** Your convenient repository for quick jottings is found in Notes.

- >> **Reminders:** Are you forgetful? Let this handy app remind you what's on your list of to-dos or in your Calendar.

- >> **Maps:** The Mac's version of Maps is similar to the Maps app on iOS devices. Go here for directions.

- >> **Photos:** This is your shoebox for storing, sharing, touching up, and applying special effects to digital images (see Chapter 14). Older Macs had a program called iPhoto, which may still reside on your computer in the background.

- >> **Messages:** Once known as iChat or, depending on the vintage, iChat AV, this application is Apple's answer to instant messaging and text messaging (see Chapter 11).

- >> **FaceTime:** The magic of video calling: That's FaceTime. Audio calls are possible too.

- >> **iTunes:** Everyone knows Apple's renowned musical jukebox, long ago expanded to movies and TV shows, too (see Chapter 13).

- >> **iBooks:** Another iOS-first feature brought over to the Mac more recently. Launch iBooks to read eBooks and shop in the iBooks Store.

- >> **App Store:** Apple's online emporium for purchasing or fetching free Mac apps from Apple (including any new versions of OS X) and programs from outside software publishers. You get system updates and updates to programs here, too. Apps for your Mac run the gamut, of course, and are segregated into business, entertainment, news, social networking, utilities, and several other categories.

- >> **System Preferences:** You can have it your way (see Chapter 5).

In addition, you may see these dock icons, depending on the age of your Mac or on what you choose to dock on the dock:

- >> **Dashboard:** The round gauge is the front end for clever little applications called *widgets*. Frankly, Apple is no longer giving A-1 treatment to the Dashboard and such widgets.

- >> **Mission Control:** Nope, it's not a place for NASA engineers (though I suspect that many of those guys and gals own Macs). In Mission Control, you can get a bird's-eye view of everything that's open on your Mac. You can summon Mission Control from the dock (if its dock icon is present) or by using an upward three-finger swipe on a trackpad or a double tap (not double-click) with a Magic Mouse. Still another way is to press Control plus the up or down arrow keys on the keyboard. (For more on Mission Control, check out Chapter 5.)

» **Photo Booth:** Go here to take your account picture or goofy images.

» **Game Center:** The place for fun and games. Sign in with your Apple ID, and keep tabs on your game apps, scores, and the old and new friends you choose to play with.

» **iMovie:** This is the place to edit videos (see Chapter 15).

» **GarageBand:** This is where you can launch your musical career (see Chapter 15).

» **Time Machine:** A clever backup feature lets you restore lost files by going back in time to find them (see Chapter 12).

And these icons appear on the right bank:

» **Stacks:** These collections of icons keep your desktop organized and tidy. In OS X El Capitan, Apple supplies a premade stack for the Downloads folder.

» **Trash:** Hey, even computer garbage has to go somewhere (see Chapter 7).

REMEMBER

You can summon a contextual menu for all your dock items. From this menu, it's a snap to remove an item from the dock, open the program in question when you log in, or show it in Finder.

Loading up the dock

Adding favorite items to the dock is as simple as dragging and dropping them there. The more icons that you drop in the dock, of course, the more congested the joint gets. Even icons deserve breathing room. To remove items, just drag them slightly outside the dock and wait for the little white poof cloud to appear. When it does, release the mouse button, and your icon has been safely removed. Don't worry — the application itself remains on the Mac.

Alternatively, you can remove a dock icon by dragging it to the Trash.

Still another method: If you have an old-fashioned two-button mouse, right-click it (or press Control on the keyboard at the same time you click, or click a trackpad with two fingers). You see an option for Options. Choose Remove from dock as one of those options.

Here's another neat stunt:

1. **Open the menu.**

2. **Choose System Preferences⇨Dock.**

3. **Select the Magnification box.**

   Now, as your cursor runs over the icons, the little pictures blow up like bubble gum.

TIP

If you're into resizing dock icons in Dock Preferences, make sure that the Magnification box is selected, and drag the Magnification slider from left (Min) to right (Max), depending on your fancy. A separate slider lets you alter the dock size.

You can also alter the size of the dock itself by clicking the line separating the programs and Stacks, and dragging it to the left or right.

And speaking of that dividing line, you can call up a menu of all dock-related commands by right-clicking or Control-clicking the line.

Docking the dock

The first time you notice the dock, it appears at the bottom of your screen. Apple doesn't make you keep it there. The dock can move to the left or right flank of the screen, depending, I suppose, on your political persuasion.

Here again in Dock Preferences, you'll see Position under Screen Settings: choose Left or Right or leave things as they are at the bottom (the default). Pardon the pun, but your dock is now dockside.

TIP

If you find that the dock is getting in the way no matter where you put it, you can make it disappear, at least until you need it again. In Preferences, select the Automatically Hide and Show the Dock box.

When the dock is hidden, drag the cursor to the bottom (or sides) of the screen where the dock would have been visible otherwise. It magically glides into view. The dock retreats to its cave when you glide the cursor away. If you find that you miss the dock after all, repeat the previous step, but deselect the box.

One other setting is worth noting in Dock Preferences. Select the Show Indicators for Open Applications box to see a little dot below a dock icon that represents an open app.

Re-opening minimized windows

Sometimes, closing a window is Draconian, especially if you intend to work in the window again a moment or so later.

You can minimize the window instead. Simply click the Minimize button (the yellow circle in the top-left corner of a window; refer to Figure 3-2). When you minimize a window, the entire thing shrivels up and lands safely on the right side of the dock (assuming that you've stuck with Minimize Windows Using Genie Effect in Dock Preferences; the alternative is Minimize Using Scale Effect, but it doesn't have the same visual impact, at least to me).

To restore the window to its full and (presumably) upright position, single-click its newly created dock icon.

WARNING

Be careful not to click Close (the tiny red circle) instead. That closes the window instead of minimizing it.

Clicking the green circle maximizes the window full screen or at least to its full potential, and clicking it again returns it to the previous size. If one of the circles appears with no color, it means that particular function is currently unavailable.

Stockpiling Stacks

I have myriad stacks of paper in my office, and in theory, all the papers in one stack are related to all the other papers in the same stack.

This same organizing principle applies to a handy feature called Stacks. *Stacks* are simply a collection of files organized by theme, and they do wonders for all you clutterholics — of whom, alas, I am one. You'll find Stacks to the right of the divider on the dock.

As I note earlier in this chapter, Apple has put together a useful premade Stack for all the stuff you may download, such as saved Mail attachments, file transfers through Messages, and files captured from the Internet with the Safari browser. In the past, Apple also provided Stacks for applications and for documents, but it no longer does so. But it's no biggie, because — as you'll see — it's a breeze to create your own Stacks.

I'm fond of the Downloads Stack in particular; it bobs up and down to let you know a new arrival is there. Before the introduction of the Stacks feature, down-loaded files had a tendency to mess up your desktop.

The icon for the Downloads Stack takes the form of the most recent item you've downloaded: a Microsoft PowerPoint presentation, Audible audio file, or whatever the item happens to be.

Opening Stacks

To view the contents of a Stack, click the Stacks icon. It immediately opens in one of three ways:

>> **Icons for the files, along with their names, fan out in an arc** (see Figure 3-9). The most recent file is at the bottom of the fan.

>> **Files and names appear in a grid** (see Figure 3-10). You can scroll through the items in the Grid view.

>> **Stacks can appear in a list.**

FIGURE 3-9: Fanning out your files.

TIP

A cool special effect: Hold down the Shift key when you click a Stack, and it opens in slow motion as a fan or a grid. If you already had a Stack open when you Shift-click another Stack, you can watch one collapse slowly while the other opens.

FIGURE 3-10:
You can blow up your Stack in more than one way.

TIP

You can dictate whether Stacks spring out as a fan, grid, or list. Right-click or Control-click the Stacks icon in the dock to instantly bring up the Stack's *contextual menu,* shown in Figure 3-11. Or hold down the left mouse button for just a second until the menu appears. From the menu, choose Fan, Grid, List, or Automatic (essentially letting the Mac choose for you) to give the Stack your marching orders. You'll notice a few other choices in this contextual menu. You can also sort the Stacks icons by name, date added, date modified, date created, or kind of file.

Adding Stacks

You can turn any folder in your arsenal into a Stack by dragging it from Finder or the desktop to the right of the dock's dashed line and to the left of Trash. It's as easy as that.

Quitting time

It's 5 p.m. (or, in my world, hours later), so it's quitting time. Here's how to punch out of a specific application:

>> Just to the right of the menu, you see the name of the program you're currently working in. Suppose that it's Safari. Click the Safari name, and

FIGURE 3-11:
A menu to control Stacks.

choose Quit Safari from the drop-down menu. Had you been working in, say, Word, you'd choose Quit Word from the drop-down menu.

>> Here's a quickie keyboard alternative: Press ⌘+Q to instantly quit the program you're using or, in the case of an application such as Word, get a chance to save the file before quitting.

>> One more way to quit: Right-click (or Control-click) an application icon in the dock and choose Quit from the contextual menu.

Getting off work was never so easy.

A Gaggle of Freebie Programs

A major fringe benefit of Mac ownership is all the nifty software you get gratis. Many of these freebie programs — notably those that used to be part of iLife — are such a big deal that they deserve entire chapters unto themselves. Buyers of recent Macs are also treated to free productivity apps from Apple: the Pages word processor, Numbers spreadsheet program, and Keynote presentation software.

In the following sections, I discuss programs of smaller stature. I'm not demeaning them; in fact, several of these *bundled* programs are quite handy to have around.

You'll find some of the programs I'm about to mention in the Applications stack in the dock, assuming that you have such a collection. Another good place to look is the *Applications folder*, accessible in several ways, as indicated here:

>> Click Applications in the Finder sidebar.

>> Choose Go ⇨ Applications.

>> Press the keyboard shortcut Shift+⌘+A.

>> Again, if you have an Applications stack, click it to see what's inside.

Staying organized

Not all of us have the luxury of hiring an assistant to keep our life in some semblance of order or just to provide a jolt of caffeine when we need it. I sure don't (sigh).

Regrettably, a Mac still can't make coffee. But it's reassuring that the computer can simplify other administrative chores. Here's how.

Contacts

You just met an attractive stranger on the way to the Apple Store, right? Contacts, which you access through the Applications folder or the Contacts dock icon, is a handy repository for addresses, phone numbers, and email addresses. You can also add a picture and note about the person ("awfully cute; owns a Mac").

After opening the program, here's how to add a Contacts entry:

1. **Click the + sign (shown in Figure 3-12).**

    Alternatively, you can open Contacts and choose File ⇨ New Card.

FIGURE 3-12:
Adding an
entry in
Contacts.

2. **Type the person's first and last names, company, phone number, and other information in the appropriate fields.**

    Press the Tab key to move from one field to the next. You can skip fields if you don't have information and add others as need be. To add space for a new mobile-phone-number entry, for example, click the + next to the field name. Or click Done.

3. **Close Contacts.**

TIP

If someone sends you a virtual address card (known as a *vCard*), just drag it into the Contacts window. If you already have an entry for the person, you'll have the option to blend the new data with the old.

TIP

You can instantly display a map to a person's house in your Contacts. Here's how:

1. **Hold down the Control key while clicking an address.**

2. **Choose Open in Maps from the contextual menu.**

    Your other options are to get directions, copy the address , and copy the Maps URL. If you stuck with Open in Maps, the Apple Maps app opens, displaying a map page of the address.

As you might imagine, Contacts has close ties to a bunch of other Mac applications that I discuss later in this book, notably Mail and Messages. You can also synchronize contacts with other computers by using your iCloud account. If you have a Yahoo! address book, you can synchronize that, too. And you can synchronize your contacts with an account that uses a Microsoft Exchange server.

TIP

If you set up accounts with Facebook, LinkedIn, or Twitter by visiting Internet Accounts within System Preferences (see Chapter 11), profile information from those accounts automatically appears in Contacts.

Creating Smart Groups

Suppose that a whole bunch of people in your Contacts app have something in common. Maybe you all play softball on weekends. (That's a good thing. Break away. Have fun. Limber up. Your computer will be waiting for you when you get back.) You can manually set up a Contacts group for all your ball-playing pals. Clicking New Group after you click the + is the easiest way to get started (or press the keyboard combination ⌘+Shift+N). You can also put together a group from selected names by first choosing those names — press ⌘ while clicking contact names to do so — and then clicking File⇨New Group from Selection. Name your new group by typing over the name in the field that by default goes by the sterile moniker "untitled group."

But there's a smarter way, known as a *Smart Group.* It's a terrific way to manage information on all your teammates in Contacts.

The key is adding a descriptive word that lumps everyone together in the Notes field — something like, say, *softball.* So whenever a new contact comes along and you type the word *softball,* he or she becomes part of your Smart Group.

To create a Smart Group from scratch, follow these steps:

1. **Choose File⇨New Smart Group.**

2. **In the Smart Group Name field, type a name for your group.**

   For this example, I typed **Weekend athletes**.

3. **Click the + and specify the group criteria by choosing them from the pop-up menus, as shown in Figure 3-13.**

Later, if a bum knee ends your softball career, you'll be able to edit or even delete the entire Smart Group.

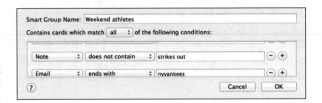

FIGURE 3-13:
Creating a
Smart Group.

Calendar

It's swell that all your friends want to join the team. But good luck figuring out a time when everybody can play.

For assistance, consult the Mac's personal calendar application, appropriately named Calendar (formerly iCal). Here's a quick look at what the Calendar app can do:

>> **Share or publish your calendar.** You can share a calendar with people on the same computer or publish it over the Internet to share with others, perhaps by subscribing to iCloud. The program can help you find a convenient time when everyone can meet.

>> **Share a calendar with the family.** In Chapter 5, I discuss an iCloud feature called Family Sharing. For now, I'll just mention that through this feature you can share appointments with other members of your clan.

>> **Subscribe to public calendars over the Internet** (movie openings, religious holidays, and so on).

>> **Display events from Facebook.** If you connect the Calendar app to Facebook, you'll see relevant Facebook events in the Calendar. Indeed, your Mac has a special relationship with the vastly popular social network. And so the Calendar may also be populated with the birthdays of your Facebook friends on the appropriate day, assuming those friends shared the date in Facebook.

>> **Track different activities** for family members or track the different phases of your own life (meetings at work, Boy Scout troop meetings for your son, and so on).

>> **Send meeting invitations** to people in and out of your workplace; Calendar is tightly integrated with the Mac's Mail program (see Chapter 10).

When you need to add an item to your calendar, click the + in the top-left corner of the Calendar app to create an appointment, typing all the particulars you know (such as **Lunch with Janie at 12:30 p.m. tomorrow at Nobu**). Your Mac fills in the basics. You can add more specific information, including the precise location, alerts, invitees, and which calendar to apply the information to.

There's even a travel-time feature that shows the driving or walking time to your next event. Your computer kindly sends you a notification when it's time to get going. But Apple doesn't stop there. You can also peek at an inline map of your event location and even receive a weather forecast that helps you figure out what to wear.

Reminders

If you need a reminder of all the things you have to do (finish writing a *For Dummies* chapter, for example), the Reminders app lets you display to-do lists. You can sort these reminders by due date, priority, the date they were created, or by title. Check out Figure 3-14 for one of the Reminders views, this one shared with my kids under the iCloud Family Sharing feature.

Through iCloud, Reminders can be pushed to all your compatible devices: other Macs, an iPhone, an iPad, an iPod touch, or a PC. You can receive notifications of reminders

FIGURE 3-14:
Remind the kids of all the things they have to do.

through Notification Center (covered later in this chapter). You can move from one Reminder list to another by swiping from left to right or from right to left on a trackpad. In a clever twist, if your Mac knows your current location or knows where you're headed, it can remind you of something when you get to your specified destination or remind you when to leave your current whereabouts.

Stickies

Walk around your office, and I'll lay odds that some of your colleagues have yellow sticky notes attached to their computer monitors. You too, huh? They're great ways to make your supervisor think you're really busy.

The Mac provides electronic versions of these notes called *Stickies.* Just like the gluey paper kind, these electronic notes let you jot down quickie shopping lists, phone numbers, and to-do items.

But virtual sticky notes have it all over their paper counterparts. Consider these stunts:

>> You can resize a Sticky by dragging the handle on the note's bottom-right corner.

>> You can import text or graphics, alter fonts and font sizes, and change colors.

>> You can check the spelling of words in the note.

>> You can create translucent Stickies to see what's behind them.

>> You can delete a note without crumpling it or crossing out its contents.

>> You won't clutter up your good-looking Macintosh computer. (You have to concoct another scheme to convince your boss how hard you're working.)

Creating a new Sticky doesn't count as work. After opening the app, choose File⇨New Note. Then start scribbling . . . um, typing.

Notes

Stickies aren't the only kind of notes on your Mac. In OS X, Apple provides a Notes app that's similar to the app on iOS devices such as the iPad and iPhone. The Notes app has a similar purpose to Stickies and, let's face it, makes the former redundant. Here's a look at what you can do in Notes:

>> Jot down quick musings, enter the amounts you spent on groceries, add frequent-flier numbers — you name it.

>> Organize notes in folders, search across all of them, display them full-screen, drag photos or attachments into them, or pin them to your desktop (just like Stickies).

>> As part of El Capitan, you can drag in documents, photos, videos, and PDFs. And you can save stuff from Maps, Safari, and other apps into Notes, and create to-do checklists.

>> Through an *Attachments browser* in the Notes app, you can easily scan all the attachments held in Notes, including sketches and audio notes.

>> Push a note to your other devices through iCloud. When you click the Action button at the bottom of a line (the Action button resembles an arrow trying to break out of a rectangle), you can share the note via email or Messages. If you double-click a note name in the list of notes, shown in the middle pane of the app in Figure 3-15 (the view when the sidebar is visible), you can open the note in its own window to keep it on your desktop even after you close the Notes app.

My advice: Take note of Notes. I think you'll end up using this handy app a lot. Even if it now means you pay far less attention to those stickies.

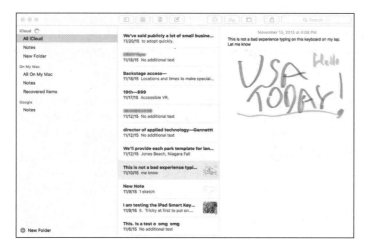

FIGURE 3-15:
Take notes.

Notification Center

Apple provides a neat way to deliver unobtrusive systemwide notifications and alerts in the top-right corner of your screen. It's Notification Center, a convenient feature borrowed from iOS. In Notification Center, shown in Figure 3-16, you can receive email alerts and peek at Calendar appointments, Reminders, Facebook notifications, and more. Inside Notification Center, you can also post an update to Facebook, share an item in LinkedIn, or send a tweet in Twitter.

FIGURE 3-16:
Notification
Center keeps
you informed.

You have a few ways to manage the notifications that you receive, which may come in the form of banners that turn up in the top-right corner of the screen and then go away after five seconds. Or they may appear as alerts that stay visible until you actively dismiss them.

>> **To see all your missed notifications in Notification Center,** click the Notification Center icon in the top-right corner of the screen. Alternatively, take two fingers to the right edge of your trackpad and swipe to the left.

>> **To temporarily turn off alerts and banners,** flip the Do Not Disturb switch at the top. Alerts and banners are brought back the next day unless you again turn the Do Not Disturb switch on. (The switch isn't visible in Figure 3-16.)

To make further decisions about which apps can notify you and how, visit System Preferences.

Tooling around for a reference

A lot of what people do on a computer is look things up, mainly through Internet search engines (see Chapter 9) and other online tools (see Chapter 11). Help is closer at hand — in the Applications folder.

Dictionary

Finding the meaning of words or phrases is as simple as typing them in a search box. Finding the meaning of life is something else altogether. The Mac supplies versions of the *New Oxford American Dictionary, Oxford American Writer's Thesaurus,* and if you choose to load it, *Oxford Dictionary of English* (British English). You can consult an Apple Dictionary to look up terms you can't find in this book. You can also visit the popular Wikipedia online encyclopedia; translate English words to Japanese, or vice versa; and add dictionaries in Chinese, Dutch, French, German, Italian, Korean, Spanish, and other languages. The computer (via text to speech) can even read a dictionary entry out loud.

TextEdit

TextEdit is a freebie word processor. Although it offers nowhere near the flexibility of an industrial-strength word processor such as Word (see Chapters 7 and 21) or Apple's own Pages, it's no slouch. You can create shortcuts for phrases you use all the time. You can make tables and lists, and apply a bunch of formatting tricks. TextEdit can even accommodate Word documents (if someone sends you one).

Calculator

Hey, if all of us could do math in our heads, we wouldn't need a calculator. The Mac supplies not one but three onscreen calculators: Basic, Scientific, and Programmer. Choose the one you need from the calculator's View menu.

>> **The Basic calculator** is for people like me who find the need to perform simple arithmetic here and there. You can use the numeric keypad on your keyboard, if it has one, or use the mouse to click the calculator's keypad.

>> **The Scientific version** adds square root, sin, cos, and other keys whose mere thought causes me to break out in hives. (Don't count on seeing me as a future author of *Math For Dummies*.)

>> **The Mac calculator** is capable of tricks that blow away even the fanciest pocket calculator, such as going online to fetch the latest currency exchange rates. You can also do quick conversions, such as going from Celsius to Fahrenheit. Explore your options under the Convert menu.

Also, you can pick the number of decimal places up to 15 digits. Any math nerds in the crowd?

QuickTime in the nick of time

QuickTime Player, Apple's onboard multimedia player, comes to the rescue when you want to watch a movie (but not a DVD), play sounds, or display pictures. QuickTime typically pops up as needed. QuickTime X lets you trim and edit videos, among other features. Under the File menu in the Quick Time Player app, you can create a new movie recording, a new audio recording, or even a new screen recording. This last option is helpful if you're trying to demonstrate something in OS X.

Preview

Preview is a versatile program that lets you view graphics files and faxes, see screen captures, convert graphic file formats (from TIFF to JPEG, for example), and handle PDFs with panache. (*PDF* is shorthand for Adobe's *Portable Document Format.*) Preview typically loads automatically as needed. If you double-click a PDF file that someone sent you, Preview is probably the program that lets you read it. You can also use Preview to rotate, resize, and crop images in one of the many file types it recognizes.

Improvements to Preview have arrived through recent iterations of OS X. Inside the app, you can access PDF documents and images from anywhere via a feature known as iCloud Drive. Prior to El Capitan, you may have taken advantage of the Documents in the Cloud feature instead, a similar idea. And you can easily share things in Preview by tapping a Share button that lets you drop documents in Messages, AirDrop, or Mail.

Throughout the book, you meet other apps and programs on your Mac.

Chapter 4

Here a Mac, There a Mac, Everywhere a Mac Mac

Which of the following describes you?

>> Based on what you already know (or gleaned from this book), you're on the righteous path toward purchasing a Macintosh computer. *The challenge now is figuring out which model makes the most sense.*

>> You already own a Mac and are looking to add a second or even third machine to your arsenal. *The challenge now is figuring out which model makes the most sense.*

>> You received this book as a gift and have no intention of buying any computer. *The challenge now is explaining to the person who gave it to you why no model makes sense (without hurting his or her feelings).*

Regrettably, I can't help anyone in the third group, but feel free to tag along anyway.

Big Mac or Little Mac?

Desktop? Laptop? Or notebook? Okay, that was a bit of a trick question, because people use *notebook* and *laptop* to refer to the same thing. So it's really desktop versus laptop/notebook.

As always, the choice comes down to lifestyle, economics, and what you do for a living. If you burn lots of frequent-flier miles, chances are that you'll gravitate to a laptop. If you tend to be home- or office-bound, a desktop may be more suitable. You generally get computing bang for your buck with a desktop; a laptop affords you mobility.

If a Desktop Is Your Poison

Buying an Apple desktop computer doesn't mean that you have to start rearranging the furniture. Sure, Mac desktops generally take up more space than Mac notebooks do. But the machines are no larger than they have to be and are so handsome that you'll want to show them off.

iMac

As shown in Figure 4-1, the *iMac* is arguably the most elegantly designed desktop computer on the planet — unless, of course, you think that's the Mac Pro (read on).

The innards of the all-in-one system — quad-core Intel Core i5 or i7 processor, memory, hard drive (and/or solid-state flash drive), and more — are concealed inside a beautiful and remarkably thin 5mm (at the edge) flat-screen monitor. You can't help but wonder where the rest of the computer is, especially if you're accustomed to seeing a more traditional tower-type PC design. Apple sells iMacs with 21.5-inch monitors (measured diagonally) or whopping 27-inch monitors, each an LED-backlit display with widescreen *aspect ratios*, a common way monitors and cinematic displays are measured. The machine is covered in glass, and comes with a Magic Mouse 2 or Magic Trackpad 2, and a Magic keyboard.

As of this writing, you can buy iMacs with or without Retina displays. The cheapest 21.5-inch iMacs have non-Retina displays with a resolution of 1920 x 1080, essentially a measure of picture sharpness. The smaller display models have 4K Retina displays, with screen resolutions of 4096 x 2304. The larger 27-inch iMac models now come only in Retina display configurations, specifically 5K Retina with 5120 x 2880 resolution. The takeaway: These displays are knockouts.

Depending on the model, and whatever extra loot you have to spend, you can outfit the iMac with up to 1TB of flash storage or up to a 3TB Fusion Drive, which combines a hard drive with flash storage. The drive determines which apps and files you use most often and keeps them in the faster flash portion.

Through several versions of the iMac, Apple moved away from the Super Drive (CD/DVD) player that was once standard on the computer. Because you're encouraged to buy most software these days online, and because you can install any operating-system updates through the Mac App Store, physical discs aren't as prevalent or necessary as they once were. Still, if you have a lot of CDs and/or DVDs lying around, you can purchase an optional external USB SuperDrive from Apple for $79, or find a cheaper alternative from another company.

The small peephole at the top of the monitor covers a built-in high-definition *FaceTime* video camera, used for FaceTime video calls, for pictures you take in Photo Booth or videos you might capture in iMovie and for other purposes.

Mac mini

Is the *Mac mini,* shown in Figure 4-2, really a desktop? After all, the mini is easily mistaken for a breadbox or a coaster on steroids. But the petite (1.4-inch-tall,

7.7-inch-square) aluminum contraption is indeed Apple's crazy — and cozy — notion of what a "budget" desktop computer is all about. At 2.7 pounds, the Mac mini is portable, but not in the same sense as a notebook you'd fly with cross-country.

Courtesy of Apple

FIGURE 4-2:
Mini-Me's favorite Macintosh.

Base configuration models start at $499, $699, and $999 and go up depending on memory and storage. But keep in mind that this is a BYOB computer — as in bring your own keyboard, mouse, and monitor. (The assumption is that you have these items already; if not, Apple will happily sell them to you, or you can opt for third-party choices.) Given its size and price, the Mac mini makes an ideal second computer and is a perfect dorm-room companion.

TIP

Because the mini has an HDMI (High-Definition Multimedia Interface) port, you can also hook it up to a big-screen TV or take advantage of a superior speaker system. The computer also has 2 Thunderbolt 2, Gigabit Ethernet, and four USB 3.0 connectors, plus an SDXC card slot (for memory cards). And it has the smarts to play back music or videos stored on other computers in your house, including Windows systems.

A Fusion Drive is an option here as well.

Mac Pro: A Mac with muscle

The redesigned, tubular Mac Pro is a computer to drool over, even if it's overkill for most readers of this book. The machine is capable of generating up to 12 cores of processing power through the Intel Xeon — a preferred system for graphics designers, video production professionals, scientists, music producers, developers, and so on. If you're not one of those folks, scram; there's a reason why it's called the Mac *Pro.* Then again, it's hard not to be seduced by the machine's powerful graphics (AMD Dual FirePro graphics processors), storage options, and multiple ports and connectors.

Going Mobile

You don't have to be a traditional road warrior to crave a notebook these days. You may need something to schlep from lecture hall to lecture hall, from your home to your office, or maybe just from the basement to the bedroom. Also, some computers are worth having (such as the MacBook Air, described shortly) just because they're so darn sexy.

In choosing any laptop, take into account its *traveling weight.* Besides the weight of the machine itself, consider the heft of the AC power cord and possibly a spare battery (though Macs of recent vintage don't let you replace the battery yourself).

One of the first decisions you have to make is the screen size. Bigger displays are nice, of course, but weigh and cost more, and you may be sacrificing some battery life. Are you getting the sense that this battery business is a big deal? It can be, which is why I offer tips (later in the chapter) on how to stay juiced.

MacBook Pro

Apple's top-of-the-line *MacBook Pro* notebook, boasting a beautiful Retina display, is shown in Figure 4-3. It comes in 13- and 15-inch versions, with models starting at $1,299 and going up to $2,499 or more, depending how you configure the machine. You can get a 13-inch MacBook Pro without the glorious Retina display for $1,099 on up. That model, unlike Retina versions that came later, still has a SuperDrive for playing optical disks, as well as a FireWire 800 connector to complement Thunderbolt. Models with Retina ditch such features but get a pair of Thunderbolt 2 connectors and the Force Touch trackpad.

FIGURE 4-3: A handsome 15-inch MacBook Pro with Retina display.

Courtesy of Apple

Constructed from a solid slab of aluminum, the MacBook Pro is fast and boasts souped-up Intel graphics (great for 3D games and videos) and long-lasting batteries.

The MacBook Pro did relinquish some features of old PowerBooks and older MacBook Pros. Yes, in most cases it ditched the optical disc drive (though it's still available as an external accessory), and the hard drive went by way of all flash storage. The Gigabit Ethernet port also went bye-bye. MacBook Pros were the first notebooks to come with a pair of Thunderbolt ports, Apple's speedy connectors, though Thunderbolt eventually made its way onto MacBook Airs as well. USB 3.0

connectors are included on the MacBook Pro and Air models, as is an HDMI port on the Pro.

Because a FireWire port is no longer available on Retina models, you'll need an optional adapter if that connector is important to you. Ambient sensors that can illuminate the keyboard when the cabin lights are dimmed on an airplane are included. If that doesn't create a mood and show the cute passenger in 12C how resourceful you are, nothing will. You can also use the glass multitouch trackpad and navigate by using some of the finger gestures mentioned later in this chapter or by using Force Touch, which relies on pressure sensitivity to dictate certain outcomes.

MacBook Air

It's hard to imagine how thin and light MacBook Airs are without seeing them and picking them up. They're dream computers to take on the road or to the coffee shop. Pictures — even the ones in Figure 4-4 — don't do them justice. Like MacBook Pros, the machines are crafted from a single slab of aluminum. The smaller models have 11.6-inch displays, weigh just 2.4 pounds, and measure just 0.68 inches at the rear before tapering to a mere 0.11 inches at their thinnest point in the front. They cost $899 or $1,099 in their base configurations.

FIGURE 4-4:
Floating on MacBook Air.

Courtesy of Apple

Larger 13.3-inch-display models also measure 0.68 inches in the rear and a hair over a tenth of an inch thick at the front. Despite the larger screen size, the machines aren't a whole lot heavier (2.96 pounds). They cost $999 and $1,199 in their base configurations.

Apple still managed to include full-size backlit keyboards, multitouch trackpads, and battery life (for wireless web surfing) that extends well beyond double-digit hours, depending on the model. (I'm writing these words on an airplane with an unplugged MacBook Air. The machine is fully charged, and the indicator says I have nearly 15½ hours of power left. Awesome!) Alas, the battery is sealed and not easily replaced.

The Airs use all-flash storage in lieu of hard drives, and because flash is expensive, storage is relatively cramped: 128GB or 256GB on both the 11.6- and 13.3-inch versions. You can go as high as 512GB of flash storage.

Any Lilliputian computer exacts compromises, and so it goes with Air. As with other models, it has no integrated CD/DVD drive, though the absence of such a drive is less concerning these days because of all the software you can fetch online, including in the Mac App Store. You'll find just a pair of USB 3.0 ports and no Ethernet connector, though you can purchase an adapter if having Ethernet is important Apple has added Thunderbolt 2 ports to the latest models, as well as the new MagSafe 2 power-port connector. The larger MacBook Air includes an SD card slot. The machines also come with 4GB of RAM (upgradable at the time of purchase to 8GB).

MacBook

Forget what I just told you about how thin and light the MacBook Air is. Yeah, it is thin and light, but when I'm speaking about the latest MacBook, I mean *really* thin and light. The machine is barely above 2 pounds, making it the lightest notebook that Apple has ever produced. With an edge that tapers from 13.1mm down to a mere 3.5mm, you won't find a thinner Mac either. This beauty of this machine, which is shown in Figure 4-5, is that it also boasts a 12-inch Retina display and an all-day battery.

Apple designed the keyboard with a butterfly mechanism that the company says is 40 percent thinner than than typical scissor-type method. I had to type on the keyboard a few times before I got used to it, and I suspect others might have a similar experience. But you do get used to it.

Apple also designed the MacBook with a USB-C power adaptor, which is based on an emerging industry-wide standard. USB-C is versatile; you can plug the connector into the computer in either orientation. My biggest gripe is that, aside from the headphone jack, USB-C is this computer's *only* connector. When the USB-C power cable is plugged into the computer, you need an adaptor to connect any accessories that rely on USB. (Perhaps this situation will change by the time you read this.)

Courtesy of Apple

FIGURE 4-5:
Now we're talking thin and light with the MacBook.

The cost as of this writing is $1299 or $1599, depending on storage and processor choices. The machine also boasts Force Touch.

Taming the Trackpad

In Chapter 2, I introduce the trackpad — the smooth, rectangular, finger-clicking surface below the keyboard that's your laptop's answer to a mouse. On the latest Mac laptops, the entire trackpad is a clickable button, and many of the latest versions also let you exploit Force Touch.

You can still use a regular mouse with a laptop, and you may prefer to do so if you're at your desk. If you're sitting in coach instead, the mouse is an unwelcome critter, especially to the passenger sitting next to you. Don't be surprised if he or she calls an exterminator (or at least the flight attendant).

The best place to train a trackpad is in Trackpad Preferences. Choose ⌘⇨System Preferences⇨Trackpad. As shown in Figure 4-6, you have numerous options for making things happen with one, two, or even three fingers by selecting the appropriate check boxes. A handy little video window helps you figure out what to do.

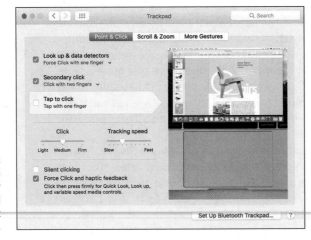

FIGURE 4-6:
The key to taming your trackpad on different laptops.

On models with Force Touch, you can click the Force Click and Haptic Feedback check box to summon Quick Look when you click and press firmly with the trackpad. You might also use Force Touch to look up the definition of a word you've highlighted.

TIP

Many other multitouch gestures were borrowed from the Mac's famous corporate cousin, the iPhone. You can zoom in on a web page in Safari or a photo in Photos by *pinching,* or placing your thumb and forefinger together on the trackpad and then pulling them apart. And with the *swipe* gesture, you can navigate web pages with three fingers by dragging from right to left to page forward and from left to right to retreat.

Here are a few more options:

>> Drag the Tracking Speed slider to change how fast the pointer moves. On Force Touch trackpad models, you can drag the Click slider in Preferences to set how much pressure you need to apply for a click (light, medium, firm).

>> Use one finger tap to click. Or for a secondary click, use one finger in either the bottom-right or bottom-left corner of the trackpad, or you can click with two fingers (the equivalent of a right-click).

>> You can show the desktop by spreading your thumb and three fingers.

>> You can rotate the screen by using two fingers.

Keeping Your Notebook Juiced

Although Apple has dramatically improved the battery life across all its notebooks, sooner or later, your battery will lose its charge, especially if Murphy (the fellow behind that nasty law) has any say in the manner. And you can be sure that you'll be without a charge at precisely the worst possible moment — when your professor is prepping you for a final exam, or when you're about to discover whodunit while watching a movie on an overseas flight. (I hasten to point out that watching a flick will drain your battery a lot faster than working on a spreadsheet.)

TIP

You may routinely keep the computer plugged in to recharge the battery. Still, Apple recommends pulling the plug periodically to keep the juices flowing. If you didn't plan on using the computer for six months or more (and why the heck not?), on older Mac laptops, you could remove the battery and store it with about a 50 percent charge. You couldn't always resuscitate a fully discharged battery that had been kept on the sidelines too long.

Okay, maybe it's time to spill the bad news: Sealed batteries mean no more do-it-yourself. You're a prisoner to the Apple battery replacement service.

Rechargeable batteries have a finite number of charging cycles, so even with the best feed and caring, they have to be replaced eventually. It's time to put the battery out to pasture when it no longer holds a charge for very long. Remember to give it an environmentally correct burial.

Don't give up the fight just yet, however. You can take steps to boost your battery's longevity. Your computer is smart about conservation. When plugged in, it feels free to let loose. That means the hard drive (if there is one) will spin around to its heart's content, and the display can be turned up to maximum brightness settings.

You can tell a Mac how to behave when it's unplugged:

» **Dim the screen.** Your laptop battery likes nothing better than mood lighting. Press F1 on the keyboard to turn down the brightness and F2 when you're ready to turn it up again.

» **Open Energy Saver** (see Figure 4-7) by clicking the battery gauge on the menu bar and then choosing Open Energy Saver Preferences from the drop-down menu. (Or choose ⌥⇧System Preferences⇨Energy Saver.) You have options to put the hard drives to sleep when possible (a swell idea), to slightly dim the display when using a battery (equally swell idea), or to automatically reduce brightness before the display goes to sleep. You'll notice other options in Energy Saver, including a slider to turn off the display when it's not used for a certain period. If you click Schedule, you can determine when the computer starts or wakes up or goes to sleep. And you can enable Power Nap, which lets the Mac accomplish certain tasks while it is asleep, such as letting Mail receive new messages and keeping contacts up to date when changes are made on other devices.

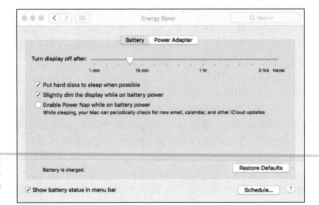

FIGURE 4-7:
Mac conservation inside Energy Saver.

» **Shut down the AirPort wireless networking feature** (see Chapter 16) if you're not surfing the Internet, sending and receiving email, or sharing files over the network. AirPort hogs power, and you shouldn't be using it anyway if you're traveling on an airplane that doesn't offer Wi-Fi.

» **Likewise, turn off the wireless settings for Bluetooth** if you're on a plane or if you just want to save some juice.

After all, given all your aspirations with your computer, the last thing you want is to run out of power.

Mac Daily Dealings

2

Chapter 5

Making the Mac Your Own

You adore your family and friends to death but have to admit that they get under your skin from time to time. They know how to push your buttons, and you sure know how to push theirs. People are fussy about certain things, and that includes you (and me).

So it goes with your Macintosh. The presumption is that you and your Mac are going to cohabit well into the future. Still, it can't hurt to get off on the right foot and set up the machine so that it matches your preferences and expectations, not some programmer's at Apple. The software you load on your system differs from the programs your best buddies install on their computers. You tolerate dozens of icons on the Mac desktop; they prefer a less cluttered screen. You choose a blown-up picture of Homer Simpson for your desktop background; your pals go with a screen-size poster of Jessica Simpson.

The Mac may share a nickname with a certain McDonald's hamburger, but an old Burger King slogan is most apt for describing your computer. As this chapter will show, you can "have it your way."

Establishing User Accounts

As much as the computer staring you in the face is your very own Mac, chances are you'll be sharing it with someone else: your spouse and kids, perhaps, if not your students and coworkers. I know you generously thought about buying each of them a computer. But then your little one needs braces; you've been eyeing a new set of golf clubs; and the truth is, your largesse has limits. So you'll be sharing the computer, all right, at least for a while. The challenge now is avoiding chaos and all-out civil war.

The Mac helps keep the peace by giving everyone his or her own user account, which is a separate area to hang out in that is password-protected to prevent intrusions. (The folks at Apple can't do much to avert fights over *when* people use the computer — though moms and dads have some control over when Junior gets to use the machine.)

Ranking user accounts

As the owner of the machine, you're the head honcho, the Big Cheese, or (in the bureaucracy of your computer) the *administrator.*

Being the Big Cheese doesn't earn you an expense account or a plush corner office with a view of the lakefront. It does, however, carry executive privileges. You get to lord over not only who else can use the machine, but also who, if anyone, gets the same administrative rights you have. You do so by creating user accounts and assigning a ranking to those accounts.

WARNING

Think long and hard before you grant anyone else these dictatorial powers. Only an administrator can muck around with system settings such as Date & Time and Energy Saver. And only an administrator can effectively hire and fire by creating or eliminating other user accounts. Naturally, an administrator can also install software.

Here's a quick look at the hierarchy of accounts:

>> **Administrator:** As outlined previously, you have almighty powers, at least when it comes to your computer.

>> **Standard:** You can't mess with other people's accounts. But you pretty much have free rein when it comes to your own account. That means you can install software, alter the look of your desktop, and so on.

>> **Managed with Parental Controls:** Consider this Mom's and Dad's Revenge. The kids may get away with murder around the house, but they can't get away with murder on the Mac.

>> **Sharing Only:** This type of account is a limited account for sharing files remotely across a network.

>> **Group:** By creating a group account, you can share files with the members of said group. It's really a type of account comprised of one or more accounts.

>> **Guest:** Willing to let the babysitter play with your Mac after putting the little ones to bed? A guest account lets her log in without a password (though you can still restrict her activities through parental controls). You can allow guests to connect to shared folders on the system. Or not. And the beauty of one of these accounts is that after a guest has logged out, traces of her stay are removed, right down to the temporary home folder created for her visit.

Creating new accounts

So now that you know about the different types of user accounts, I'll discuss more about setting up one. To create a new account for one of your coworkers, say, follow these steps:

1. **Choose ⬢⇨ System Preferences and then click the Users & Groups icon.**

   Alternatively, you can click your username in the upper-right corner of the screen, mouse down to Users & Groups Preferences and then click that item, or get to System Preferences through its dock icon.

   It's worth remembering how you get to System Preferences because you'll be spending a lot of time there in this chapter.

   The Users & Groups window that appears is shown in Figure 5-1.

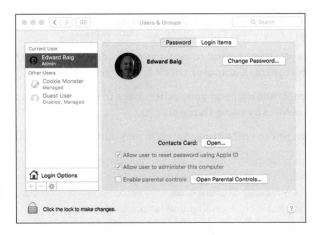

FIGURE 5-1: Change account preferences here.

2. **If the Password tab (as opposed to Login Items) isn't highlighted, click it.**

3. **Click the + in the lower-left corner (right there below the list of names).**

If the + appears dimmed, you have to click the padlock at the bottom of the screen and enter your username and password to proceed. (You'll encounter this padlock throughout System Preferences and must click it and enter an administrative password before being allowed to make changes.)

4. **In the screen shown in Figure 5-2, do the following:**

a. *From the New Account pop-up menu, choose one of the account designations listed in the preceding section (such as Administrator, Standard, or [as shown here] Managed with Parental Controls).*

b. *Enter a full name, an account name, a password, the password verification, and (if you choose) a password hint in the blank fields shown. You can also go with an iCloud password. If this is a Managed with Parental Controls account, click the age box and make a selection (4+, 9+, 12+, 17+).*

FIGURE 5-2:
Add a new account here.

For help in choosing a password, click the key next to the password field. You may want to give a coworker or other person sharing an account the ability to enter his or her own password and username, of course.

c. *Click Create User.*

You're taken back to the Users & Groups window.

5. **Unless you have a good reason to do otherwise, deselect the Allow User to Administer This Computer check box (refer to Figure 5-1).**

6. **(Optional) Allow one of your other users to set his own Apple ID and to reset his password by using that Apple ID.**

7. **(Optional) Turn off automatic login on your computer, if you want to.**

This option presents itself when you click Login Options in the sidebar on the left. Click on the administrator (your) name in the Automatic login field or the name of any other account holder for whom you will extend automatic logging in privileges. Or choose Off if that is your preference.

You can leave the remaining steps to the new account holder — letting him or her choose an identifying picture, for example.

8. **Click the Picture thumbnail.**

   It shows your mug or a picture of an object — say, a butterfly or a tennis ball. You're taken to the screen outlined in the next step.

9. **Select the small image that will be displayed next to the username when the account holder logs on to the computer.**

   You can click the archery target, piano keyboard, gingerbread cookie, luscious lips, or other goofy iconic images presented in the Users & Groups window (under Default). But account holders may well want to choose one of their own images. You can do this from your iCloud Photos collection, or you can let them snap a new image as follows:

   a. *Select Camera in the list that appears after you click the Picture thumbnail in the Users & Groups window.*

      Other options here are Default, Recents, iCloud Photos, Faces, and Linked.

      The Face Time camera on the front of your Mac (or on the Apple monitor if you have one) launches. You see what the camera sees in a small window.

   b. *Click the camera icon that shows up just under the window displaying your own face.*

      After a three-two-one countdown, your mug (or the other account holder's mug) is captured. You can drag a slider to zoom in on the image you just shot and even apply Photo Booth effects (see the next section).

   c. *If you're satisfied with the result, click Done, and that image will serve as the account picture.*

      If you're not satisfied, click Cancel to reshoot.

Entering the Photo Booth

Remember when you and your high-school sweetheart slipped into one of those coin-operated photo booths at the five-and-dime? Or maybe it was your mom or dad's high-school sweetheart. Don't worry — I'm not telling what went on behind that curtain. Years ago, you or your parent probably confiscated the evidence: a strip with all those silly poses.

Silly poses are back in vogue. Apple is supplying its own photo booth of sorts as a built-in software feature on your Mac. You can produce an acceptable account picture to use when, say, you're exchanging instant messages (see Chapter 11).

Apple's Photo Booth and the photo booth of yesteryear — and of today, because you still see them around — have some major differences. For starters, you don't have to surrender any loose change with Apple's version. What's more, you don't have to hide behind a curtain (which is kind of too bad). And that old-fashioned photo booth can't match Apple's other stunts: making movie clips or having your mug appear in front of a *moving* roller coaster or other fluid backdrop.

Taking a Photo Booth picture

Open Photo Booth by clicking its name in the Applications folder, clicking its dock icon, or clicking its Launchpad icon. You can snap an image right away merely by clicking the oblong red shutter button below the large video screen that serves as a viewfinder, as shown in Figure 5-3. When you do so, a three-two-one countdown ticks off. On zero, the display flashes, and your portrait is captured.

FIGURE 5-3:
It's a snap: the main Photo Booth view.

Take a movie clip   See Special Effects menu

Take a still picture   Shutter button

Take four quick pictures

But consider your other options. Take a gander at the three little icons in the lower-left corner of the screen. Here's what they do:

>> If you click the leftmost icon and then click the shutter button, Photo Booth takes four successive snapshots in a row, right after the three-two-one countdown. The just-captured images appear in a single "four-up" snapshot, showing your four poses. You've activated *burst mode.*

>> Clicking (or dialing) the icon in the middle sticks with the one-shot approach, following the same three-two-one countdown.

>> Making use of the icon on the right puts Photo Booth in video mode. After the countdown, the computer starts making a little video, complete with audio. You have to click the shutter button again (now a stop button) to cease recording. A red digital counter reminds you that you're still shooting.

You can remove any of the still images or videos you've captured in Photo Booth by clicking a thumbnail of those images and clicking the circled X that appears on the upper-left corner of the thumbnail.

Applying special effects

So far, I've told you how to capture straightforward images (assuming that you didn't stick your tongue out). Now the real fun begins. You can summon your inner mad scientist and apply a series of warping effects. Here's how:

1. **Click the Effects button (refer to Figure 5-3).**

    A *Brady Bunch*–like grid appears, with each square revealing a different effect, some silly and some creepy, just like the screen shown in Figure 5-4.

FIGURE 5-4:
How goofy (or creepy) can you get? Applying effects in Photo Booth.

2. **Click a square to preview the potential effect in a much larger window.**

    Or, if you don't like this set of effects, click the arrows on the screen to display a new set.

    You can make it look as though the picture was taken with a thermal camera or an X-ray, or drawn with a colored pencil. You can turn the image into pop art worthy of Warhol or make it glow radioactively. You can apply a chipmunk effect or a love-struck image in which red hearts float around your head. And you can place yourself in a mirror image reminiscent of the Doublemint Twins from the old gum commercials.

TIP

When you click some effects (such as bulge, squeeze, or twirl), you see a slider that you can drag with the mouse to tweak the level of distortion.

3. **Now you can proceed by doing one of the following:**

- To choose the previewed effect, click the Camera button to snap the picture.

- To see another effect in this set, click the Effects button again and make your selection. Once more, click the Camera button when you're ready to capture the image.

- To revert to the normal view, click Effects and then the middle of this tic-tac-toe grid. Again, click Camera when you're ready.

Admiring and sharing Photo Booth photos

The pictures and movies that you make in Photo Booth turn up at the bottom of the Photo Booth program in an onscreen photo strip. To admire an image, just click the corresponding thumbnail.

You also have several options for sharing the picture or movie with others. Click the Share button and choose among the following options:

» Make the image your account picture or Contacts picture.

» Drop the image into a message.

» Email the picture through the Mac's Mail application.

» Send the image to your Photos picture library.

» Share it through Facebook, Twitter, or Flickr.

» Make the image available to a nearby Mac through AirDrop.

TIP

Further, you can drag the image to your desktop. Or export the thumbnail by selecting it and choosing Photo Booth ⇨ File ⇨ Export). That way, you can use the image file in a third-party application or web-based email client.

Using Parental Controls: When Father (or Mother) Knows Best

Suppose that one of the new accounts you create is for your impressionable offspring, Cookie Monster. As a responsible parent, you want to set limits to keep him out of trouble. And as a responsible Mac owner, you want to keep him from unwittingly (or otherwise) inflicting damage on the computer.

It's time to apply *parental controls*. Presumably, you already set up Cookie Monster as a managed account with parental controls. If not, choose the proper user account — Cookie Monster, in this example — and select the Enable Parental Controls check box in the Users & Groups window in System Preferences. When you do so, Cookie Monster's account goes from being a regular standard account to a managed account, with you as the manager.

After you've created your youngster's account, you're ready to open Parental Controls and have your say about what he or she can and can't do on your Mac. In the Users & Groups window, click Open Parental Controls. Alternatively, click Parental Controls in System Preferences. Either way, you end up in the same place. In the Parental Controls window, shown in Figure 5-5, select Cookie Monster's name in the list on the left. Now, protective parent, you can do lots of things.

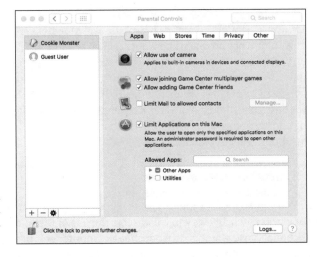

FIGURE 5-5:
Parental controls may protect your kid and your computer.

Here, I dive in to the five tabs at the top of the window:

>> **Apps:** In this section, parents can cherry-pick the apps that their kids can use and also place restrictions on the use of the Camera, Game Center, and Mail apps. Mom or dad might decide that the kids can participate in Game Center,

but not let them join multiplayer games or add Game Center friends. Parents can also limit the contacts who can engage their children via Mail.

» **Web:** By selecting this tab, you allow unrestricted access to websites or limit access. If you click Customize, you can list your own approved sites, as well as those you don't deem kosher. You can also restrict web access so that all Cookie Monster supposedly gets to see are clean sites. Apple makes the decision on your behalf if you select the check box titled Try to Limit Access to Adult Websites Automatically. You can view sites that meet Apple's approval and, if you agree, select Allow Access to Only These Websites. (Discovery Kids, Disney, PBS Kids, National Geographic – Kids, Scholastic.com, and Smithsonian Institution are among the sites that made Apple's list.)

I know you trust your kid. All the same, you want to ensure his safety by getting a good handle on his online behavior. Click the Logs button to find out which websites your child visited, which he tried to visit but were blocked, which applications he used, and who in Messages he chatted with. You can summon logs for one day, one week, one month, three months, six months, or one year. Or you can subpoena all the records. You can group logs by date or by website, contact, or app. The option to click Logs also appears on the Apps and People tabs.

» **Stores:** You can disable iTunes Store, iTunes U, and iBooks Store. But even if you allow your little ones to access such stores, you can restrict the type of content they can fetch and purchase based on a ratings system for movies, TV shows, books, and apps. You can also keep music with explicit lyrics off-limits.

» **Time Limits:** It's not only a matter of who Cookie Monster would like to interact with or what programs he wants to play around with; it's also a matter of when you let him do so. By dragging the sliders shown in Figure 5-6, you can establish weekday and weekend time restrictions. In other words, you can prevent access to the Mac when it's time for him to go beddy-bye, choosing different times on school nights and weekends. Cookie Monster gets a fair warning shortly before shutdown time so that he can save his work. He also gets the opportunity to plead for more time.

» **Privacy:** Here you can manage privacy preferences and limit access to Cookie Monster's data.

» **Other:** You can do lots of other things to try and keep your child safe and sound. On this catch-all tab, you can disable the use of Dictation, hide profanity in Dictionary, prevent the kid from changing printer settings, limit CD or DVD burning, and prevent him from changing his password. Or choose Simple Finder, which limits this managed account to a simple, barebones desktop, with three folders in the Simple Finder version of the dock for My Applications, Documents, and Shared, plus Trash.

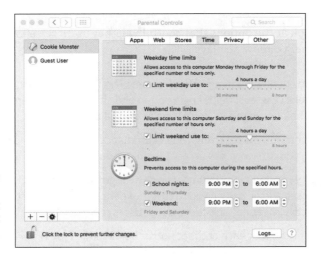

The Lowdown on Logging In

You can create user accounts for any and all family members or visitors who will be using a particular Mac, and you can control how they log in. In this section, I describe how:

1. **Choose ⏵System Preferences.**

2. **Choose Users & Groups and then click Login Options at the bottom of the left pane, below the list of all the account holders on your system.**

   If need be, click the padlock, and enter a username and administrative password. After you're in, you see the window shown in Figure 5-7.

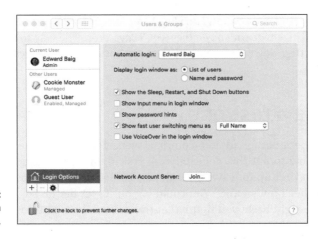

Here's a look at the options that control whether users see a login window and, if so, what that window displays:

>> **Automatically log in a particular user:** This is likely yourself. To make it happen, select the Automatic Login option and choose the appropriate person from the pop-up menu. You'll have to enter a password.

WARNING

If the computer is set to log you in automatically, any user who restarts the Mac in your absence has access to your account.

>> **Display (or don't display) users on the login window:** If, at login, you'd like to see a login screen with a roster of people alongside pictures for their respective accounts, select the List of Users radio button.

If you prefer that each account holder be forced to type his or her own username and password in the appropriate boxes on the login screen (the most secure method of keeping interlopers at bay), select the Name and Password radio button.

After you've set these account preferences and it's time for you (or others) to log into the Mac, press Enter (or Return) or click the account picture after entering the username and/or password to actually log in. If you type the wrong password, the password text box wobbles as though it's having a momentary seizure. Type it wrong a few more times, and any password hints you previously entered appear (provided that you chose that option). If you can't remember it, you may have to reset your password using your Apple ID.

. . . And logging out

Say that you're ready to call it quits for the day but don't want to shut down the machine. At the same time, you don't want to leave your account open for anyone with prying eyes. *Baig's Law: Just because your family, friends, and coworkers are upstanding citizens doesn't mean they won't eavesdrop.* The way to shut down without really shutting down is to choose ⇨ Log Out or use the keyboard combination Shift+⌘+Q.

Pulling a fast one

Now consider another all-too-common scenario. You're in the middle of working when — how to put this delicately? — last night's pasta exacts revenge. Nature calls. As you get up to leave, your spouse comes running in, asking, "Honey, can I quickly check my email?" You could log out to let her do so, but because you're going to be right back, you figure that there has to be a better way. The better way is called Fast User Switching.

To take advantage of Fast User Switching, you must have previously selected the Show Fast User Switching Menu As check box in the Login Options window (refer to Figure 5-7). You can display this menu as a full name, account name, or an icon.

After you enable Fast User Switching behind the scenes, here's how to take advantage of the feature while using your Mac:

1. **To let your spouse (or any other user) butt in, click your username in the upper-right corner of the screen.**

A list of all account holders appears.

2. **The person can click his or her name and type a password.**

Like a revolving door, your entire desktop spins out of the way while the other user's desktop spins in.

When you return moments later, you repeat this procedure by choosing your name and entering your password. Your desktop twirls back into view, right where you left off.

Letting Someone Go

Sometimes, being the boss really does mean being the bad guy. The Mac equivalent of terminating someone is deleting the person's user account from the system. Here's how to axe an account:

1. **Choose ⇨ System Preferences, and then select the Users & Groups option.**

2. **Click the padlock (it's at the lower left of the window) to permit changes.**

3. **Select the name of the person getting the pink slip.**

4. **Click the – button below the list of names.**

5. **In the dialog that appears, you can make a few choices:**

Clicking Delete User wipes the account from the system, but you get to choose one of the following:

- Save the person's home folder in a disk image (in an appropriately labeled Deleted Users folder).

- Leave his or her home folder where it was in the Users folder.

- Delete the home folder.

The last option is reserved for users who were particularly naughty (and whose files you don't need).

Changing Appearances

This section is all about making the Mac look pretty. No hair products, intense workout routines, or high-end clothing labels are required. Here, I'm talking about the color schemes, screen savers, and other settings you can adjust to make your Mac look good to *you*.

Altering buttons menus, and windows

Are you not too keen on the look of the buttons, menus, and windows currently residing on your Mac?

Choose ⌥ System Preferences and then click General. In the resulting window, you can alter the menus and the colors of those buttons, and apply other cosmetic touches. You can decide, for example, whether to show scroll bars or determine the behavior that occurs when you close documents and windows.

TIP

One of the options to consider is Use LCD Font Smoothing When Available. Font smoothing reduces jagged edges of some fonts.

Setting your wallpaper and screen saver

Is the wallpaper that Apple's interior designers put behind your desktop attractive enough but not to your taste? You can rip it down and start anew.

Choose ⌥ System Preferences and open the Desktop & Screen Saver window. With the settings here, you can really start putting your stamp on the place.

Make sure that the Desktop tab is selected, as shown in Figure 5-8. Click Desktop Pictures or Solid Colors. Various design swatches appear on the right side of the window. Best of all, this pane isn't like a salesperson showing you swatches in a home decorating store. To see what a finished remodeling job will look like, all you have to do is click.

The design categories on the left include listings for pictures, albums, and events from your Photos library (see Chapter 14). Clicking these options lets you choose one of your own images for the desktop background. Apple's designer collection has nothing over masterpieces that include your gorgeous child. You can also select images from your Pictures folder.

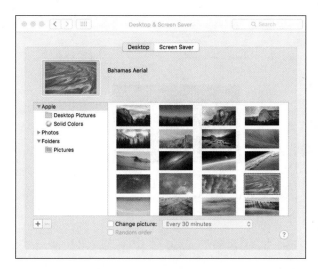

FIGURE 5-8:
Become your
own interior
decorator.

Choosing a screen saver

Screen savers are so named because they were created to save your screen from a ghostly phenomenon known as *burn-in*. Whenever the same fixed image was shown on a screen over long periods, a dim specter from that image was permanently etched on the display. Burn-in isn't much of an issue anymore, due to the prevalence of LCD and LED displays, but the screen-saver moniker survived. Today, the value of the screen saver is strictly cosmetic, in the same way that you may choose a vanity license plate or a ringtone for your cellphone. Along those lines there's a plethora of screen savers that can be downloaded out on the Internet, from movies, TV shows, musical artists, on and on. The following steps walk you through the Screen Saver pane on the Mac:

1. **Choose ⌥ System Preferences and then click Desktop & Screen Saver.**

2. **In the box on the left, shown in Figure 5-9, click one of the screen savers.**

   You can choose among such effects as Shifting Tiles and Sliding Panels. You can eyeball screen savers in the small preview area to the right.

   Here's a quick look at some screen saver options:

   - If you want to show pictures, choose one of the slideshow screensavers.

   - If you want to know what words such as *soporific* and *flume* mean, choose the Word of the Day screen saver. It's not as pretty as some other options, but at least it'll boost your vocabulary.

   - Love music? Consider Apple's iTunes Artwork screen saver, shown in Figure 5-10. This handsome grid of 40 album covers from your iTunes music library is constantly changing; every 3 seconds, one of the album cover pictures is swapped for another picture.

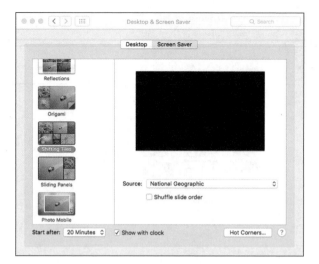

FIGURE 5-9:
Beautifying your display with a screen saver.

FIGURE 5-10:
This iTunes Artwork screen saver is off the charts.

3. **If you chose a slideshow screen saver, you can pick the source of the pictures by clicking the pop-up menu below the preview area.**

   National Geographic images are particularly stunning, but I also recommend Cosmos and Nature Patterns.

   If you want to use your own pictures, select the folder of pictures you want the slideshow to display.

   Click the Shuffle Slide Order check box to make the pictures appear in random order.

4. **If you want to display the time with your chosen screen saver, select the Show with Clock check box.**

5. **Choose a time for the screen saver to kick in from the Start After pop-up menu.**

Your choices range from 1 minute to 1 hour (or Never, which kind of renders the whole idea of a screen saver beside the point).

You can choose slideshows from your own pictures as screen savers, using various special effects, including one modeled after the work of documentary filmmaker Ken Burns.

Tidying Up with Mission Control

Things can get untidy on the Mac desktop, too, especially as you juggle several projects at once. At any given time, you may have opened System Preferences, Dictionary, Calendar, an email program, numerous word processing documents, and then some. Windows lie on top of windows. Chaos abounds. You've fallen into the dark abyss that is multitasking.

Apple has the perfect remedy for MDLS (Messy Desktop Layered Syndrome). The antidote is *Mission Control*, shown in Figure 5-11, and it's as close as the F3 key on current Apple keyboards, (F9 or fn+F9 on older keyboards, or the keyboard combination of Control+up arrow key). Mission Control provides a unified view of everything on your system: Dashboard, any open desktops, full-screen applications that are open, plus other apps that are open. The very top area in Mission Control is known as the *Spaces bar*.

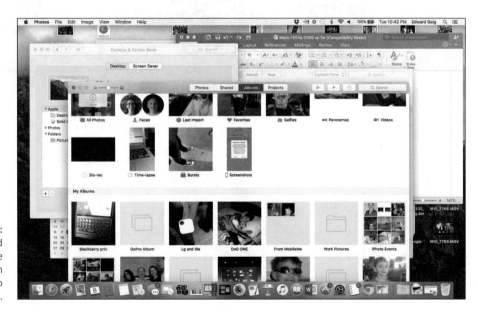

FIGURE 5-11:
A cluttered desktop before putting Mission Control to work.

TECHNICAL STUFF

Mission Control essentially merges features that were introduced by Apple in earlier versions of OS X. One of those features, called Exposé, lives on within Mission Control. The other feature is called Spaces.

Go ahead and press F3 now. All previously open but obstructed windows emerge from their hiding places, like crooks finally willing to give themselves up after a lengthy standoff. All the windows are proportionately (and simultaneously) downsized so that you can temporarily see them all at once, as shown in Figure 5-12.

Desktop is currently open

Click to add new desktop

Click to enter Dashboard

Open full-screen apps currently open

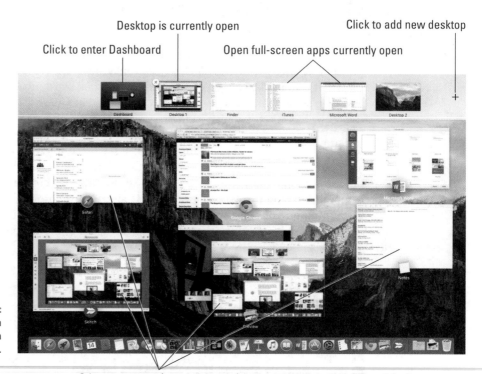

FIGURE 5-12:
Mission Control in action.

Other open apps (non-full screen)

In addition to the F3 (or older F9) method, you have other ways to summon Mission Control:

>> Swipe up with three fingers on a trackpad.

>> Click the Mission Control icon on the dock.

>> Click the Mission Control icon in Launchpad.

>> Double-tap (but not double-click) on a Magic Mouse or Magic Mouse 2.

TIP

In El Capitan, open windows in Mission Control view are neatly arranged in a grid. In the upper-left portion of the Mission Control screen, you see a thumbnail window representing Dashboard, a repository for handy widgets that reveal the time, the weather, and other information. (This is the case if you've selected the Dashboard As Space option in the Mission Control section of System Preferences.) When you're done with Mission Control, swipe three fingers down on the trackpad or double-tap the Magic Mouse. You can also click the desktop that you want to go to or one of the windows representing the application you want to work on. See the upcoming sections for details.

Working on multiple desktops

To the right of Dashboard on the top row is a thumbnail with a blue border around it. That's the desktop that you're currently working in. Adjacent to that desktop window are windows for any open full-screen apps or documents that you have going at the moment, and any other desktop environments that you may be working in. (The *full-screen* feature enables the app in question to take over the entire screen; click the green gumdrop in the upper left of an app window to go full-screen.)

If you find that the desktop you're working on is too cluttered, drag a window to the top of the screen to enter Mission Control and reveal the Spaces bar.

Now, while you're in the Spaces bar area, move the cursor all the way to the upper-right corner of the screen. Click the + to open a new desktop, which appears as a mini representation inside Mission Control of that new desktop. You can drag an application window or icon to move it to the new space. You must leave Mission Control to see the "real" full-screen desktop.

This begs the question of why you'd want a new desktop in the first place. The answer is simple: You may want to keep only those programs and windows related to a distinct pastime in one dedicated location. Apple once handled this feature in Spaces, which lets you display only the stuff required to tackle the projects at hand. Spaces is now part of Mission Control, too.

So maybe you're an emailin', web-surfin' kind of dude. Maybe you're putting together a family scrapbook. And maybe you're writing a *For Dummies* book in your spare time. Either way, you may want desktops or Spaces dedicated to those vocations.

To remove an extra desktop after your assignment is complete, roll your cursor over the desktop thumbnail in Mission Control until a circled X appears. Click the X to make the desktop go away.

Navigating application windows

Below this top row of desktop thumbnails are all the application windows that you're using at the moment (not those that you were using in full-screen mode). If you move the cursor over one of the visible windows, you see a blue border framing the window. To bring that window front and center while leaving the other Mission Control windows as they are for the moment, press the spacebar on your keyboard. Alternatively, point to the window you want to bring to the front (to work on), and click inside the window or press F9 or F3 (depending on your keyboard).

Mission Control is good for a few other stunts, and these are the default keys that make them happen:

» **F10 (Control+F3 on newer keyboards) or Control+down arrow on the keyboard:** Opens all the windows in the application you're currently using. If you're working on a document in TextEdit, for example, any other open documents in the program are also brought to the front lines.

» **F11 (⌘+F3 on new keyboards):** Hides all windows so that you can admire the stunning photograph you chose for your desktop.

Customizing Misson Control

If you have something the keys you're using for Exposé, open System Preferences, choose Mission Control, and assign alternative keys. And if you have something against keys in general, you can arrange to have the Mac do its thing by moving the cursor to one of the four so-called Hot Corners of the screen. For example, you can make Mission Control appear by moving the cursor to one of the designated corners.

To make a Hot Corner active, click the Hot Corners button inside Mission Control System Preferences. Click any of the four Hot Corner buttons that you see upon doing so, and choose one of the pop-up options for the Hot Corner you've selected to summon application windows, your desktop, Dashboard, Notification Center, or Launchpad. You can also start or disable a screen saver from a Hot Corner, or put the display to sleep from one.

TIP

You can designate your Hot Corner choices (assuming that you want to take advantage of the feature) on the Desktop & Screen Saver pane of System Preferences after selecting the Screen Saver tab and again clicking the Hot Corners button.

Take a gander at some of your other Mission Control options within System Preferences. You can select check boxes to show Dashboard as a Space, to automatically rearrange Spaces based on most recent use, to switch to a Space with open windows for a given application, and to group windows by application. And you can check a box that lets you give more than one display its own assigned Space.

Splitting Windows

One of the key principles for any kind of personal computer is multitasking, the capability to run a number of apps at the same time. With the Split view feature that arrived as part of El Capitan, you can display two running apps side-by-side and have the combination of the two take up the entire screen. Maybe you want your Mail app right next to your Calendar, as shown in Figure 5-13. Or maybe you want to reference the web while choosing a place to eat as you compose a message.

Here's how it works. Click and hold the green full-screen button in the upper left corner window on the first of the two apps you want to display on the screen. While continuing to hold down the green button drag the open app windows to one side of the screen. The app claims half your display.

Now repeat this action with a second app. The second app automatically takes residence in the second half of your Mac display.

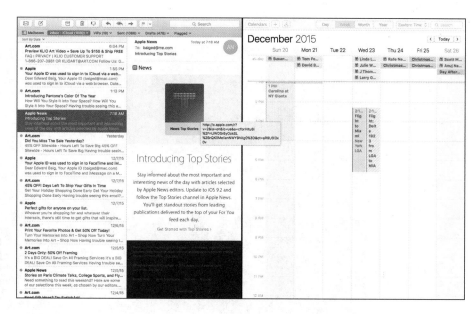

FIGURE 5-13: Displaying apps side-by-side can be convenient.

You can resize these app windows by dragging the mouse pointer to the vertical border between the two so that the pointer turns into a straight line with tiny arrows at either end. You can now drag one of the visible windows in either direction, making it bigger while the other window becomes narrower.

TIP

You can also create a Split view from Spaces bar. Merely drag an app window onto a full-screen thumbnail in the Spaces Bar to make it happen.

To exit Split view altogether, click the green full-screen button again.

Launching Launchpad

If you have an iPhone or iPad, the iOS-inspired Launchpad app launcher on your Mac looks awfully familiar; it's a screen decorated with colorful icons, as shown in Figure 5-14. Click an icon to launch the underlying program. If you have lots of programs on your system, you soon end up with multiple Launchpad screens. The max number of icons displayed on any single Launchpad screen is 35.

To move from one Launchpad screen to another, just swipe with two fingers in either direction. Or click a dot below all the icons; each dot signifies one of your Launchpad screens. You can also move from one Launchpad screen to another (or from one icon to the next) by using the keyboard shortcuts, ⌘+left arrow and ⌘+right arrow.

Launchpad Search field

FIGURE 5-14:
Launchpad is a jumping-off point for your apps.

You can find a single app if it's not immediately visible on the screen by typing its name in the search box provided at the top of each Launchpad page. As you type letters in this search box, Launchpad reduces the number of icons shown to only those that might make a match.

You can also organize icons into folders simply by dragging one icon on top of another. The idea is that you'd put all related icons in the same folder — one for your photography-related programs, say, and another for productivity apps. (See Figure 5-15 for an example.) As you do, Apple takes a stab at what it thinks the folder name should be, but don't fret if you're not happy with the given title. Click the title inside the folder and type an alternative name more to your liking.

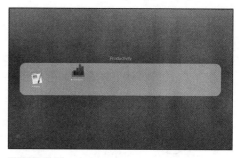

FIGURE 5-15:
Dragging productivity apps into a folder.

System Preferences: Choosing Priorities

You may be wondering what's left. I've already dug inside System Preferences to alter the desktop and screen saver, establish parental controls, muck around with Mission Control, and then some. But as Figure 5-16 shows, you can still do a lot more. I explore some of these options here and some in other chapters.

FIGURE 5-16:
Doing it my way through System Preferences.

Date and time

In System Preferences, you can change the appearance of the clock from a digital readout to an analog face with hands. If you choose a digital clock, you can flash the time separators — or not. You can display the time with seconds, use a 24-hour clock, or both. You can even have the Mac announce the time on the hour, the half hour, or the quarter hour and customize the voice you hear (with male or female voice options). And you can display (or not), the day of the week, as well as the date and time from the menu bar at the top of the screen. Finally, you can choose the time zone or let the Mac set the time zone automatically, using your current location.

TIP

You find Date & Time preferences within System Preferences. Alternatively, you can reach those preferences by clicking the time display at the right end of the menu bar.

Displays

If you are hunky-dory with what your display looks like, feel free to ignore this section. Read on if you're the least bit curious about resolution and what changing it will do to your screen.

Resolution is a measure of sharpness expressed by tiny picture elements, or *pixels*. *Pixels* is such a nice-sounding word that I always thought it would make a terrific name for a breakfast cereal — something like Kellogg's Sugar-Coated Pixels. But I digress.

TECHNICAL STUFF

Apple really does try to make this stuff simple, so you see a default setting that's meant to be best suited for your computer. On a MacBook Pro with Retina display, for example, the resolution that Apple has selected is Best for Retina Display. If you deselect that check box and choose Scaled instead, you see other options for showing off larger text or a setting that shrinks everything so that you have more space on the screen.

By contrast, on a MacBook Air without Retina display, you can leave the default Best for Display option selected. If you go with Scaled, you see resolution choices written out as 1440 x 900, 1280 x 800, 1152 x 720, 1024 x 768, and so on. The first number refers to the number of pixels horizontally, and the second number is the number of pixels vertically. Higher numbers reflect higher resolution, meaning that the picture is sharper and that you can fit more things on the screen. At lower resolutions, the images may be larger but fuzzier (though this depends on your monitor). The resolution options you see in System Preferences vary according to the Mac you have. Lower resolutions also *refresh,* or update, more quickly, though you'll be hard-pressed to see this on most modern monitors. As it happens, the refresh rate doesn't mean boo on iMacs or laptops with LCD or flat-panel displays.

If you select Scaled, an option on newer Macs, instead of seeing the resolution written out as numbers, you will see small thumbnails and descriptors: Larger Text, Default, and More Space.

You can also calibrate the color that a Mac displays. Best advice: Play around with these settings if you must. More often than not, you can leave well enough alone.

If you own an AirPlay–capable display, such as an Apple TV, you can adjust those settings here, too. For more on AirPlay, read Chapter 17.

REMEMBER

This seems as good a place as any to note that Apple provides the flexibility to use multiple displays in any manner you choose. You might go full-screen on two or more displays, or go full-screen on one and go with a desktop view on another. Each display connected to your computer can have its own menu bar, dock, Mission Display bird's-eye view, and so on without your having to worry about configuring each one.

Sound

Ever wonder what the Basso sound is? Or Sosumi or Tink? I'd play them for you if this were an enhanced e-book, but because it isn't, check out these and other sound effects in System Preferences. You'll hear one of them whenever the Mac wants to issue an alert. Sound Preferences is also the place to adjust speaker balance, microphone settings, and pretty much anything else having to do with what you hear on the Mac.

App Store

Apple hasn't forgotten about you just because you've already purchased one of its prized computers. From time to time, the company issues new releases of programs to add features it won't make you pay for, to *patch* (fix) bugs or to thwart security threats.

You can have the Mac check for automatic software updates, including system data files and security updates. If you choose, the Mac will fetch important updates in the background and bother you only when the program update is ready to be installed. You can have updates installed automatically.

Apple also makes system and third-party software updates available through the Mac App Store. In App Store Preferences, you can select an option to automatically download apps purchased on other Macs, as long as you're using the same Apple ID on those other Macs. Through Notification Center, you'll be notified when a system update is available.

Accessibility

Some physically challenged users may require special help controlling the Mac. Choose Accessibility in System Preferences, and click the option that you need assistance with, under such broad categories as Vision, Media, Hearing, and Interacting. Some of these items are visible in Figure 5-17.

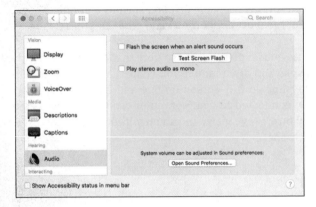

FIGURE 5-17: Accessibility preferences.

Among the options, you can arrange to

>> Turn on the Mac's screen reader, VoiceOver, to hear descriptions of what's on your display. By opening this utility, you can change the default voice.

>> Enhance the contrast or alter the display from black on white to white on black.

>> Flash the screen when an alert sound occurs.

>> Zoom in on the screen to make everything appear larger, or enlarge the mouse pointer if you have trouble seeing it.

>> Use a Slow Keys function to set a delay between when a key is pressed and when the result of that key press is accepted. If you can't easily press several keys at once, use Sticky Keys to press groups of modifier keys (Shift, ⌘, Option, and Control) in a sequence.

Your computer can recognize most Braille displays the moment you plug them in. OS X can recognize wireless Bluetooth displays in Braille. If you or a member of your family has a disability, I recommend checking out these and other potential Accessibility options that can help make your or their experience with the Mac more enjoyable.

You can call upon an Accessibility pane no matter what you're doing on your Mac. On the keyboard, press ⌘+Option+F5 to summon this helpful toolkit or to get to the aforementioned Accessibility preferences.

TIP

Chapter 6

El Capitan: No More Feline Fetish

The late Apple cofounder and CEO Steve Jobs was apparently fond of big cats. Before Apple unleashed Mavericks, Yosemite, and El Capitan, previous versions of OS X software carried such *purr-fect* monikers as Cheetah, Puma, Jaguar, Panther, Tiger, Leopard, Snow Leopard, Lion, and Mountain Lion. (Apple used the code words *Cheetah* and *Puma* internally.)

In choosing to name the latest versions of OS X after Northern California scenery, Apple eschewed Lynx, Siamese, and any other cat names while apparently ushering in a new kitty-free era of Golden State–inspired descriptors.

As strong a release as it is, the name *OS X* just doesn't have the bite that *El Capitan* does, not to mention *Mountain Lion* or any of the other giant-feline nicknames used through the years. But *X* (for *ten*) is the most celebrated use of Roman numerals this side of the Super Bowl. You already know that if you've been using an older Mac. Read the next section and beyond to find out how to climb onto El Capitan.

Upgrading to El Capitan

El Capitan actually represents OS X version 10.11. Apple used to update its operating system every 18 months to 2 years, give or take. The company now plans to bring out a new iteration of its operating-system (OS) software more on a yearly basis, often with a boatload of new features and identified by an increased decimal point. Many of the features are under the hood.

During the year, Apple makes interim tweaks to its operating system. You know when this happens because the OS takes on an extra decimal digit. At this writing, Apple is up to OS X version 10.11.3 (pronounced "ten dot eleven dot three"). I wonder how many features must be added before Apple changes the designation to OS XI.

To check out the version of Mac software running on your system, choose ⇨ About This Mac. Choose ⇨ Software Update to see whether the OS is up to date (and, for that matter, other Mac programs). You are taken to the Mac App Store, where such updates are delivered. You need to click the Update tab once in the store. It's also the only supported way to upgrade the very operating system, should you still own a Mac running Yosemite or some other earlier version of OS X.

If you already own a Mac, the cost of an OS X upgrade is nothing. That's right: free, *nada*, gratis, however you want to put it. Compare free with the $19.99 you had to pay a few years ago to migrate from Lion to Mountain Lion.

To upgrade to El Capitan, your Mac must meet the minimum requirements. Macs from 2009 and on are good to go, as are some models from 2007 and 2008. The general requirement is a Mac running Snow Leopard (version 10.6.8 or later), with at least 2GB of memory and 8.8GB of available storage. You can upgrade from a machine running Leopard, too, but you will have to first migrate to Snow Leopard and then to El Capitan.

Searching with Spotlight

Part of what makes OS X so powerful is *Spotlight,* the marvelous desktop search utility that debuted with Tiger and improved with subsequent versions of OS X. Search is a big deal. A computer isn't much good if you can't easily lay your hands on the documents, pictures, email messages, and programs you need at any particular moment. When most people think about searching on a computer, they probably have Google, Yahoo!, Bing, or some other Internet search engine in mind. Internet search is a big deal too, of course, and I spend some time discussing it in Chapter 9.

But the lines are blurring. So while the searching I have in mind here largely involves the contents of your own system, Spotlight reaches out into cyberspace too. And through enhanced *Spotlight suggestions* that arrived with El Capitan, the feature got a lot smarter. For instance, you can get

- » Sports scores by entering the name of a team

- » Stock results by entering a ticker symbol or company name

- » Web video from services such as You Tube, Vimeo, and Vevo

- » Public transit directions in select areas

- » Weather information for your local area or another city

Over time, Mac users accumulate thousands of photos, songs, school reports, work projects, contacts, calendar entries — you name it. Spotlight helps you locate them in a blink. It starts spitting out search results before you finish typing.

REMEMBER

What's even better is that Spotlight can uncover material in documents and files. That's incredibly useful if you haven't the foggiest idea what you named a file.

You can use Spotlight by following these steps:

1. **Click the magnifying-glass icon in the upper-right corner of the menu bar.**

Or press ⌘ and the spacebar simultaneously. (Select the check box for Spotlight in System Preferences if the shortcut doesn't work.) The Spotlight search box appears.

2. **Enter the word or phrase you want to search for.**

The instant you type the first letter, a window shows up, displaying what Spotlight considers to be the most likely search matches. The search is immediately refined as you type extra keystrokes, as shown in Figure 6-1.

Say you're planning a tropical vacation and remember that your cousin Gilligan emailed you a while back, raving about the beach on some deserted Pacific island. You can open the Mac Mail program and dig for the missive among the dozens that Gilligan sent you. (Evidently, he has a lot of time on his hands.) But it's far simpler and faster to type Gilligan's name in Spotlight.

Or maybe you want to give Gilligan a quick buzz. Without Spotlight, you would probably open your contacts to find your cousin's phone number. The faster way is to type **Gilligan** in Spotlight and then click his name next to Contacts in the results window. Contacts opens, displaying Gilligan's contact page.

Rummaging through your stuff

Spotlight is built into the very fabric of the operating system. Quietly, behind the scenes, Spotlight indexes, or catalogs, most files on the computer so that you can access them at a moment's notice. The index is seamlessly updated each time you add, move, modify, copy, or delete a file.

TECHNICAL STUFF

Moreover, Spotlight automatically rummages through *metadata,* the information about your data. Digital photographs typically capture the following metadata: the camera model used to snap the image, the date, the aperture and exposure settings, whether a flash was used, and so on. If a friend emails you pictures taken with a Sony camera, for example, you can quickly find those images — as opposed to, say, the pictures you took with your own Canon — by entering the search term *Sony.*

TIP

Spotlight is one confident sucker. It boldly takes a stab at what it thinks is the *top hit,* or search result you have in mind. The top hit in Figure 6-1, for Chief Lite Officer, isn't necessarily what I was looking for. So Spotlight's track record is pretty good but not perfect. If it guesses right, click the Top Hit entry or press Return or Enter. That launches the application in question, opens a particular file, or displays the appropriate folder in Finder. As is often the case, you'll find a shortcut. Press ⌘ and Return to launch the top hit.

Spotlight is arguably the zippiest way to launch an application. Just start typing its name in the Spotlight search field, and the application should show up as the top hit after only a few letters (and sometimes a single keystroke). Press Return to launch the program.

As you roll the cursor over the Spotlight list, a window appears to the right of the list, showing the photo, email, or whatever file is the object of your search.

As noted previously, Spotlight isn't always going to get the top hit right, so it also displays a number of other matches — just how many depends on the scope of the search and the size of the Spotlight window. You can stretch or resize that window to see more results, a capability added with El Capitan. You can also move that window around the screen; the next time you summon Spotlight, the window will be where you left it. To return it to its default position, click and hold down on the Spotlight icon in the upper-right corner of the display.

Results are segregated into categories (Applications, Documents, Folders, PDF Documents, Maps, Music, Mail & Messages, Images, Movies, Bookmarks, Suggested Website, and so on). Again, just click an item to launch or open it.

Click at the bottom of the list to search the web as a whole or to narrow your search for your chosen topic (beach, in this case) to the Wikipedia online encyclopedia.

As I mentioned, some searches yield quite a few possible outcomes. That's what the Show All in Finder option at the bottom of the list (not visible in Figure 6-1) is all about. Clicking Show All in Finder doesn't, in fact, show you everything. Most of the time, your screen wouldn't be nearly big enough. Instead, Show All opens a separate Finder window like the one shown in Figure 6-2. As you are about to see, it's a pretty powerful window indeed.

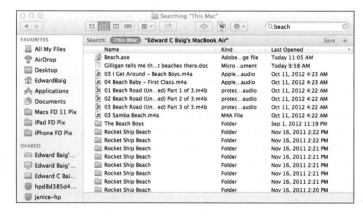

FIGURE 6-2:
Spotlighting the Spotlight results in a Finder window.

TIP

If you get a flood of results in Finder and aren't sure which result is the one you're looking for, Spotlight is a good spot to use the Quick Look feature (see Chapter 3). Just click the Quick Look icon and . . . well, have a quick look at the sorted files until you find the proper one.

You can't search every internal file with Spotlight or, for that matter, display them through Quick Look — at least, not without a software add-on called a *plug-in.* FileMaker databases and Adobe InDesign and QuarkXPress documents are among the files that are in this category.

Intelligent searching

You can customize search results in numerous ways by telling Spotlight where to search and by telling it, in precise detail, the criteria to use in that search.

Look over here

I'll start with where to look. If the contents you're searching for reside on the Mac before your very eyes (as opposed to another on your network), make sure that the Search: This Mac button (refer to Figure 6-2) is the one you choose.

The button to its immediate right changes depending on what you have high-lighted and what you are searching. Back in Figure 6-2, you see All My Files, also displayed under Favorites in the navigation tree on the left. Choosing either option tells Spotlight to look nowhere else but that folder (and its subfolders).

Sometimes, the next button shows any other computer on your network for which you have sharing rights. In Figure 6-2, my MacBook Air is visible even though the Finder window shown resides on my iMac.

The Shared option doesn't appear if no other Mac is on your network with File Sharing turned on. Indeed, you have to set up the computers so that they're in a sharing mood (see Chapter 17 for more).

Search this, not that

Now that Spotlight knows where to set its sights, it's time to tell it exactly what you're looking for. Do you want Spotlight to search for an item by its filename? Or do you want it to hunt for nuggets buried somewhere deep inside those files? Remember that in searching for something, you don't necessarily want to cast too wide a net.

The best way to start (and likely uncover what you're looking for) is to use your own words: "Find the presentation I worked on Tuesday that covered the job selection process," for example, or "Find the images I opened last week."

Of course you can also narrow results by entering as specific a search term as possible right off the bat. As you plan your vacation, typing **beach** will probably summon the email message Gilligan sent you. But because Spotlight finds *all* files or programs that match that text, results may also include Microsoft PowerPoint presentations with a beach theme, pictures of your family by the seashore, and songs on your storage drives sung by the Beach Boys. Typing **Gilligan** and **beach** together helps you fine-tune your search.

TIP

If you know the type of item you're looking for, such as Gilligan's email as opposed to his picture, you can filter the search in another way. Enter the search term followed by *kind*, a colon, and the file type you're looking for, as shown here:

```
Gilligan kind:email
```

Other `kind` keywords include `application`, `contacts`, `images`, `music`, and `presentations`. The `kind` keywords date back to OS X Tiger, when Spotlight was introduced. Such keywords have since been expanded, so now you can use a label such as `author` (as in `author:baig`) or `width` (as in `width:768-1024`).

Here are a few other advanced Spotlight techniques:

» **Boolean query:** You can enter a search phrase using AND, NOT, or OR (in caps, as shown) within parentheses. So you can type **(Mary Ann OR Ginger) NOT Mrs. Howell** to bring up references to either of the first two castaways but not the millionaire's wife. You can substitute a hyphen (-) for NOT, as in *vacation - island,* to indicate that you don't want to see any trip pictures from your tropical adventures.

» **Dates:** By entering **kind:message created 3/11/14**, you can search for an email you sent on March 11 wishing a pal a happy birthday. You can also enter a range of dates, as in **kind:images date 3/11/14 - 3/15/14.**

» **Quotes and phrases:** When you place quotation marks around a particular phrase, Spotlight searches for that exact phrase. If you're looking for a song with *Blue Sky* in it, put quotes around the phrase (as in *"Blue Sky"*) to have Spotlight look for that precise match. Otherwise, Spotlight searches for anything with the words *blue* and *sky* in it.

» **Look Up:** In Chapter 3, I introduce Dictionary as one of the freebie programs that come on a Mac. Thanks to Spotlight, you can get to the word you want the meaning of in a hurry. Type the word you have in mind in the Spotlight search field, and along with all the other results, Spotlight gives you a Look Up option. Click Look Up, and Spotlight takes you to Dictionary.

» **Calculator:** Spotlight can solve a math problem for you without your having to summon the Calculator program. Just type the problem or math equation in the search box, and Spotlight serves up the result. To divide 654 by 7, for example, all you need to do is type **654/7**, and Spotlight provides the answer (93.428571429).

» **Web history:** Spotlight follows you around the web — sort of. That is, it indexes the names of sites you've recently visited. Just enter a search query that relates to a site you want to return to.

Searching your way

As the boss, you can specify which categories appear in Spotlight search results. To do so, open Spotlight Preferences by clicking it at the bottom of the Spotlight results window or in the main System Preferences window. With the Search Results tab selected, you can select or deselect the types of items you want Spotlight to search, as shown in Figure 6-3.

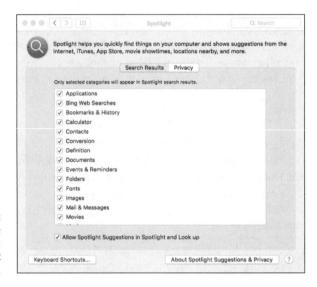

FIGURE 6-3:
Focusing the limelight on Spotlight Preferences.

If you click the Privacy tab, you can prevent Spotlight from searching particular locations. Click the Add button (+) or drag folders or disks into the Privacy pane to let Spotlight know that these items are off-limits. Spotlight removes any associated files from the index and prevents you from searching items in the directory in question.

Using Smart Folders

When you go to all the trouble of selecting specific attributes for your search query, you may want to revisit the search in the future — incorporating the latest information, of course. Let's presume that, when you conducted your Spotlight search, you clicked Show All in Finder. The Finder Spotlight window that appears has a handy Save button at the upper right. And that Save button has an important wrinkle that's worth expanding on.

Traditionally, the files on your computer are organized by their locations on your storage drive. *Smart Folders* change the organizing principle based on the search criteria you've chosen. These folders don't give a hoot where the actual files that match your search criteria reside on the machine; the files stay put in their original locations. You are, in effect, working on *aliases* of (shortcuts to) those files. (See Chapter 7 for more on aliases.)

What's more, behind the scenes, Smart Folders are constantly on the prowl for new items that match your search criteria. In other words, they're updated in real time.

To create a Smart Folder from an existing search, click that Save button in the Finder window (In Figure 6-2, left, the Save button is shown in the upper right.) Alternatively, in Finder, choose File⇨New Smart Folder to create a new Smart Folder.

In the Finder window that appears, click the + to choose criteria for your Smart Folder, such as the kind of file that will be in your folder (Documents in Figure 6-2, left) and the timeframe you're looking at (Last opened date). From here on, your Smart Folder gets updated in real time.

When you click Save, you can specify a name and destination for your newly created Smart Folder, as shown in Figure 6-4, right. If you want, select the Add to Sidebar check box to easily find the Smart Folder you just created.

FIGURE 6-4: Here's the Smart Folder dialog.

TIP

A premade Documents folder in your home folder contains, um, your documents. You can easily access the folder by clicking Documents in the sidebar. But you may want to create a simple Smart Folder containing all the documents you've worked on in the past seven days. Give it an original name — I dunno, something like *What a Hellish Week!*, the name I chose for the example in Figure 6-4. In any case, all your recent stuff is easily at your disposal. Your older documents will pass new arrivals on their way out.

Fiddling with Dashboard Widgets

When you're using your Mac, most of the time you'll likely be engaged with some full-blown (and sometimes pricey) software application — even if you take advantage of a relatively narrow set of features. The wordsmiths among you couldn't subsist without Word or some other big-time word processor. You graphic artists live and breathe Adobe Photoshop. But sometimes, all you want is a snippet of information: the temperature, a stock quote, or a phone number.

That's what a gaggle of mini applications known as *widgets* are all about. Indeed, these lightweight programs might serve a useful and singular purpose, from letting you track an overnight package to finding out whether your favorite team covered the spread. Frankly, you can perform many of these tasks through the web or other programs on your desktop, but widgets add a dose of convenience and flair. Indeed, fronted by large, colorful icons, widgets come at you en masse when you summon the Dashboard, a screen that lies on top of your desktop. Nothing underneath is disturbed.

Before moving on, however, I have to tell you that although the Dashboard is still around (as are widgets), Apple has largely ignored the feature in recent of OS X versions.

To open Dashboard, swipe with three or four fingers to the right on the trackpad or click the Dashboard icon on the dock (if the icon is there). Or press F12 (on older keyboards) or F4 (on newer Apple keyboards) to summon Launchpad and then click the Dashboard icon. Pressing the function key again closes Dashboard. You can exit by clicking the right-pointing arrow inside a circle at the lower-right corner of the screen.

To get you started, Apple supplies a collection of basic widgets: Calculator, Clock, Calendar, and Weather. Another 1700 or so widgets, many of great interest, are available online. You can embark on a widget hunt at www.apple.com/downloads/dashboard. Another way to get there is to right-click (or Control-click) the Dashboard icon on the dock and then choose More Widgets from the contextual menu.

When you call up Dashboard, only the widgets you previously used and haven't closed appear onscreen, right where you left them. The rest of the widgets in your collection are hanging out behind the scenes. Click the + button in the lower-left corner of the screen to access them. If you want to enlist one of these backstage widgets, just click its icon, and it appears on the grand Dashboard. You can also drag one widget on top of another to place the widgets in a folder, just as described in Chapter 5.

If you want to move any of your widgets backstage again, click the dash inside a circle. An X button appears on all the widgets. Click the X on the widget you want to usher out of the way.

Chapter 7

Handling All That Busy Work

In professional football, the skill-position players — quarterbacks, running backs, and wide receivers — get a disproportionate amount of the glory when a team wins and assume most of the blame when they fall on their collective fannies. But any halfway-competent field general will tell you that those in the trenches typically determine the outcome.

Sure, you want to draw up a razzmatazz game plan for your Mac, probably something involving stupendous graphics and spine-tingling special effects — a high-tech flea-flicker, to keep it in the gridiron vernacular. After all, you bought the computer with the intention of becoming the next Mozart, Picasso, or at very least Steve Jobs. (What — you expected Peyton or Eli Manning?)

But for this one itty-bitty chapter, I'm asking you to keep your expectations in check. You have to make first downs before you make touchdowns. Forget heaving Hail Marys down the field. You're better off grinding out yardage the tough way.

In coach-speak, the mission of the moment is to master the computing equivalent of blocking and tackling: basic word processing and the other fundamentals required to get you through your daily routine.

Practice these now. You can pour the Gatorade on my head later.

Form and Function: The Essentials of Word Processing

I'm old enough to recall life before word processors. (Hey, it wasn't *that* long ago.)

I can't possibly begin to fathom how we survived in the days before every last one of us had access to word processors and computers on our respective desks.

Pardon the interruption, but I'm not thrilled with the preceding sentence. It's kind of wordy and repetitious. Permit me to get right to the point.

I can't imagine how any of us got along without word processors.

Thanks. Much more concise.

The purpose of this mini editing exercise is to illustrate the splendor of word processing. Had I produced these sentences on a typewriter (you remember those?) instead of a computer, changing even a few words would hardly seem worth it. I would have to use correction fluid to erase my previous comments and type over them. If things got really messy, or if I wanted to take my writing in a different direction, I'd end up yanking the sheet of paper from the typewriter in disgust and begin pecking away anew on a blank page.

Word processing lets you substitute words at will, move entire blocks of text around with panache, and display characters in various typefaces or specific fonts. You won't even take a productivity hit swapping typewriter ribbons (or swapping out balls with different fonts) in the middle of a project, though (as the next chapter reveals) you will at some point have to replace the ink in your printer.

REMEMBER

Before running out to buy (or subscribe to via Office 365) Microsoft Word (or another industrial-strength and expensive) word processing program for your Mac — and I'm not suggesting that you don't — it's my obligation to point out that Apple includes a respectable word processor with OS X. Actually, it includes two word processors, if you purchased a recent Mac. There's the Pages word processor, and there's TextEdit, which calls the Applications folder home. TextEdit will be your classroom for much of this chapter.

Creating a document

REMEMBER

The first order of business in using TextEdit (or pretty much any word processor) is creating a new document. There's really not much to it. It's about as easy as opening the program itself and then clicking the New Document button in the bottom-left corner of the TextEdit window. The moment you do so, a window with a large blank area in which to type appears, as Figure 7-1 shows.

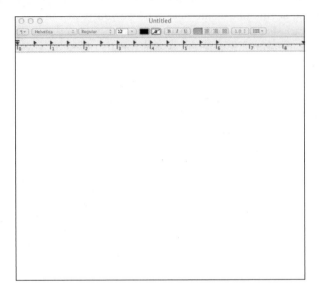

FIGURE 7-1: In the beginning was a blank page.

Have a look around the window. There at the top, you see *Untitled* because no one at Apple is presumptuous enough to come up with a name for your yet-to-be-produced manuscript. I get around to naming (and saving) your stuff later. In my experience, it helps to write first and add a title later, though scholars may disagree.

Notice the blinking vertical line at the upper-left edge of the screen, just below the ruler. That line, called the *insertion point,* might as well be tapping out Morse code for "start typing here."

Indeed, friends, you've come to the most challenging point in the entire word processing experience, and believe me, it has nothing to do with the software. The burden is on you to produce clever, witty, and inventive prose, lest all that blank space go to waste.

Okay, get it? At the blinking insertion point, type with abandon. Something original like

It was a dark and stormy night.

If you type like I do, you may have accidentally produced

It was a drk and stormy nihgt.

Fortunately, your amiable word processor has your best interests at heart. See the dotted red lines below *drk* and *nihgt* in Figure 7-2? Those lines are TextEdit's not-so-subtle way of flagging likely typos, presuming that you've left the default Check Spelling As You Type option activated in TextEdit Preferences. That presumption seems like a safe one, because you're at the beginning of this exercise. (You can also have TextEdit automatically correct your spelling mistakes by checking that option in Preferences, but for the moment, stick to the default.)

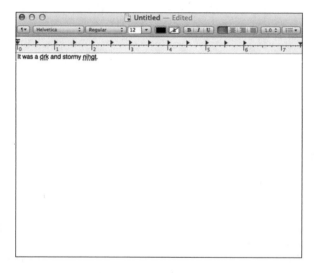

FIGURE 7-2:
Oops! I made some mistakes.

You can address these snafus in several ways. For one, you can use the computer's Delete key to wipe out all the letters to the left of the insertion point. After the misspelled word has been quietly sent to Siberia, you can type over the space more carefully. All traces of your sloppiness disappear.

Delete is a wonderfully handy key. I'd recommend using it to eliminate a single word such as *nihgt*. But in this little case study, you have to repair *drk* too. And using Delete to erase *drk* means sacrificing *and* and *stormy* as well — kind of overkill, if you ask me.

Back to football. It's time to call an audible. Here are a few quick options:

>> Use the left arrow key (on the lower-right side of the keyboard on keyboards lacking a numeric keypad) to move the insertion point to the spot just to the right of the word you want to deep-six. No characters are eliminated when

you move the insertion point that way. Only when the insertion point is where it ought to be do you again hire your reliable keyboard hit man, Delete.

>> Eschew the keyboard and click this same spot to the right of the misspelled word; then press Delete.

>> You need not delete anything. You can merely place the insertion point after the *d* and type an *a*.

TIP

Now try this helpful remedy. Right-click (or Control-click) anywhere on the misspelled word. A contextual menu of suggestions appears, as shown in Figure 7-3. Choose the correct word, and voilà — it instantly replaces the mistake. Be careful in this example not to choose *dork*.

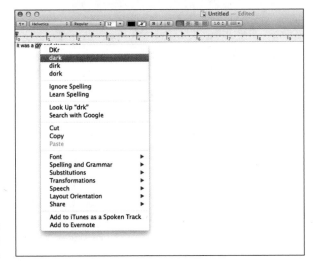

FIGURE 7-3:
I'm no dork. I
fixed it.

Selecting text in a document

You can try another experiment. Double-click a word. See what happens. It's as though you ran a light-blue marker across the word. You've *highlighted*, or *selected*, this word so that it can be deleted, moved, or changed.

Many times, you want to select more than a single word. Perhaps you want to select a complete sentence, a paragraph, or several paragraphs. Here's how to highlight a block of text to delete it:

1. **Using the mouse, point to the block in question.**

2. **Press and hold down the left mouse button or click and hold on the trackpad, and drag the cursor (which bears a slight resemblance to the Seattle Space Needle) across the entire section you want to highlight.**

The direction in which you drag the mouse affects what gets highlighted. If you drag horizontally, a single line is selected. Dragging vertically selects an entire block. You can highlight text also by holding down Shift and using the arrow keys.

3. **Release the mouse button or trackpad when you reach the end of the passage that you want to highlight, as shown with *Once upon a time* in Figure 7-4.**

4. **To wipe out the selected text immediately, press Delete.**

Alternatively, start typing. Your old material is exorcised upon your very first keystroke and replaced with the new characters you type.

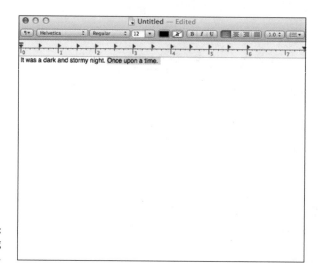

FIGURE 7-4: Highlighting text.

TIP

To jump to a specific line of text, choose Edit⇨Find⇨Select Line. Then enter the pertinent line number, and click Select. Or to jump ahead, say, five lines, add the + symbol, as in +5. To jump backward five lines, enter −5 instead. In both instances, click Select.

To select several pages of text at once, single-click at the beginning portion of the material you want to select and then scroll to the very bottom. While holding down the Shift key, click again. Everything between clicks is highlighted.

TIP

Now suppose that you were overzealous and selected too much text. Or maybe you released the mouse button a bit too soon, so that not enough of the passage you have in mind was highlighted. Just click the selected area to deselect it, and try again.

Here's another screwup: This time, you annihilated text that, upon further review, you want to keep. Fortunately, the Mac lets you perform a do-over. Choose Edit➪Undo Typing. The text is miraculously revived. Variations of this life-saving Undo command appear in most of the Mac programs you encounter. So before losing sleep over some silly thing you did on the computer, visit the Edit menu and check out your Undo options.

Dragging and dropping

In Chapter 3, I discuss dragging and dropping to move icons to the dock. In this chapter, you drag an entire block of text to a new location and leave it there.

TIP

Here's how to drag and drop text with a mouse:

1. **Select a passage in one of the ways mentioned in the preceding section.**

2. **Anywhere on the highlighted area, click and hold down the mouse button.**

3. **Roll the mouse across a flat surface to drag the text to its new destination.**

4. **Release the mouse button to drop off the text.**

   If you hold down the Option key, you can drag a copy, which allows you to duplicate a passage without having to cut and paste (see the next section).

Using a trackpad to select or highlight text takes a different skill.

1. **Press and hold the surface of the trackpad with your index finger.**

2. **Then, without lifting your index finger, drag your middle finger along the surface to select the material you have in mind.**

3. **Once selected, remove your finger.**

4. **Place the cursor anywhere over the selected text and again press and hold the surface of the trackpad.**

5. **Drag the text to the new destination.**

6. **When it's in the correct spot, release your finger to drop off the text.**

You aren't restricted to dragging and dropping text in the program you're working in. You can lift text completely out of TextEdit and place it in programs such as Word, or Pages — Apple's own word processing program for (among other things) producing spiffy newsletters and brochures.

Alternatively, if you know that you'll want to use a text block in another program at some point in the future — you just don't know when — drop it directly onto the Mac Desktop (see Figure 7-5) and call upon it whenever necessary. Text copied to the Desktop is shown as an icon and named from the text in the beginning of the selection you copied. Moving text in this manner to an external program or the Desktop constitutes a Copy command, not a Move command, so the lifted text remains in its original location.

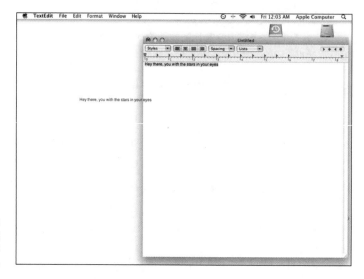

FIGURE 7-5:
Dropping text on the Desktop.

Cutting and pasting

Cutting and pasting lifts material from one spot and moves it elsewhere without leaving anything behind. (In the typewriter era, you literally cut out passages of paper with scissors and pasted them onto new documents.)

After selecting your source material, choose Edit⇨Cut (or press the keyboard alternative ⌘+X). To paste to a new location, first navigate there, click the spot and then choose Edit⇨Paste (or press ⌘+V). If you want to match the style of the text you're moving, click Paste and Match Style instead.

REMEMBER

The Cut command is easily confused with the Copy command (⌘+C). As the name suggests, the latter copies selected text that can be pasted somewhere else. Cut clips text out of its original spot.

The very last thing you copied or cut is temporarily sheltered on the Clipboard. It remains there until it's replaced by newer material that you copy or cut.

If you can't remember what you last placed on the Clipboard, open Finder and choose Edit⇨Show Clipboard.

Changing the font

When typewriters were in vogue, you were pretty much limited to the typeface of the machine. Computers being computers, you can alter the appearance of individual characters and complete words effortlessly. I'll start with something simple.

In TextEdit, take a gander at the tiny *B, I,* and *U* buttons on the toolbar above the ruler. They stand for *Bold, Italic,* and *Underline.* (You see these same choices on the Font submenu, located on the Format menu in TextEdit.) Try these buttons now. Click the I, and highlighted text becomes *text.* Next, try B for Bold. Highlighted text becomes **text**. Now try U for Underline. Highlighted text becomes text.

I recommend using keyboard shortcuts in this instance. Just before typing a word, try pressing ⌘+I for *italics* or ⌘+B for **bold**. When you want to revert to normal type, just press those respective keyboard combinations again.

Making words bold or italic is the tip of the proverbial iceberg. You may want to experiment with other choices on the Font menu (found in the Format menu). You can make text take on a faint tint (Outline). You can change the kerning (spacing), ligatures (the stroke that joins adjacent letters, according to the Dictionary on the Mac), baselines, or character shape.

For a more dramatic statement, you might dress up documents with different *fonts,* or typefaces.

Open the Format menu, and choose Font⇨Show Fonts. The window in Figure 7-6 appears. You can change the typeface of any highlighted text by clicking a font listed in the pane labeled Family. Choices carry names such as Arial, Chalkboard, Courier, Desdemona, Helvetica, Papyrus, Stencil, and Times New Roman.

Unless you wrote your graduate thesis on *fontomology* (don't bother looking up the word; it's my invention), no one on the *For Dummies* faculty expects you to have a clue about what any of the aforementioned fonts looks like. I sure don't. Cheating is okay. Peek at your document to see how highlighted words in the text change after you click different font choices.

As usual, another way to view different fonts is available. In the lower-left corner of the Fonts window, click the icon that looks like a gear or cog, and choose Show Preview from the menu that appears. You'll be able to inspect various font families and typefaces in the preview pane that appears above your selection. To revert to the status quo, click the gear icon again and then choose Hide Preview from the menu that appears (see Figure 7-7).

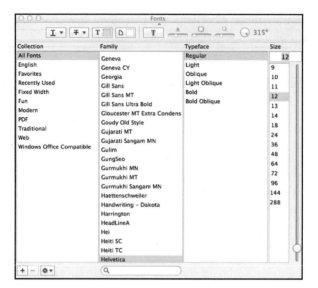

FIGURE 7-6:
A fonts
funhouse.

Hide/show font preview   Previewing your font

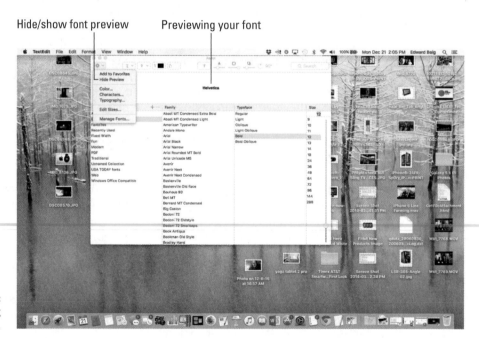

FIGURE 7-7:
Previewing
your fonts.

TECHNICAL STUFF

You can also preview the type size of your chosen font, as measured by standard units called *points*. In general, 1 inch has 72 points.

Revealing the Font Book

You likely have more than 100 fonts on your computer, if not a lot more. Some fonts were supplied with TextEdit; others arrived with other word processing programs. You may have even gone on a font hunt and added more yourself from the Internet. At the end of the day, you may need help managing and organizing them.

That's the purpose behind an OS X program called *Font Book,* located in the Applications folder. It's shown in Figure 7-8. Think of Font Book as a gallery that shows off all your finest fonts. Indeed, fonts here can be grouped into *font collections,* shown in the left pane. Choices include English, Fixed Width, Fun, Modern, PDF, Traditional, and Web. The Traditional collection, for example, assembles classic fonts with names such as Baskerville, Copperplate, and Didot.

Add fonts   Disable selected fonts

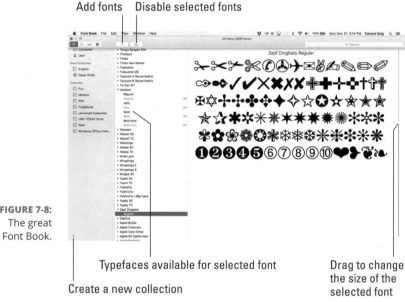

FIGURE 7-8:
The great Font Book.

Typefaces available for selected font

Drag to change the size of the selected font

Create a new collection

You can create your own font collections by clicking the + at the bottom-left corner of the screen, or by choosing File ⇨ New Collection and typing a name for the collection. Then just drag fonts from the Font column into your new collection.

By clicking a name in the Font column, you can sample what your font of choice looks like in the pane on the right. Drag the slider (labeled in Figure 7-8) to the right of that pane to adjust the type size of the fonts you're sampling.

ALL IN THE FONTS

Admit it — you're curious about the genealogy of the font named Zapf Dingbats. Me, too. For that matter, you may be wondering about the roots of other fonts on the system. Hey, it's your computer; you have a right to know. At the top of the display, click the circled *i* button (or press the keyboard shortcut ⌘+I), and the Font Book window reveals all, including the full name of a font, the languages in which it's used, and any copyright and trademark information. As best I can tell, Zapf Dingbats wasn't created by Archie Bunker. If you want to, choose Preview➪Hide Font Info when you're done.

TIP

If you're like most mortals, you'll use a small set of fonts in your lifetime, although the more adventurous among you may find yourself adopting fonts with funky names such as Ayuthaya and Zapf Dingbats. (See the nearby "All in the fonts" sidebar.)

You can disable the fonts that you rarely or never use by clicking the little box with the check mark above the Font list (labeled in Figure 7-8). The word *Off* appears next to the font's newly dimmed name. If you change your mind, click that box again (it no longer has a check mark) or choose Edit➪Enable *font you disabled.* Don't worry if you come across an application that requests a disabled font. OS X will open the font on your behalf and shut it down when you close the program.

If you want to add fonts to the machine, click the adjacent + button and browse to the font's location on your computer. You can also open new fonts you've downloaded or purchased with the Font Book application simply by double-clicking them.

TIP

When a yellow triangle appears next to a name in the Font list, duplicates of that font family are installed. To eliminate doubles, select the font in question and choose Edit➪Look for Enabled Duplicates. Copies that aren't in use are automatically deactivated.

Changing colors

Too often, we get bogged down in the black-and-white of things. But the Mac is about jazzing things up, with pizzazz and color. And so it goes inside TextEdit, making your documents sing with different hues.

Select the text you want to add a dash of color to, and choose Format➪Font➪Show Colors. Alternatively, use the keyboard shortcut Shift+⌘+C, or click the *color well* on the toolbar (which is likely employing black to start) and click Show Colors.

A Colors window appears inside your document, fronted by a circle with different hues inside it. Click anywhere in the circle to go with your preferred color. At the top of the Colors window, you also see small icons. Click one of them to move from the color-circle view to a grayscale slider or to a color palette, spectrum, or crayon view. When you click any of the various color choices, you see a bar in the window in the color that you've just selected. You also see your chosen color reflected in the color well. If you click the color well, a grid with more color options appears. Click a color inside that window to make a new color selection.

Click the other icons in the Colors window for different views on adding color, including one that shows colored pencils.

Printing fonts

You can also preview a font family (or families) in Font Book by printing them. You can display these fonts in three ways, depending on which of the three Report Type options you choose from a pop-up menu. The menu appears after you choose File ⇨ Print. (If you don't see the menu, click the Show Details button in the Printer dialog.) These Report Type options are

- **Catalog:** Numbers and letters in the sample fonts are printed alphabetically (in uppercase and lowercase). Drag the Sample Size slider to alter the size of the sample text.

- **Repertoire:** All the font glyphs or special symbols are printed in a grid. This time, you can drag a Glyph Size slider.

- **Waterfall:** Waterfall is the Niagara Falls of font printing. An entire font alphabet is printed in increasingly larger sizes until no more room exists on the printed page. You can choose the sample sizes of the text.

Formatting your document

Fancy fonts aren't the only way to doll up a document. You have important decisions to make about proper margins, paragraph indentations, and text tabs. And you must determine whether lines of text should be single- or double-spaced (or in some other interval, such as one-and-a-half spaces).

Okay, you're back in the TextEdit classroom. Set your margins and tab stops by dragging the tiny triangles along the ruler.

Just above the ruler, almost all the way to the right side, is a pop-up menu with a number in it, showing 1.0 by default. This is the Line and Paragraph Spacing pop-up menu. Leaving it at 1.0 separates the lines in the way you're reading them in this paragraph: single-spaced.

If you go with 2.0, the line jumps down to here, and the next line

jumps down to here. Yep, that's double-spaced.

You can also space lines somewhere between 1 and 2 lines, like say, 1.5 lines.

TECHNICAL STUFF

The control freaks among you (you know who you are) may want to choose Spacing⇨Show More, which displays the dialog shown in Figure 7-9. Now you can precisely determine the height of your line, the way the paragraphs are spaced (that is, the distance from the bottom of a paragraph to the top of the first line in the paragraph below), and other parameters, according to the points system.

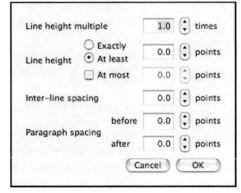

FIGURE 7-9:
When it has to look just like this.

Here are other tricks that make Text-Edit a capable writing companion:

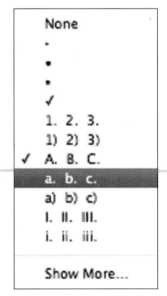

>> **Aligning paragraphs:** After clicking anywhere in a paragraph, choose Format⇨Text, and choose an alignment (Left, Center, Justify, or Right). Play around with these choices to determine what looks best. You can also click the corresponding alignment buttons above the ruler.

>> **Writing from right to left:** I suppose this one's useful for writing in Hebrew or Arabic. Choose Format⇨Text⇨Writing Direction and then click Right to Left. Click again to go back the other way, or choose Edit⇨Undo Set Writing Direction.

>> **Locating text:** You can use the Find command on the Edit menu to uncover multiple occurrences of specific words and phrases and replace them individually or collectively.

>> **Producing lists:** Sometimes, the best way to get your message across is to put it in list form, kind of like what I'm doing here. By clicking the Lists pop-up menu — it's all the way to the right above the ruler — you can present a list with bullets, numbers, Roman numerals, uppercase or lowercase letters, and more, as shown in Figure 7-10. Click Show More for more options. As an alternative,

FIGURE 7-10:
Formatting a list.

you can summon the list by clicking Format⇨List. Keep clicking the choices until you find the one that makes the most sense.

>> **Creating tables:** Then again, you may want to emphasize important points by using a table or chart. Choose Format⇨Table. In the dialog that appears (see Figure 7-11), you can select the number of rows and columns you need for your table. You can select a color background for each cell by clicking the Cell Background pop-up menu and choosing Color Fill, and then choosing a hue from the palette that appears when you click the rectangle to the right. You can drag the borders of a row or a column to alter its dimensions. You can also merge or split table cells by selecting the appropriate cells and then clicking the Merge Cells or Split Cells button.

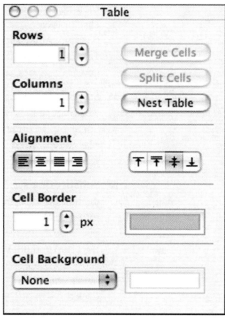

FIGURE 7-11:
Creating a table.

>> **Using smart quotes:** Publishers sometimes try to fancy up books by using curly quotation marks rather than straight ones. Somehow, curly is smarter than straight. Whatever. To use smart quotes in the document you're working on, choose TextEdit⇨Edit⇨Substitutions⇨Smart Quotes. To use curly quotes in all docs, choose TextEdit Preferences, click New Document, and select the Smart Quotes check box. If you've already selected smart quotes but want to go with straight quotes inside a document you're working on, press Control+' (apostrophe) for a single quotation mark or Control+Shift+' (apostrophe) for a double quotation mark.

>> **Converting to smart dashes:** You can automatically convert double hyphens (--) to em dashes (—) as you type. Choose TextEdit⇨Edit⇨Substitutions⇨ Smart Dashes. Head to TextEdit Preferences to use smart dashes in all your written masterpieces. Pressing Option+- (hyphen) on the keyboard gives you an en dash (–).

>> **Using smart links:** You can set things up so that any time you type an Internet address (see Chapter 9) in a document, it acts as a link or jumping point that takes you to that web page. Choose TextEdit⇨Edit⇨Substitutions⇨Smart Links to use a smart link in the document you're working on. Or visit TextEdit

Preferences, click New Document, and select the Smart Links check box to make this feature permanent.

>> **Making transformations:** You can decide after the fact to make text uppercase or lowercase or to capitalize the first letter of every word that makes up a passage. After selecting the text you want to transform in this manner, choose TextEdit⇨Edit⇨Transformations and then choose Make Upper Case, Make Lower Case, or Capitalize.

>> **Starting speaking:** Your loquacious Mac can read text aloud. Select what you want read to you, choose TextEdit⇨Edit⇨Speech, and then choose Start Speaking. To end the filibuster, choose Stop Speaking. You can also tell your Mac to type what you say, as I explain in the upcoming section, "Speaking what's on your mind."

>> **Substituting symbols and text:** You can type **(r)** to summon ® or type **(c)** to produce ©, but you can also build similar shortcuts on your own: perhaps (PC) for *Personal & Confidential* or (FYI) for *For Your Information.* I created one for my byline so that when I type **(ECB)**, I get *Edward C Baig* instead. Such shortcuts go beyond TextEdit; they also work in the Mail, Messages, Notes, and Safari applications. To see which shortcuts Apple has created on your behalf — or to configure your own shortcuts — choose System Preferences⇨Keyboard⇨Text. Click the + to add your own shortcuts.

>> **Conversing with Calendar:** TextEdit automatically detects dates and times when you move a pointer over them in a document. And when it does, a pop-up menu appears, allowing you to create a new event in the Mac's Calendar program (see Chapter 3) or to show the date in question in Calendar. TextEdit can recognize a specific date and time, such as *March 11* or *5 p.m.,* but it can also figure out the meaning of text such as *next Tuesday* or *tomorrow.* To turn on date and time recognition for the document you're working in, choose Edit⇨Substitutions⇨Data Detectors. To do it for all documents, select the option in TextEdit Preferences.

>> **Conversing with contacts:** Data detection also works with contacts and addresses. When you hover your cursor over an address in a TextEdit document, the pop-up menu that appears lets you create or add the address to your Contacts, display a map of the location (inside Safari, which opens or the Maps app), or show the address in blown-up text. Simply make sure that data detection is turned on (see the preceding paragraph for instructions). Now aren't you impressed by all that your freebie Mac word processor can do?

TIP

You can even do more with TextEdit. If you're using a trackpad, try this neat trick: Pinch or unpinch (as I like to call it) to zoom in or out of the characters on the screen.

If you want to use TextEdit as a type of Mac equivalent of the simple Notepad program in Microsoft Windows, choose Format⇨Make Plain Text. Doing so removes the ruler and the visible text formatting tools.

Speaking what's on your mind

In OS X, you can speak wherever you might otherwise type, be it inside TextEdit or in numerous other apps. To turn on this Dictation feature, press the function (fn) key on your keyboard twice or choose Edit⇨Start Dictation. (You can choose other shortcuts in Dictation & Speech preferences.) Dictation isn't always perfect, but in a relatively noise-free environment, it should do just fine. And make sure your Mac has an appropriate microphone or other input device.

WARNING

When you dictate, your words are recorded and sent to Apple, where everything gets converted to text (ideally, with minimal errors). But other information is also sent to Apple, including your first name, nickname, and contacts. The idea is to help Apple understand what you meant to say, thus improving the accuracy. If you find this arrangement troubling, you can turn off Dictation. In System Preferences, click Dictation & Speech; then click Off in the Dictation section. Apple deletes your user data and any recent stuff that you recorded.

TIP

If you select Use Enhanced Dictation, you can use dictation without Internet access and also get continuous dictation with live feedback. However, you must download a 1.2 GB file.

As noted in Chapter 5, you can also restrict access to Dictation in parental controls.

Saving your work

You've worked so darn hard making your document read well and look nice that I'd hate to see all your efforts go to waste. Yet in the cruel world of computers, that's precisely what could happen if you don't take a second to save your file. A second is all it takes to save a file — but you can lose everything just as fast.

Stable as it is, the Mac is a machine, for goodness sakes, and not immune to power failures or human foibles. Odd as it may seem, even tech authors pound a calamitous combination of keys from time to time.

All the work you've done so far exists in an ethereal kind of way, as part of *temporary* memory. (See Chapter 2.) Don't let the fact that you can see something on your computer monitor fool you. If you shut down your computer, or if it unexpectedly crashes (it's been known to happen even on Macs), any unsaved material resides nowhere but in another type of memory: your own.

So exactly where do you save your work? Why, on the *Save sheet,* of course (see Figure 7-12). It slides into view from the top of your document when you choose File⇨Save or press the keyboard combo ⌘+S.

Do you want to keep this new document "Untitled"?

You can choose to save your changes, or delete this document immediately. You can't undo this action.

Save As: Dark and Stormy

Tags:

Where: ✏ TextEdit — iCloud

Delete   Cancel   Save

FIGURE 7-12: Everyone needs a file saver.

Way back at the beginning of this chapter, I mention that Apple wouldn't dare name a file for you except to give it the temporary moniker *Untitled.* Well, this is your big chance to call the file something special by filling in a title in the Save As field. Go ahead and name it something like Dark and Stormy.

When you click the Save button, the contents of Dark and Stormy are assigned to a permanent home on your Mac's hard drive or SSD (solid-state drive), at least until you're ready to work on the document again.

But there's more: You also get to choose the folder in which to stash the file. In Figure 7-12, you see the default option to save the file to iCloud, Apple's online locker. Doing so lets you access the document from any computer connected to the Internet. You need an iCloud account for this option, of course, but that account is free.

If you'd rather keep the file closer to home, you can save it to your Documents folder or any other folder on your computer. You can choose among several other possible destinations, as becomes clear when you click the arrows in the Where field, revealing various drop-down options. You can stuff your manuscript in any existing folder or subfolder in the sidebar or create one from scratch by clicking the New Folder button and giving the folder a name.

TECHNICAL STUFF

Confession time: I've been holding back. When you christened your opus Dark and Stormy, little did you know that you were actually giving it a slightly longer name: `Dark and Stormy.rtf`. The little suffix, or *extension,* stands for *Rich Text Format,* one of the file format types that the Mac makes nice with. You could have saved the file as a Rich Text document or in various Microsoft Word formats instead (with the `.doc` or `.docx` extension). Or you could have chosen HTML, the language of the web. (I discuss the Internet in see Chapter 9.) Apple doesn't want to bog you down with all this information, so you won't see these extensions routinely.

TIP

OS X in all its wisdom provides a safety net for saving. In other words, you can now save TextEdit documents automatically. Even with autosave protections, it's a good idea to save often as you work on documents. You just never know what will happen.

Securing, copying, and otherwise managing your file

If you click the name of a document in the title bar, you see an option to lock the file or to prevent you or anyone else from making inadvertent changes. As a separate protective measure, you can prevent a file from being edited, period. Choose Format⇨Prevent Editing. (You can undo this, of course.)

Let me point you to other options on the File menu: Duplicate, Rename, Move To, and Revert To. If you choose Rename, for example, you can save a document under a new name.

The Rename option isn't the only one that's self-explanatory. You can choose Move To and Duplicate to move the file to another folder or destination or to duplicate or make a copy of it.

Choosing Revert To lets you browse the last-opened version of the file in question or to browse all versions of the file (which summons all the earlier iterations of the file, presented in an interface similar to the Time Machine feature, which I address in Chapter 12).

Tagging a File

You also have the option to tag a file — a potentially indispensable feature that makes it easy to find a document you've created or to organize all your files by project. I created a Wiley tag for the files I produced for this book, for example.

You can tag iCloud documents or documents that reside on the Mac. Tags work with other types of files, too, including pictures. When you click a tag name in Finder, you can find the files you've assigned to that tag. You can also search for a tag in the Finder search box.

So how do you assign a tag? When you save a file (as discussed earlier in this chapter), you see a Tags field in the Save dialog that appears (refer to Figure 7-12). Clicking in that field summons a list of any recent tags you've set up, along with color-coded tab options that Apple supplies. (Under the tabs list, click Show All if you don't see those options.) Click one or more of the tags to assign those tags to your file. You can assign multiple tags as well. I might tag a photo file used in this book as a Mac FD pic and also put it in a separate Wiley tag. If any of your current tag names is no longer relevant, you can give it a new tag name. Of course, any existing files that have the old tag name will now get the new tag moniker.

That's not the only way to assign or create a new tag. In Finder, select a file and click the Tags button (see Figure 7-13). Then either click an existing tag name or type a new name. Tags appear in the sidebar, with the most recently used tags appearing at the top.

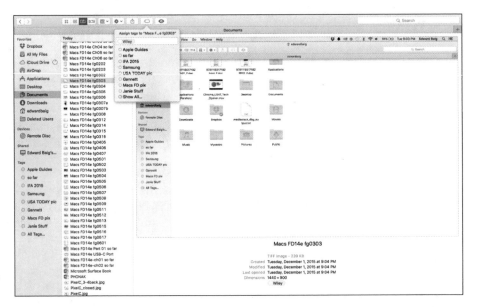

FIGURE 7-13:
Tag your
(file is) it.

Making Revisions

Your Dark and Stormy file is safe and sound on your hard drive, on your SSD, or in the iCloud. But after you down a few chill pills overnight, you have a brand-new outlook on life in the morning. You're past your brooding period. You want to rework your inspiration's central theme and give it a new name: Bright and Sunny.

Back to TextEdit you go. To rename a document, merely click its title in the title bar of the document. The existing title appears highlighted in blue in a Name field. Type your new name over the old name to make the change. Alternatively, choose Rename under the File menu. The title again gets highlighted in blue, except that this time it remains in the title bar of the document. As before, type the new name over the old one to complete the name change. Simple, right?

Because your document is only as permanent as the last time you saved it, remember to save it early and often as you make revisions, even taking into account the fact that some autosaving magic is at work in the background. Besides, TextEdit isn't the only program in which you'll want to save your work, so I figure it's a good idea to get you into the habit; you never know when disaster might intervene. Along the way, you can rename your best seller as I told you: by clicking the title inside the new document and by typing a new name where the old name was. You'll still have the previous version under the old name.

TIP

As always, your Mac tries to assist you in these matters. The computer makes the assumption that if you worked on a document yesterday or the day before, you may want to take another stab at it today. And to prevent you, Oh Prolific One, from having to strain too hard digging for a document you may want to edit, choose File⇨Open Recent. Your freshest files will turn up in the list. Just click the name of the document you want to revisit.

Perhaps the fastest way to find a file you want to revise is to use the Spotlight tool. Choose Spotlight by single-clicking its icon in the upper-right corner of the screen, and type the name of the manuscript that requires your attention. Chapter 6 explains how Spotlight works in more detail.

It goes without saying that making revisions goes a lot further than just typing a new name for the document. So go crazy; tackle the project with abandon. Make up down or down up. What was Dark and Stormy yesterday is Bright and Sunny today.

Taking Out the Trash

Like much else in life, documents — if not entire folders — inevitably outlive their usefulness. The material grows stale. It takes on a virtual stench. It claims storage space you could put to better use.

Yes, it's time to take out the trash. Here's how:

» Use the mouse to drag the document's icon above the Trash icon on the dock. Release the mouse button when the Trash icon turns black.

» As usual, you have a keyboard alternative: ⌘+Delete. Or you can choose File⇨Move to Trash.

You'll know that you have stuff in the Trash because the icon shows crumpled paper. And just like you do with your real-life trash bin, you want to empty it from time to time, lest your neighbors complain.

To do so, choose Finder⇨Empty Trash or press ⌘+Shift+Delete. A warning pops up (see Figure 7-14), reminding you that after your trash is gone, it's gone for good. (Even then, you may be able to get it back by purchasing data-recovery software or hiring an expert.)

FIGURE 7-14:
Think before trashing.

Never Mind: Retrieving What You've Tossed

It's pretty easy to pull something out of the Trash, provided that you didn't take that last Draconian measure and choose the Empty Trash command. It's less smelly or embarrassing than sticking your hands in a real trash bin. Click the Trash icon on the dock to peek at its contents. If you find something worth saving after all, drag it back onto the Desktop or to the folder where it used to reside. Even easier: right-click or Control-click the trashed file name and choose Put Back.

If you take advantage of Apple's Time Machine (see Chapter 12), you can also retrieve the file through the backup service.

Making an Alias

You can create an *alias* of a file to serve as a shortcut for finding it, no matter where it's buried on your Mac. To understand what an alias is, it helps to understand what it's not. It's not a full duplicate of a file. (If you want to create a full duplicate, press ⌘+Shift+D or choose File⇨Duplicate.)

Instead, you're effectively copying the file's icon, not the file itself, meaning that you're barely using any disk space. Clicking an alias icon summons the original file no matter where it's hanging out on the computer — even if you've renamed the file.

Why create an alias in the first place? Perhaps you're not sure where to place a file that you can easily justify putting in any number of folders. If you have a document titled Seven Dwarfs, it may belong in a folder for Snow White, one for Bashful, one for Doc, and so on. Because the Mac lets you create multiple aliases, you can effectively place the file in each of those folders (even though you and I know that it really resides in only one place).

To create an alias, highlight the original icon and press ⌘+L or choose File ➪ Make Alias. You can also drag an icon out of its file window or to another location inside the window while you hold down the Option and ⌘ keys.

As you can see in Figure 7-15, the alias looks like a clone of the original icon, except that the alias suffix is added to its name and a tiny arrow appears in the lower-left corner of the icon. Clicking either icon — the original or the clone — brings up the same file.

FIGURE 7-15:
In this example, the alias icon sits to the right of the original file.

TIP

If you want to find the location of the original file, highlight the alias icon and choose File ➪ Show in Enclosing Folder.

To get rid of an alias, drag it to the Trash. Doing so doesn't delete the original file. If you deleted the original file separately, however, the alias can't bring it back.

Chapter 8

Printing and Scanning

Computers are supposed to bring relief to pack rats. The idea that you can store documents and files in their electronic state on your hard drive or solid-state drive (SSD), or in iCloud — thus reducing physical clutter — has widespread appeal. A few trees may breathe a sigh of relief, too.

There's been a lot of buzz over the years surrounding the potential for a paperless society. Perhaps pulp-industry executives, who've seen paper production decline of late, are beginning to lose sleep over the possibility.

But paper isn't going away any time soon. Fact is, you want to pick up something tangible for your own edification and convenience. And you want hard copies to show people. It's better to hand Grandma printed pictures of the newborn than to pull out a computer (or other gizmo) to show off your latest bundle of joy. What's more, even in the age of email and electronic filings, you still usually print documents and reports for employers, teachers, financial institutions, and (sigh) the Internal Revenue Service.

Which reminds me: Despite wonderful advances in state-of-the-art printers, the counterfeiters among you will find no helpful hints in this chapter about printing money.

Choosing a Printer

What are those state-of-the-art printers? So kind of you to ask. Today's printers generally fall into two main camps: *inkjet* and *laser,* with the differences coming down to how ink makes its way onto a page. (Yes, you can find other variations, especially for photo printing — *dye sublimation* or *dye sub,* anyone?) Printers vary by speed, features, resolution (sharpness), output quality, and price. And at least in some circles, 3D printing is all the rage, though as of this writing not quite a mass market option for a home consumer.

Popular models are produced by Brother, Canon, Epson, Hewlett-Packard, Lexmark, and Samsung, but you can buy printers from a host of competitors.

Believe it or not, you can still find an el-cheapo, hand-me-down *daisy-wheel* or *dot-matrix* printer on eBay and elsewhere (and some manufacturers still make new ones that work with modern Macs). But these so-called *impact printers* are most definitely *not* the state-of-the-art kind that I have in mind, and the assumption here is that you aren't using such a printer.

Inkjets

Inkjet printers consist of nozzles that squirt droplets of ink onto a sheet of paper. Models may be equipped with a single black cartridge and a single color cartridge, or they may contain several color cartridges. (Where's that magenta cartridge when I need it?)

Most of you, I suspect, will end up with inkjet printers. They're the least expensive to buy, with some rock-bottom models costing as little as $30.

WARNING

Bargains aren't always what they seem, however. The cost of ownership of inkjet printers can be exorbitant. You must replace pricey ($30 or so) ink cartridges on a routine basis — more often if you spit out lots of photographs of your pet kitten Fluffy. So an inkjet printer's cost per page tends to be considerably higher than that of its laser cousins.

Having said that, inkjets generally are the most flexible bets for consumers, especially those who demonstrate shutterbug tendencies. Besides using standard-size 8½ -by-11-inch paper, some inkjet models can produce fine-looking 4-by-6-inch color snapshots on glossy photographic paper. (Photo paper, I'm obligated to point out, is expensive too.)

Granted, black text produced on an inkjet won't look nearly as crisp as the text produced by a laser, though it can be quite decent just the same. Under certain conditions, some inks bleed or smudge. But for the most part, the quality of inkjets is perfectly acceptable for producing, say, family newsletters or brochures for your burgeoning catering business. And if you stick to better-quality paper, what you print might even rival consumer laser printers (see the next section).

Lasers

It's somewhat remarkable that a focused laser beam can produce such excellent-quality graphics. Then again, if lasers can correct nearsightedness and can be used to perform other medical miracles, perhaps printing isn't such a major deal after all.

Laser printers use a combination of heat, toner, and static electricity to produce superb images on paper. Such printers, especially color models, used to fetch thousands of dollars. To be sure, you'll still find prices for some models in the stratosphere. But entry-level color lasers now cost less than $100 in some cases.

However affordable they have become in recent years, lasers still generally command a premium over inkjets, but they're far more economical over the long term. Toner cartridges are relatively cheap and don't need to be replaced very often. A highly efficient laser may cost a couple of cents per page to operate — a small fraction of what an inkjet costs to run.

TIP

Some newer smart printers from certain manufacturers can automatically reorder ink or toner when you're running low, using services such as Amazon Dash Replenishment.

Lasers remain staple printers in corporate offices. Businesses appreciate the photo copier–like output and the fact that lasers can handle high-volume printing loads at blistering speeds. The machines typically offer more paper-handling options as well. On the other hand, they consume far more electricity than most inkjets do, making them less "green."

All-in-ones

Printers print, of course. But if your Mac is the centerpiece of a home office, you probably have other chores in mind: copying and scanning, for example, and faxing too. An *all-in-one* model, otherwise known as a *multifunction* printer, can provide some combination of these tasks. Most multifunction workhorses in homes are inkjet-based, but in home offices, it's common to find multifunction lasers.

It's cheaper to buy a single multifunction device than several stand-alone devices. That lone machine takes up less space, too.

Down side: If your fax, copier, or scanner goes on the fritz, you may also have to live without a printer while the multifunction unit is under repair.

Connecting and Activating a Printer

Almost all printers compatible with OS X — and that includes most printers sold today — connect to your Mac through the Universal Serial Bus (USB) port that I discuss in Chapter 2 or through wireless options. So much for unretiring the printer in the attic that connects through what's called a *parallel* port.

Just make sure your printer includes a USB cable (or buy one if it doesn't) before you purchase your printer. After you get home, here's how you set up a printer with a USB connection:

1. **Plug the printer into an AC wall jack.**

2. **If you're not exploiting a wireless connection, plug the USB cable into the USB port on the Mac, and make sure that it's connected snugly to the printer itself.**

3. **Turn on your printer.**

   The thing is warmed and ready for action.

OS X big-heartedly assembled most of the software drivers required to communicate with modern printers. Chances are that yours is one of them. You still may want to install the software that came with the printer. OS X makes sure that your printer driver is as fresh as can be by periodically checking for updates; these updates show up as a software update inside the Mac App Store. If for some reason your printer falls through the cracks with regard to updates, visit the printer manufacturer's website. If you try to print and don't see your printer listed among your output options, as I explain in the next section, that's a pretty good sign that you need to install your printer drivers yourself.

As I mentioned, the good news is that not all printers require a cord, that is, other than the cord that plugs into a power outlet. Again, most printers these days are compatible with Wi-Fi or Bluetooth. Configuring wireless or wired (through Ethernet) networked printers is a tad more complicated, and varies by model and printer manufacturer. Generally speaking if you're going with a Wi-Fi printer, you'll need to know the SSID or Wi-Fi network name, and the network password if (as there should be) there is one. Consult Chapter 17 for more on networking.

Ready, Set, Print

You have ink. You have paper. You have a USB cable or wireless. You're antsy. Time's a-wasting. I sense impatience. I'll jump to the task at hand.

For now, I'll assume that you've connected a USB printer. Open the Mac's trusted word processor, TextEdit. Then follow these steps:

1. **Open the document you want to print.**

2. **Choose File➪Print or press ⌘+P.**

REMEMBER

   Even though you're doing this exercise in TextEdit, you'll find the Print command on the File menu across your Mac software library. The ⌘+P shortcut works across the board too.

   The Print dialog shown in Figure 8-1 appears, though what you actually see may vary depending on the program you're printing from and the printer you're calling on.

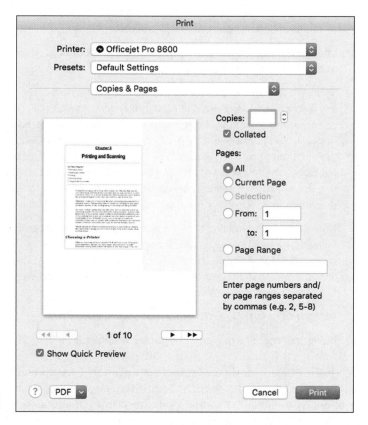

FIGURE 8-1:
Fit to print?

3. **Click the Printer pop-up menu and select your printer, if available.**

   The printer you want to use must be turned on, of course.

If your printer isn't listed in the Printer pop-up menu, follow these steps:

a. *Select the pop-up menu's Add Printer item.*

The Add dialog (essentially, an Add Printer setup window) opens.

b. *If your printer appears in the list, select it (if it's not already selected). Click Add, and you're golden. Continue with Step 4.*

c. *If your printer isn't listed, click the printer-connection type icon at the top, and make the appropriate selection.*

Choices include Default, IP (an Internet printer), and Windows. When you make your choice, the Mac searches for available printers.

d. *Highlight the printer you want to use and then click Add.*

Alternatively, you can choose Select Printer Software from the Use pop-up menu to find a specific model, if available.

4. **Choose among the bevy of options in the Print dialog, which are too numerous to show in one figure.**

Select which pages to print. All is the default, but in most cases you can give any range by tabbing from one From box to the other. And in some apps you can enumerate the specific page to print. Click where indicated to select the paper size and print orientation, which you can examine in a quick preview of the document you want to print. You get to select the number of copies you need and whether you want the pages to be collated. You can decide whether to print a header and footer. And you can choose whether to save your document in Adobe PDF format (along with other PDF options).

Note that this Print dialog differs a bit from program to program. In the Safari browser, for example, you can choose whether to print backgrounds — an option that doesn't appear in the TextEdit dialog. In TextEdit, one of the choices lets you rewrap the contents to fit the page. You may have to click Show Details to see some of these additional options.

5. **When you're satisfied with your selections, click Print.**

If all goes according to plan, your printer will oblige.

TIP

Even if the Mac instantly recognizes your printer, I recommend loading any Mac installation discs that came with the printer, assuming you have an optical drive on or for your Mac. Otherwise visit the printer manufacturer's website. Why bother? Your printer is already printing stuff. The answer is that the disc may supply extra fonts (see Chapter 7), as well as useful software updates.

It wouldn't hurt to also visit the printer manufacturer's website to see whether updated printer drivers are available.

Printing it your way

The Mac gives you a lot of control of how your printer will behave and how your printouts will look.

You may have noticed another pop-up menu in the Print dialog just below the orientation icons that TextEdit is displaying. If you click that menu, a gaggle of other choices present themselves, some of which are shown in Figure 8-2 and described in the following bulleted list.

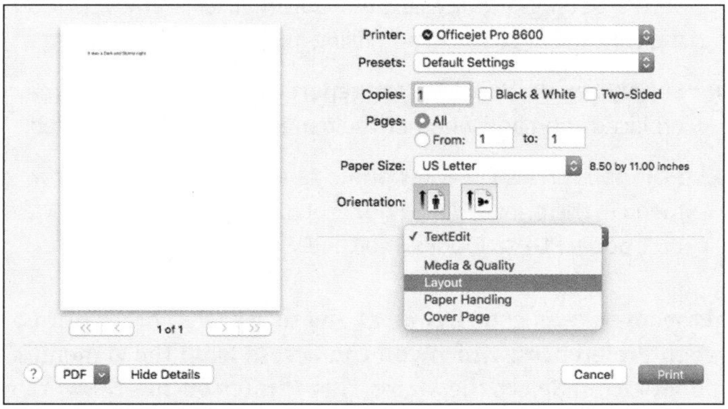

Printer:
Officejet Pro 8600
Presets:
Default Settings
Copies:
1
Black & White
Two-Sided
Pages:
All
From:
1
to:
1
Paper Size:
US Letter
8.50 by 11.00 inches
Orientation:
✓ TextEdit
Media & Quality
Layout
Paper Handling
Cover Page
1 of 1
PDF
Hide Details
Cancel
Print

FIGURE 8-2: Choosing a print layout.

Clicking an item calls up a sheet where you can specify the settings you want. (Some listed options are specific to your printer or the application in use, and the menu for these options may appear in different places in the dialog for different programs.)

Here's a quick rundown of options you may see and what you'll see when you select each one:

- **Layout:** You can select the number of pages to be printed on a single sheet of paper and determine the way those pages are laid out. You can choose a page border (Single Thin Line, Double Hairline, and so on). And you can turn two-sided printing on or off, provided that your printer can handle such a task.
- **Color Matching:** Choose this setting to select ColorSync Profiles (from Apple and others). Thus, you can match the color on the screen to the color you are printing.
- **Paper Handling:** You can choose to print only odd- or even-numbered pages or to print pages in reverse order. You can also scale a page so that it fits a legal- or letter-size sheet, an envelope, or a variety of other paper sizes.
- **Cover Page:** Pretend that you work for the CIA. Then print a cover sheet stating that everything else you're printing is classified, confidential, or top secret. (Yeah, like they're not going to look.)

- **>> Paper Type/Quality:** This option clues the printer in on the type of paper you loaded (inkjet, transparency film, greeting card, brochure, and so on). You also get to choose the print quality. A fast draft uses less ink than printing at the spiffiest, or best, quality. If your printer has more than one tray (a main tray and a photo tray, for example), you can also choose the source of the paper to use. In the Advanced Print options section, you can adjust the volume of ink that's used.

- **>> Borderless Printing:** Tell your printer to print without borders. Or not.

- **>> Real Life Digital Photography:** If you're printing pictures, you can tweak several settings. Choices include automatically removing red-eye, enhancing the contrast of pictures, and filling in dark areas of photos.

- **>> Supply Levels:** Your Mac can report which ink cartridges may need to be replaced soon and whether the paper tray needs to be filled.

- **>> PDF:** You can also preview prints as a PDF, which gets its own drop-down menu in the printer dialog box. You can open a PDF in Preview, save a file as a PDF, add a PDF to iBooks, mail a PDF, and more.

This seems like as good a time as any to see what other print options await you in System Preferences, which you can access from the ● menu. Click the Printers & Scanners icon. Select the Share This Printer on the Network check box if you're willing to share the printer with other computers in your house or office, a setting you can fine-tune by clicking Sharing Preferences. You'll also find the following options:

- **>> Print Queue:** Click the Open Print Queue button to check the status of any current printing jobs, among other things.

- **>> Options & Supplies:** You can make sure that you have the current printer driver and check to see if you have an ample supply of inks. If you're low on, say, cyan, you'll get a Low Ink indicator. You can even order from the Apple Store, if it happens to stock the ink you seek.

- **>> Printer utility:** In System Preferences, click the Printers & Scanners icon and then click Options & Supplies (see the preceding paragraph). Click the Show Printer Webpage button. You'll see more useful data on the connected printer. On the HP printer connected to my Mac, for example, I can clean the print heads and align the print cartridges. You can check out fax settings (fax logs, fax forwarding, and so on), assuming that your printer doubles as a fax machine.

Previewing your print

Before you waste ink and paper on an ill-advised print job, make sure that your documents meet your lofty standards, which means that the margins and spacing look spiffy, and you have a clean layout with no *widows* or *orphans.* That's publishing-speak for a lonely word or two on a line of text all to itself.

As you've already seen, the Mac lets you sneak a peek in the small preview window that appears in the Print dialog in TextEdit (and other programs). If you're satisfied with the preview, go ahead and click Print. If not, go back and apply the necessary changes to your documents.

One more nice thing about printing on your Mac: The various programs you work in may offer you lots more custom printing options. You can print a CD jewel-case insert in iTunes (see Chapter 13) or a pocket address book, mailing label or envelopes in Contacts.

When Printers Stop Printing

As sure a thing as you'll get in computing is that sooner or later (but probably sooner), your printer will let you down. I've already hinted at why.

Running out of ink or toner

Ink is perishable, especially in an inkjet printer. The symptoms are obvious. The characters on a page get lighter and lighter each time you print, to the point where they become barely legible. The software that came with your printer may give you an estimate on how much ink you have left each time you print. You can also check supply levels (on some printers, anyway) by clicking the Options & Supplies button in the Printers & Scanners section of System Preferences and then clicking Supply Levels. Alternatively, you can click Supply Levels in the Print dialog.

Running out of paper

Unless you make a habit of peeking at your printer's paper tray, you won't get a fair warning when your paper supply is exhausted. The rule of thumb is that you'll run out of paper the hour before an important term paper is due (or a legal brief or journalism deadline is due; feel free to insert your own catastrophe). Wherever you buy your ink and paper, I recommend having a spare set around. And do keep a close eye on your ink levels.

Sometimes, a printer stops working for no apparent reason. In the Print Queue or Print Jobs window try clicking Resume or Resume Printer. You can summon this window to see any pending (or incomplete) print jobs by clicking on the Printer icon that appears in the dock after you click Print. You can also visit the Print Queue in

System Preferences. If all else fails, turn off and restart your printer. You might also check your printer's manual for options to clean the printing heads on your inkjet printer and other basic maintenance that can help your printer run like new again.

Hooking Up a Scanner

As with printers, connecting a *scanner* is no big deal. It usually hooks up through USB, although you have a variety of wireless options as well. More than likely, you may gain a scanner as part of a multifunction, or all-in-one, device. Scanners are kind of antiprinters, because you already have a printed image that you want to reproduce on your computer screen, such as receipts, newspaper clippings, or photo slides and negatives. Stand-alone scanners may cost less than $50, though you pay a lot more as you add features.

You can open your scanner by clicking Printers & Scanners in System Preferences, clicking the Scan tab, and choosing Open Scanner. If you click Scanner in the aforementioned Print Queue, you can tinker with the software provided by your scanner manufacturer. The software may let you remove dust or scratches from an image and restore faded colors.

Your scanner can also team up with the onboard Apple Image Capture program, in the Applications folder. After launching Image Capture, select your scanner in the list on the left side of the window, and choose a document-feeding scanner or a flatbed or transparency-type scanner.

TECHNICAL
STUFF

You can choose whether to store scanned images in a folder (Pictures, Desktop, Documents) or have a separate application on the Mac (such as Preview, Photos, or Mail) handle the post-scanning chores. And you can choose the format for your scan (JPEG, TIFF, PNG, JPEG 2000, GIF, BMP, PDF). For more advanced scanning options — color restoration or image correction, for example — click Show Details and apply your changes. If you already see a screen with more detailed options, click Hide Details to truncate the window.

When everything is to your liking, click Scan to fire up the scanner. Image Capture works with scanners that have OS X software drivers, as well as some TWAIN-compatible models.

TIP

In recent versions of OS X, you can scan, view, and make corrections of scanned images in the Preview application. In Preview, choose File ⇨ Import from Scanner.

3

Rocketing into Cyberspace

IN THIS PART . . .

Take your Mac on a spin through the Internet.

Master the minutia of reading, writing, and sending email.

See what Messages, social media, and FaceTime have to offer.

Find out how to keep your Mac safe and secure.

Chapter 9

Stairway to the Internet

Remember what life was like before the middle half of the 1990s? Before this nebulous thing called the Internet changed only *everything?*

Way back in the Dark Ages, people routinely set foot in record stores to buy music. Students went to the library to do research. Folks paid bills with checks and read newspapers on, gosh, paper. They even picked up the telephone to gab with friends. How *passé.*

Nowadays, such transactions and exchanges take place gazillions of times a second on the Internet. Cyberspace has become the place to shop, meet your soul mate, and conduct business. It is also a virtual playground for the kids.

You can fetch, or *download,* computer software, movies, and all kinds of other goodies. You may even get the stuff for free. Let your guard down, however, and you can also lose your shirt. (You really have to question how you won the Sri Lankan lottery when you never bought a ticket.)

Nobody in the early days of the Internet could have envisioned such a future. What eventually morphed into the Net (or the cloud, as it's commonly referred to nowadays) was invented by the nerds of their day: 1960s Defense Department scientists. They constructed — in the interest of national security — the mother of all computer networks.

Hundreds of thousands of computers were interconnected with hundreds of thousands more. The friendly face of cyberspace — what became the *World Wide Web*, or *web* for short — was still decades away.

TIP

Has this somehow passed you by? Forget about fretting if you haven't boarded the cybershuttle just yet. Getting up to speed on the Internet isn't as daunting as you may think. You can enjoy a perfectly rewarding online experience through your Mac without ever deciphering the Net's most puzzling terms — everything from *domain names* to *file transfer protocols.* And you certainly don't have to stay up late cramming for any final exams.

But the Internet is not for people who cherish siestas, either. It's as addictive as nicotine. Expect a warning from the Surgeon General any day now: Spending time online is hazardous to your sleep cycle.

Feeling brave? Want to take the online plunge anyhow? The rest of this chapter clues you in on how best to proceed.

Dialing In

At home, you can find your way online in two main ways, both of which involve getting chummy with an important piece of computer circuitry: the *modem.* I address *dialup* modems here and *broadband* modems in the next section.

Dialup used to merit a longer discussion, but such modems are yesterday's news. Apple hasn't sold a Mac with an internal modem since the Intel switch-over. If you do have an older model with an internal modem, you only need to locate the phone jack on the back or side of the computer. A little phone icon lets you know you've arrived at the right place. You can buy an optional dialup modem that connects to a USB port on the machine. Either way, connect one end of a standard phone cord to the modem jack and the other end to the wall jack where your telephone was connected.

Taking the Broadband Express

If the traditional dialup modem is the local, broadband is the express. Who can blame you for wanting to take the fast train? After you've experienced a fast hookup, you'll have a difficult time giving it up.

DSL, cable . . .

Broadband service comes in several flavors nowadays. Depending on where you live, you may have a choice of all, some, or none of the various alternatives. All broadband types have dedicated modems that reside outside the computer. In some (but not all) cases, a technician will come to your house (generally for a fee) and connect a broadband modem to the service you've selected. But more and more folks do it themselves. The options are:

» **Cable modem:** Sometimes, cable modem is the fastest of the broadband choices — if you don't have access to FIOS or a super-speedy fiber connection, discussed later in this list — and the one that may well make the most sense if you already subscribe to cable TV. The reason is that your cable company is likely to cut you a small break on the monthly fee, especially if you also opt for its phone and TV service. The connection involves hooking up the cable TV cord to the modem.

» **DSL:** Like dialup, DSL (which stands for *digital subscriber line*) works over existing telephone lines. But DSL's big difference from dialup is that it lets you prowl the Internet and make or receive phone calls at the same time. Also, DSL, like a cable modem, is leagues faster than a dialup modem, though usually slower than cable. As with cable, deals can be had if you take on service from the same company that supplies your regular phone service.

» **FIOS:** In this speedy fiber-optic broadband network offered by Verizon, hair-thin strands of glass fiber and laser-generated light pulses transmit data. Verizon was expanding its FIOS network at this writing, but its availability remains somewhat limited.

» **Google Fiber and AT&T GigaPower:** Think broadband Internet on steroids. These rival connections are still available only in select markets. Under the blazing speeds promised here — up to 1 gigabit per second — you might be able to download two dozen songs in less than a second, a TV show in three seconds, and a high-definition movie in under 36 seconds.

» **Cellular broadband:** Several wireless technologies can speedily access the Internet when you're out and about with a Mac laptop, and they work through high-speed cellular networks. Wireless broadband inroads were made a few years ago by Verizon and Sprint through a geeky-sounding technology known as *EV-DO (Evolution-Data Optimized* or *Evolution-Data Only,* depending who you ask). These are *3G* (third-generation) wireless networks. But faster *LTE (Long-Term Evolution)* and other *4G* (fourth-generation) wireless cellular networks are now common.

You may be able to plug in optional cellular modems to exploit these networks or use a wireless model such as MiFi, made by Novatel Wireless, creating a *mobile hotspot*. You typically have to commit to a data plan, often for two years, to take advantage of the portable modems, but at this writing, some providers were relaxing the contractual restrictions. Data plans might run you about $50 a month on top of any other cellular charges you incur, but prices vary and are in a constant state of flux. Coverage can be spotty, though, and depending on the strength of the wireless signal, this option might come closer to dialup than to other broadband alternatives in terms of speed. You might also be able to tap into a mobile hotspot off your cellular phone.

>> **Satellite:** A satellite may be your only alternative to dialup if you live in the boondocks. You get the Internet signal the same way you receive satellite TV: through a dish or an antenna mounted on or near your house. If you go the satellite route, make sure that your modem can send, or *upload,* information as well as receive, or *download,* it. Upload speeds typically are much pokier than download speeds, and satellite service in general is sluggish compared with other broadband choices, with the possible exception of cellular. (Uploading and downloading are components of all modem types.) Satellite also commands higher up-front costs than cable or DSL because you have to shell out for the dish and other components.

>> **Public Hotspots:** You may be able to find a public hotspot in your town or neighborhood. Try the library or maybe a local park. I reckon, though, that most of you are going to want Internet access at home. And public hotspots aren't always secure.

Always on, always connected

Broadband is far more liberating than dial-up ever was because you have a persistent, always-on connection, at least as long as the Mac itself is turned on and your modem or Internet router (which lets you share the connection across numerous computers and devices) doesn't punk out. You won't have to compete with your teenagers for access to the only phone in the house. Web pages get updated. Emails and instant messages usually arrive in a blink. So do social networking statuses. And you can share your Internet connection with other computers in the house (see Chapter 17).

Let Me In

This whole Internet business has one more essential piece: deciding on the outfit that will let you past the Net's front gate. That company is called an *Internet service provider,* or *ISP* for short. You'll invariably have to slip this gatekeeper a few bucks each month, though sometimes, paying annually lowers the price of admission.

Many ISPs — such as AOL, AT&T, Charter, Comcast/XFINITY, Cox, EarthLink, MSN, and Verizon — are large, well-known enterprises. But tiny, unfamiliar companies may also serve the bill.

As always, you'll find exceptions. You may not have to shop for an ISP if your employer provides the Internet *gratis,* for example. Students often get complimentary access on college campuses, though the costs are likely buried in tuition.

If you signed up for broadband, chances are that you've already met your ISP because it's the cable or phone company that set you up. But if you're playing one company off against another, take into account the ISP's customer service, fee structure, and whether they offer any extras, perhaps email accounts or parental controls.

Going on a Safari

It's virtually impossible to ignore the web. Practically every business, school, hospital, restaurant, and other institutions you deal with, research, or come across has a web page. So do the sports teams you follow and the media properties you read. Lots of individuals have web pages too. Web addresses are plastered on billboards, business cards, and the covers of books like this one.

Just browsing

TECHNICAL STUFF

Technologists have an uncanny knack for making simple things hard. They could ask you to make a phone call over the Internet. But if they told you instead to make a *VoIP (Voice over Internet Protocol)* call, they'd pretend to be really smart. So it's unbelievably refreshing to discover that to browse or surf the web, you need a piece of software that's called . . . um, a *web browser.* (Okay, they might have called it a web surfer.)

Because you had the good sense to purchase a Mac, you're blessed with one of the best browsers in the business. It's aptly named *Safari* because much of what you do in cyberspace is an expedition into the wild, unless your revisionist take on this has to do with the Beach Boys hit "Surfin' Safari" (see Figure 9-1 for one view of Safari and some of its icons).

Taming Safari means getting fluent with the concept of a web address, or what those aforementioned technologists dub a *URL (Uniform Resource Locator).* I told you, these guys can't seem to help themselves.

And URLs or Internet addresses end with a suffix, typically .com (pronounced "dot com"), .edu, .gov, .net, or .org. What you type between is often an excellent indicator of where you'll end up on the web. So typing www.usatoday.com takes you to the nation's largest newspaper, typing www.espn.com leads to a popular sports destination, and so on. You enter the URL in the *Smart Search field* at the top of the browser window (labeled in Figure 9-1). As you will discover, it's called the Smart Search field because in addition to entering URLs in this field, you can also enter search queries. As a web page loads, a blue bar fills the address field to let you know that the page is coming.

Web addresses usually begin with www. but that prefix is no longer the defacto nomenclature or in most cases required. So typing, say, ESPN.com (rather than www.ESPN.com) will get you to the sports site.

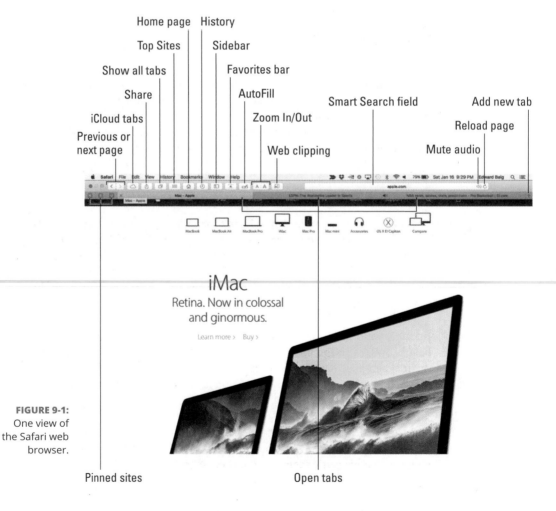

FIGURE 9-1:
One view of the Safari web browser.

Financial institutions and other companies sometimes begin a web address with `https://` instead of `http://`. This prefix indicates that encryption is used to make communication to or from the site more secure (in theory, anyway).

Smart addressing

The crash-resistant web browser is intelligent about recognizing addresses. When you start entering an address in the Smart Search field, Safari takes a stab at what it deems is the most likely match, presented at the top of the menu shown in Figure 9-2 as the Top Hit. A single click takes you there. This smart-addressing feature goes a step further by also listing other possible outcomes, culled from your bookmarks, history, and iCloud Tabs — topics you read about later in this chapter.

FIGURE 9-2: More often than not, the Smart Search field gets you where you need to go.

You enter Google (or other) search queries in the same unified Smart Search field where you enter a web address. I get to more about search in a few pages.

Clicking links

Web surfing would be tedious if you had to type an address each time you wanted to go from one site to another. Fortunately, the bright minds who invented Safari and other browsers agree.

On the Safari *toolbar,* you typically see a series of buttons or icons to the left of the address box where you enter the URL. The buttons you see and the order in which they appear vary, depending on how you customize the browser. (Refer to Figure 9-1 for a look at some of these buttons.) If you want to always see the toolbar when in the full screen, select Always Show Toolbar in Full Screen in the Safari View menu.

The left- and right-facing arrow buttons function as the Back and Forward buttons, respectively. So clicking the left arrow transports you back to the last page you were looking at before the page that's currently displayed. Click the right, or Forward, button to advance to a page you've already looked at but backed up from.

TIP

Click the toolbar icon that looks like a house, and you go to your starting base, or *home page.* But you won't see it by default, as in earlier versions of Safari, unless you choose to add it to the toolbar. To do just that (or add other missing icons), choose View⇨Customize Toolbar, and drag your favorite items onto the toolbar. If you prefer, drag the default set of icons onto the toolbar.

A home page of course is the Web destination you land on the first time you fire up a browser. It's no coincidence that Apple chose one of its own web pages as the default Safari starting point. That way, it can promote the company and try to sell you stuff. As you might imagine, home pages are valuable pieces of screen real estate to marketers. Everyone from AOL to Google to Yahoo! would love you to choose its portal as your start page. Fortunately, changing Safari's home page is simple. Choose Safari⇨Preferences; click the General tab of the Preferences dialog; and then type the web address of your page of choice in the Homepage field, as shown in Figure 9-3.

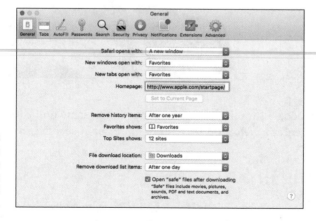

FIGURE 9-3:
You can change the home page in Safari Preferences.

You'll notice that some text on various web pages is underlined or highlighted in blue (or some other color) or both. That format means that the text is a *link*. As you move the mouse pointer over a link, the pointer icon changes from an arrow to a pointing finger and a new URL might appear at the bottom of the screen. Clicking a link takes you to another page (or another location on the same page) without having to type any other instructions.

Some links are genuinely useful. If you're reading about a Green Bay Packers game, for example, you may want to click a link that leads to, say, the career statistics of quarterback Aaron Rogers. But be wary of other links, which are merely come-ons for advertisements.

Using bookmarks

Odds are that you'll rapidly get hooked on a bevy of juicy web pages that become so irresistible you'll keep coming back for more. I won't ask, so you need not tell. It's downright silly to have to remember and type the destination's web address each time you return. Create a *bookmark* instead. The easiest way to add a bookmark is to click the Share button on the toolbar (refer to Figure 9-1). From the menu that appears, click Add Bookmark. Alternatively, choose Bookmarks⇨Add Bookmark in Safari or press the keyboard shortcut ⌘+D.

TIP

You can also add bookmarks for multiple tabs or open pages. Choose Bookmarks⇨Add Bookmarks for These *X* Tabs, with *X* representing the number of open tabs or web pages. I have more to say about tabs later in this chapter, too.

When you use one of the preceding methods to add a bookmark, a dialog appears, as shown in Figure 9-4, asking you to type a name for the bookmark you have in mind and to choose a place to keep it for handy reference later.

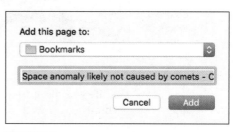

FIGURE 9-4:
Where to book your bookmarks.

TIP

You'll want to return to some sites so often that they deserve VIP status. Reserve a spot for them in Safari's Bookmarks marquee, otherwise known as the *favorites bar.* It used to be called the *bookmarks bar* and you might still see it referred to that way. When you choose to display the favorites bar, it is situated below the browser's smart search field (it is not shown in Figure 9-1). You can drag a URL right onto the favorites bar, assuming the bar is showing.

Click the pop-up menu to find other places to land the new bookmark.

You can stash bookmarks in folders — essentially, menus of bookmarks segregated by whichever categories make sense. But if the bookmarks or favorites bar is indeed your chosen destination, you have an expeditious alternative to placing your new bookmark on the bar: Drag the little icon to the left of the address in the Smart Search field directly onto the bookmarks bar to place it in the precise spot on the bar where you want it.

Clicking the Show All Bookmarks icon lets you manage all your bookmarks.

As alluded to earlier in this section, you can group bookmarks in menu folders or collections, viewable in the Safari sidebar. If you decide to bookmark the Internet Movie Database web page, for example, you may decide to place it in an Entertainment folder, as shown in Figure 9-5. Whenever you want to pay a return visit to the site, you can find it in the sidebar under the Entertainment folder and click the bookmark.

FIGURE 9-5:
Where to
manage
bookmarks.

Despite your best organizational skills, your list of bookmarks and collections may become so . . . well, overbooked that it becomes far less functional. I practically guarantee that you'll tire of at least some of the sites now cluttering your bookmarks closet. To delete a bookmark, you can drag it out of the Favorites bar. Or ⌘-click one or more bookmarks names in the sidebar, and then press Delete. If you change your mind, choose Edit⇔Undo Remove Bookmark.

Pinning websites

If you're on a Mac with El Capitan or later, you can pin favorite websites to the tab bar so that they're easily accessible. Such sites are humming in the background, even when you're not actively using them.

To pin a site, right-click (or Control-click) the tab for that site and choose Pin Tab. As an alternative, you can pin a site by dragging its tab all the way to the left of the tab bar. A pinned tab is represented by the first letter in the site's name. For example, in Figure 9-1, the *S* represents Slack and the *U* represents the *USA TODAY* site.

To un-pin a site, right-click the tab for the site and choose Unpin Site.

Employing the tools of the trade in Safari

Safari is capable of performing other neat tricks. I describe some of them in the following sections.

Pop-up blocker

Tolerating web advertising is the price we pay for all the rich web resources at our disposal. The problem is that some ads induce agita. The most offensive ads are *pop-ups,* those hiccuping, nightmarish little windows that make you think you woke up in the middle of the Las Vegas Strip. Pop-ups have the audacity to get between you and the web page you're attempting to read. Turning on the pop-up blocker can shield you from such pollutants. Choose Safari Preferences⇨Security, and select the Block Pop-up Windows check box. Once in a great while, a pop-up is worth viewing; to turn off the pop-up blocker, simply repeat this exercise.

TIP

In the Security section of Safari Preferences, you can also enable or disable plug-ins, some of which have been associated with some security vulnerabilities such as installing diabolical malware.

Meantime, when Apple unveiled Yosemite, it added support for technology known as WebGL, which lets developers render interactive 3D graphics experiences without the need for special plug-ins. But if you are concerned about WebGL from a security standpoint — and I'm not suggesting you should be — choose the sites that you'll allow to use WebGL on your Mac.

WARNING

Keep in mind that Safari sometimes uses plug-ins to show off or play music, pictures, and video. Be aware that disabling any of these options may make the web pages you frequent misbehave.

Find

Now suppose that you want to find all mentions of a particular term or phrase on the web page you're looking at. Choose Edit⇨Find or press ⌘+F. Type the word you want to find, and Safari highlights all occurrences of the text. Apple's not leaving anything to chance; the rest of the page is dimmed so that you can more easily make out those highlighted words. The number of matches is also displayed, as are arrows that let you go to the next or previous occurrence of the word.

SnapBack

Sometimes, you get carried away surfing, either while searching Google or just browsing the web. In other words, you move from page to page to page to page. Before you know it, you're in never-never web land. You can certainly keep clicking the Back button until you return to your starting point. Apple once provided an orange SnapBack icon in Safari that appeared in the right side of the then-separate address field and Google search box, letting you return to square one without those excess clicks. The icon is gone, but you can still take advantage of the SnapBack feature by pressing the keyboard combination ⌘+Option+S or choosing History ⇨ Search Results SnapBack.

Filling out forms and passwords

Safari can remember your name, address, passwords, and other information. So when you start typing a few characters in a web form or other field, the browser can finish entering the text for you, provided that it finds a match in its database. Choose Safari ⇨ Preferences ⇨ AutoFill, and select the items you want Safari to use (such as info from your Contacts card). If several choices match the first several letters you type in a form, a menu appears. Press the arrow keys to select the item you have in mind and then press Enter.

Safari can also automatically fill in your web passwords, provided that you were authenticated by entering your system password. To take advantage of this option, make sure that the User Names and Passwords check box is selected in the Auto-Fill section of Safari Preferences. You can also autofill credit card information and information for other forms.

iCloud keychain

Apple lets you exploit a feature called iCloud Keychain, which keeps those usernames, web passwords, credit-card numbers, and most Wi-Fi names and passwords up to date, no matter which compatible devices you're using. The Mac is one of the compatible machines I have in mind, obviously, but you can keep passwords and other data up to date when you use Safari on an iPad, iPhone, or iPod touch, all encrypted for security purposes.

To take advantage, make sure that iCloud Keychain is turned on. To do so, open System Preferences, click iCloud, and select the Keychain check box. Enter your Apple ID password when you're prompted. When you try to enable iCloud Keychain on a second Mac (or other compatible device), a window pops up, asking you to request approval. Meanwhile, a notification appears on the other devices using iCloud Keychain, requesting authorization for this additional machine. Enter your password again, and click Allow (assuming, of course, that you do allow it). If no other devices are available, you can enter a previously established security code. You can enter a mobile phone number to receive a text to verify your identity.

Tabbed browsing

Suppose that you want to peek at several web pages in a single browser window instead of having to open separate windows for each "open" page. Welcome to the high art of *tabbed browsing.* Choose Safari⇨Preferences and then click Tabs. The window shown in Figure 9-6 appears. Place check marks next to each of the settings you want.

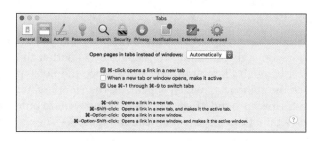

FIGURE 9-6:
Keeping tabs:
the tabbed
browsing
window.

Now, each time you ⌘-click, you open a link in a new tab instead of a window. To toggle from one open web page to another, just click its tab. The tabs appear just below the bookmarks bar. If you press Shift+⌘-click, you can open a new tab and make it the active tab.

To open a new tabbed window, choose File⇨New Tab or press ⌘+T.

TIP

To rearrange the way tabs appear, just drag them in any order.

Tab view

If you have a trackpad, you can take advantage of a neat stunt called Tab view, which is roughly similar to how you view tabs in Safari on the iPhone. This stunt also works with the Magic Mouse or Magic Mouse 2. Alternatively, click the Tab View button (labeled in Figure 9-1 earlier in this chapter).

When you pinch in to zoom, your open tabs line up one next to another, as shown in Figure 9-7. Your open tabs on other devices are also visible (see the next section). Click + to add a new tab for a new site. Click the tab itself to leave Tab view and bring the web page represented by the tab to the forefront.

FIGURE 9-7:
Pinch in to see
your live
web pages.

Muting audio

If you are running several websites simultaneously and you want to quiet down a noisy site, you could go searching from one tab to another to find the open loud tab. However, through El Capitan, you can silence the noise using a far simpler method. Click the audio icon, which appears in the Smart Search field when sound is playing in the background. If you decide that you want to unmute the audio, just click the icon again. (You can see that icon in Figure 9-1.)

iCloud tabs

As you probably suspect, Mac owners are fans of Apple in general, so they may well own other Apple products, such as the iPhone smartphone, iPad tablet, or iPod touch media player. Assuming all those Apple playthings are connected to iCloud, they can take advantage iCloud Tabs. The purpose of this feature is straightforward. If you're browsing Safari on one of your iCloud devices — including, of course, any other Macs you happen to own — you can see the last web pages you visited on those devices when browsing Safari on the machine you're currently using. And that means you can pick up right where you left off.

iCloud Tabs also work if you use the Windows version of Safari and have the iCloud control panel installed on that computer.

REMEMBER

To use iCloud Tabs, an iPhone, iPad, or iPod touch must be running iOS 6 or later.

Click the iCloud Tabs icon (labeled in Figure 9-1 earlier in this chapter) to summon a list of those open tabs. The beauty of iCloud Tabs is that you can view the pages on those other devices even if Safari is turned off or the device itself is out of action. The exception to the rule occurs if you turn on the Private Browsing feature, which you read about later in this chapter.

Benefiting from History

Suppose that you failed to bookmark a site and decide to return days later. But you can't remember what the darn place was called or the convoluted path that brought you there. Become a history major. Safari logs every web page you open and keeps the record for a week or so. Consult the History menu to view a list of all the sites you visited on a particular day during the week. Choose History⇨Show History. You can even search for a site you visited by typing a keyword in the Spotlight search field.

TIP

If you're wigged out by this Internet trail, you can always click Clear History to wipe the slate clean. Or choose the General tab of Safari Preferences and indicate whether you want to remove all traces of history after one day, one week, two weeks, one month, or one year — or to handle this cleanup job manually.

Top sites and favorites

As you may have gathered from this history discussion, Safari is watching you. It records how often you head to favorite websites. It knows when you last visited. But don't worry; it's all to your benefit. And with the Top Sites feature, it's even easier to return to your top online landing spots. In the Top Sites view, the sites you frequent most are laid out beautifully, as shown in Figure 9-8, with the name of the site or web page at the bottom of each thumbnail.

FIGURE 9-8: Finding your way through Top Sites.

Meantime, if you click the Favorites button in the upper-right corner of the Top Sites display (the star icon labeled in Figure 9-8), you can shift to a Favorites view, which shows a grid of icons for your favorite sites. In fact, whenever you open a new tab, you'll see Favorites.

To return to this Top Sites view after you've departed, click the Top Sites button (labeled in Figure 9-1 and Figure 9-8).

As you might imagine, the thumbnails shown in the Top Sites view change as your browsing habits change. But you can also customize the Top Sites page and choose the number of sites that are displayed at any time.

To change the layout of the Top Sites view, mouse over a thumbnail you want to move, and press and hold the mouse button (or trackpad). Now you can drag the thumbnail to a new location on the Top Sites layout, with the other thumbnails politely moving aside to make room.

You can also make room for more than the default dozen sites in the Top Sites layout. Open Safari Preferences, and click the General tab. From the Top Sites pop-up menu, choose either 6 sites or 24 sites. If you made the change and prefer the way things were, choose 12 sites to return to the default.

As you mouse over a Top Sites thumbnail, you see an X and a pin icon in the upper-left corner of the thumbnail. If you want to pin a site so that it always remains in the Top Sites view, click the pin. Alternatively, click the X if you want to remove the site from Top Sites.

Sharing what you read

Apple makes it a breeze to share whatever you're looking at or reading with friends or followers, care of the Share button that resides inside many apps. So it goes in Safari. Sharing favorite web pages is as easy as clicking that Share button. Check out Figure 9-9 to see your menu options. I've already discussed bookmarks, and I get to the Reading List option shortly.

Also note the other ways that you can share the page you are reading: You can email the web page, share it as an instant message, or post it to Twitter or the popular Facebook or LinkedIn social network. You can also add the website to shared links, or share it as a note or in a reminder. And if you click More, your options expand, including an option to share with third parties as a custom *extension*.

FIGURE 9-9:
Summoning
your sharing
options.

Figure 9-10 shows the *Share sheet* for Facebook. You have some room to type (or dictate) a message indicating the reason you're sharing this web thingy in the first place. Click the Friends pop-up menu to determine which of your Facebook pals get to see the attached link and your message. At your discretion, click Add Location to share where you are (or, more to the point, where your Mac is) when sending the page.

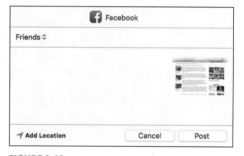

FIGURE 9-10:
Sharing a page on Facebook.

Clutter-free reading

Articles you read online are all too frequently surrounded by advertisements, banners, menu bars, and other distractions. What would it be like to read web pages without the excess visual noise? Stop wondering. The Reader feature can place you in a temporary ideal reading environment. Most of, if not all, the clutter is stripped away.

To make that happen, click the Reader button (the four horizontal lines on the left edge of the Smart Search field) to transform a story like the *USA TODAY* article shown on the left side of Figure 9-11 to the way it appears on the right side of the figure. Use the trackpad or mouse to scroll up or down the length of the article.

Click Reader button to see only the text

FIGURE 9-11:
Read a web
article with
clutter or
without.

You can enlarge or decrease the text by clicking the corresponding little *A* or big *A* icon, and also change the font.

REMEMBER

The Reader button appears only when Safari detects an actual article.

Offline reading

Though it may be filled with countless riches, the web doesn't do you much good if you lack a connection to the Internet. But now you can catch up on your reading even without that connection by saving web pages to the offline reading list. Click the aforementioned Share button, and choose Add to Reading List. Safari saves all the pages of the article you're reading, not just the single page you happen to be viewing when you click the Add to Reading List option. Or click the One-Step Add button (+) just to the left of the Smart Search field, which has the same effect. The + button appears only when you move your cursor into the Smart Search field.

TIP

The Reading List may be terrific for . . . well, offline reading. But it's also a convenient way to store articles that you want to keep around.

When you're ready to read the article — again, with or without an active Internet connection — click the Show/Hide Sidebar icon to the left of the favorites bar. It's labeled in Figure 9-1.

You notice three buttons at the top of the sidebar. The first is for bookmarks (covered earlier in this chapter). The third is for Shared Links, which I get to in the next section. And the middle is for the Reading List, which I'm talking about here. You already know what a bookmark is — think of the Reading List somewhat differently. It is a list of specific articles or webpages that you've saved to read later, even when you're offline.

Click the Reading List icon — the one that resembles a pair of reading glasses — so that it's highlighted. Scroll up or down the list that appears (shown in Figure 9-12), and click the article you want to read. To remove an article after you've read it, roll the mouse over the story in the Safari sidebar and click the X that appears inside a small circle. Or swipe from right to left on an article in the sidebar and click Remove.

FIGURE 9-12:
Reading without an Internet connection.

Click Unread to list the articles that you haven't gotten to yet. If you have a lengthy reading list, you can search for the article you have in mind by entering a search query in the search box provided for that purpose. Click the Show/Hide Sidebar icon again to make the list disappear, or click the Bookmarks or Shared Links button to display such lists instead of the Reading List.

Shared links

As you've gathered by now, the Internet has become a very social place, and a good many social folks like to share the stuff they read or stumble upon. When the Safari sidebar is visible, and you highlight Shared Links, you can see Internet links from people you follow on Twitter, as well as from the contacts or influencers you pay attention to in LinkedIn, and view any comments they've made along the way. Scroll up or down the Shared Links list to view more. Click Subscriptions at the bottom of the Shared Links list to add accounts and feeds to follow.

Although Shared Links are refreshed periodically, you can force the issue by choosing View➪Update Shared Links. (Sorry to say that there's no keyboard shortcut.)

When you click a Shared Link in the Safari sidebar, the site or page in question appears in the browser window. You can retweet the link from within that window, assuming that you, too, think it's worth sharing.

Private browsing

TIP

I was just telling you how people like to share, and now I'm going to tell you how to do anything but. Instead, you want to go incognito. Hey, maybe you *do* have something to hide. Perhaps you're surfing in an Internet cafe, or just possibly you're being paranoid. Whatever. Turn on a hush-hush Safari feature called *Private Browsing* by choosing Safari⇨New Private Window. (Or choose the keyboard shortcut, Shift+⌘+N). Now Safari won't add the web pages you've visited to the History menu (though you can still use the Back and Forward buttons to return to sites you've been to). When Private Browsing is turned on, AutoFill is turned off, searches aren't added to the pop-up menu in the Smart Search field, and web cookie preferences are also deep-sixed. (I explain cookie files later in this chapter.) Your tabs don't show up on other devices, and if you take advantage of the Handoff feature (see Chapter 16) on your Mac, your private browsing will not be handed off to other Macs or iOS devices.

To remind you when you're browsing privately, the Smart Search field is shaded gray. Close the private window, open a new (non-private) window, or switch to a previously opened non-private window to once again turn your browsing session into an open book or, if not quite that, at least a session whose steps you can retrace later.

Do not track

While I'm on the subject of privacy, you can ask a website not to track you by clicking the Ask Websites Not to Track Me option in the Privacy section of Safari Preferences.

Web clipping

In Chapter 6, I introduce you to Dashboard widgets — those handy little apps for looking up phone numbers or getting sports scores. Safari lets you create your own by clipping out a section of a favorite web page. The beauty is that you're giving birth to a live widget that gets refreshed whenever the underlying web page is updated.

In Safari, navigate to the web page you want to transform into a dashboard widget; then click the Web Clipping button (labeled in Figure 9-1, earlier in this chapter.) The button isn't visible by default. When you click the button, the screen dims except for a resizable white rectangle that appears. The rectangle automatically wraps around various portions on the page that seem like a natural section you may want to clip. You can reposition this rectangle so that another section gets highlighted. And if Apple still doesn't highlight the portions you have in mind, click inside the rectangle to bring up handles that appear on its edges. Drag these handles with your mouse until the rectangle is expanded to encompass the complete section you want to snip out for your widget.

When you're satisfied, click Add, which appears in the upper-right corner of the web screen that you're clipping. The Dashboard appears, with your newly created widget. You can apply cosmetic changes to the widget by clicking the small *i* button in its lower-right corner. The *i* appears only when you roll your mouse over the widget. When you do so, the widget flips around, and you can select a new border for your widget by clicking one of the small pictures representing a themed edge and then clicking Edit. Now you can change the size of the widget, revealing more content, or to drag its content to a new place.

TIP

Sometimes, a widget plays sounds. If you want sound to play only when you've summoned Dashboard, select the Only Play Audio in Dashboard check box.

Make a web picture your desktop picture

Ever come across a stunning picture on the web that you wish you could make your own? Go right ahead. Right-click (or Control-click) the picture in question, and choose Use Image as Desktop Picture from the contextual menu that appears.

WARNING

If you choose a low-resolution image, it will look lousy blown up as your desktop background.

Choosing a search engine

In Chapter 6, I focus on the wonders of searching your Mac through Spotlight. And with Spotlight Suggestions, searching has only improved. Spotlight can deliver stock quotes, sports scores, the weather, and a whole lot more. But what about searching all these plum pickings on the Internet while avoiding all that's rotten? An Internet search engine is the best place to begin. This useful tool scans web pages to find links based on instances of the search terms you enter. Most folks start with Google, which happens to be the default search engine on your Mac.

Anyone who is anyone — and that may as well include you — uses Google. Google has become so popular that it's often treated as a verb, as in "I Googled [something]." It's also why Google's founders have become richer than Croesus.

Haven't the foggiest idea who Croesus was? Just Google the name, and you'll soon discover how this sixth-century (BC) Lydian monarch managed to amass a fortune without launching an IPO.

The slowpoke way to Google something is to visit www.google.com. Type your search query — *Croesus*, in this example — and click the Google Search button.

Safari, however, provides a faster alternative. Just enter your query in the Smart Search field you've been using to type web addresses.

Then again, you may prefer an alternative search engine. On the Mac, you can substitute Yahoo!, Bing, or DuckDuckGo. To do so, open Safari Preferences, click the Search tab, and make your selection from the Default Search Engine pop-up menu.

TIP

Before I leave this discussion of Safari, I'm obliged to tell you that as special as it is as a browser, you can use other browsers, including Mozilla Firefox and Google Chrome. I encourage you to give these and others a try.

Chapter 10

Delivering the Goods on Email

Electronic mail is a blessing and a curse.

Why you can't live without email: Messages typically reach the person to whom they're addressed in a few seconds, compared with a few days for *snail mail*. (That's the pejorative label geeks have tattooed on regular postal mail.) You won't waste time licking envelopes, either.

Why email drives you batty: It won't take long before you're likely buried under an avalanche of messages, much of it junk mail, or *spam*.

Not that any mail system is perfect. You can only imagine the snide comments heard in the day of the Pony Express: "Love that I got my tax refund and Sears catalog, but the stench on that steed. . ."

If you're an email tyro, you discover the basics in this chapter. But even those who have been sending electronic missives for years might be able to collect a useful nugget or two.

Understanding Email

In broad terms, *email* is the exchange of messages over a communications network, typically the Internet, but also a network within an organization.

To use email, you need

>> **An email *account:*** These accounts are traditionally offered by employers; schools; or Internet service providers (ISPs). You may get your email through tech biggies such as AOL, AT&T, Comcast, EarthLink, Google, Microsoft, and Yahoo!

>> **Email *software:*** These programs send, receive, and organize email messages for your account. Of course, you won't need special software (beyond your web browser) if you're using web-based email.

Apple includes such an application with OS X, and there can't be any doubt about what the program does. It's aptly named Mail.

To access Mail, single-click the icon that looks like a stamp on the dock. If for some reason the icon isn't there, open Mail inside the Applications folder.

Sending and reading email through the Mac's Mail program is a breeze, after you set the thing up.

Setting Up a New Email Account

Mail setup has gotten ever simpler through various versions of OS X. I've listed several steps in this section, but if you're setting up such mainstream accounts as AOL, Gmail, or Yahoo!, among others, you need not go beyond the second step.

To set up a new email account, follow these steps:

1. **Open Mail by clicking the Mail icon on the dock or by double-clicking Mail in the Applications folder.**

First-timers are greeted with a Welcome to Mail window. Later, you see the Choose a Mail Account Provider when you click Add Account below the main Mail menu. If you're a member of Apple's iCloud service (see Chapter 12), Mail automatically established an account for you, using information you provided in setting up your Mac.

If you're not a member of iCloud and want to set up a mainstream email account automatically, or if you want to set up a new account in addition to iCloud from the Add Account window, proceed to Step 2.

ALTERNATIVES TO THE MAIL PROGRAM

TIP

If you already have Microsoft Office or some other third-party software, you can continue to send and read mail in such applications as Microsoft Outlook (Microsoft Entourage, in older versions of Office for the Mac).

What's more, you can continue right along on the Mac if you've been sending and receiving email on other computers through web accounts such as

- Google's Gmail
- Microsoft's web-based Hotmail or Outlook
- Yahoo! Mail
- AOL (the outfit that popularized the phrase "You've got mail!")

Ditto for just about any other email account you may come across.

Having one or more web-based email accounts is nice:

- You get the tremendous advantage of being able to access mail from any Internet browser (on a Mac, PC, or Linux machine, or a smartphone or tablet).
- Popular web email accounts are free and loaded with gobs of storage.

2. **Do one of the following:**

- If you have one of the popular email accounts — such as AOL, Google (Gmail), or Yahoo! — merely click the name of any of these providers; enter your name (if it's not already there and requested), current email address, and password in the fields provided; and then click Sign In. When Apple sees an email address from a provider it's familiar with, you can click Set Up and are pretty much finished. Oh, Apple asks along the way if you also want to set up your contacts, calendars, messages, notes, and reminders, if your provider includes those with your account. Click Done after you've checked each appropriate option.

- Click Other Mail Account to enter an email address that may be unfamiliar to Apple. You enter your full name, email address, and password and click Create.

  If all goes well, you're done. You can skip to choosing the options available to you with this account (Mail, Notes, and so on).

  If Apple still doesn't recognize the account, you must configure the account manually. Click Next and then go to Step 3.

3. **Fill in the general information required in the next screen, and click Next.**

You're transported to a window to enter your Incoming Mail Server information, select the IMAP or POP button, and fill in the Outgoing Mail Server information. Check with your ISP if you're not sure how to fill in the information.

The incoming mail server is where your messages are retrieved.

4. **Click Sign In.**

If you provided the proper credentials, you're typically good to go on, though you may be asked some security-related questions related to using *Secure Sockets Layer (SSL)*. If this account is a work account, ask one of the company's information technology specialists (assuming that you have one) to help.

If Mail can't verify the account, Apple may serve up a warning that you may be putting confidential information at risk.

TECHNICAL STUFF

At certain points during the preceding steps, the Mail program tests the information you provide to make sure that the settings are correct. Setting up additional mail accounts involves repeating these steps.

Before You Click Send

Sending email is really a snap. With the Mail program open, do one of the following:

>> Choose File⇨New Message

>> Press the keyboard alternative ⌘+N

>> Click the New Mail icon on the Mail toolbar — the one that shows what appears to be a writing instrument inside a square.

Again, if Mail isn't open, click the stamp icon on the dock.

TECHNICAL STUFF

A window like the one shown in Figure 10-1 appears.

Addressing your missive

With the New Message window on your screen, you're ready to begin the process of communicating through email with another human being.

The handiest way to address an email depends on whether your recipient is in your contacts (see Chapter 3).

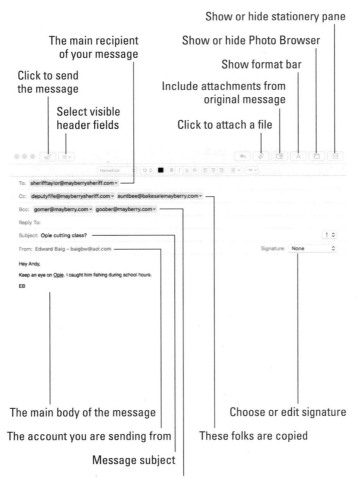

Show or hide stationery pane

Show or hide Photo Browser

The main recipient
of your message

Show format bar

Click to send
the message

Include attachments from
original message

Select visible
header fields

Click to attach a file

The main body of the message

Choose or edit signature

The account you are sending from

These folks are copied

Message subject

These folks are copied but can't see who else is copied

FIGURE 10-1:
How to send
an email
message.

Contacts non-members

If you're sending a message to someone who isn't already in your contacts, there's just one way: In the To box, *carefully* type the recipient's email address.

WARNING

If you type even a single letter, number, or symbol incorrectly, your message won't be deliverable (you should get a bounce-back notification) or, worse, will be dispatched to the wrong person.

As you start banging out an email address, the Mac tries to be helpful. It fills in the name and address of the person it thinks you're trying to reach (culled from your Contacts app). Don't worry if the wrong name shows up at first. Keep typing until Apple guesses correctly or you've entered the full address manually.

If you're sending mail to more than one recipient, separate the addresses with commas.

If you want to send mail to folks who aren't the primary addressees of your letter, type the addresses for these people (again separated by commas if you have more than one) in the Cc *(carbon copy)* field.

Contacts members

You have an alternative way to add an email address, provided that your recipient already resides in your Contacts app. In the address field of the New Message window, click the circled + that summons your contacts. Then, in Contacts, just double-click the name of the person to whom you want to send mail, and the Mail program takes care of the rest. Your contacts are categorized appropriately; All AOL, All iCloud, All Google, and so on, or listed under All Contacts. The real names of these contacts appear in the To box (or Cc box); you won't see their actual email addresses. You'd see the name Tony Soprano rather than boss@sopranos.com, for example. Have no fear; under the hood, Apple is making all the proper arrangements to send your message to the rightful recipient.

You may want to keep the recipients' list confidential. (The feds need not know where Tony's mail goes.) You can do so in two ways:

>> You can send mail to a group in your contacts (see Chapter 3) just by typing the group name in the To field. Mail automatically routes mail to each member's email address. To keep those addresses private, choose Mail ⇨ Preferences, and select Composing. Make sure that the check box titled When Sending to a Group, Show All Member Addresses is *not* selected.

>> To keep private the addresses of recipients who aren't members of the same group, click the little arrow to the left of the Account field in the New Message window, and choose Bcc Address Field. (*Bcc* stands for *blind carbon copy*.) Everyone included in the list will get the message, but they won't have a clue who else you sent it to in the Bcc list.

Composing messages

Keep a few things in mind before pounding out a message. Although optional, it's good email etiquette to type a title, or subject, for your email. In fact, some people get right to the point and blurt out everything they have to say in the Subject line (*Lunch is on at noon*, for example).

To write your message, just start typing in the large area provided below the address, Subject, and From (whichever email account) lines. You can also paste passages (or pictures) cut or copied from another program.

The standard formatting tools in your word processor are readily available. You can make words **bold**, *italic,* or <u>underlined,</u> and add spice to the letters by using fancy fonts.

TIP

If the format bar with the B, I, or U buttons isn't visible, either

>> Click the Format button (labeled in Figure 10-1).

>> Choose Format ⇨ Style, and then choose bold, italic, underline; select options that make letters bigger or smaller; or choose Show Fonts to display different typefaces (or press ⌘+T) via the Fonts window shown in Figure 10-2.

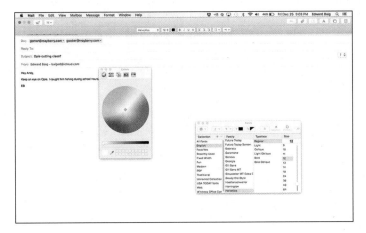

FIGURE 10-2:
Changing fonts and colors in your emails.

Choose Format ⇨ Show Colors (or press Shift+⌘+C) to alter the hues of your individual characters by summoning the Color Wheel shown in Figure 10-2. By clicking on any of the colors within this wheel, you can change text characters to that color.

WARNING

Most of us shouldn't make a habit out of using colored text. It raises the spam rating of your message and may delay or impede the delivery of your message.

Choosing stationery

It's nice that you can dress up an outgoing message with fancy fonts and different colors. But there's dressing up email and then there's *dressing* up email, and the OS X crowd can apply just the right visual tonic to outgoing messages.

Apple provides nearly three dozen spiffy stationery templates as part of OS X, covering most major occasions and organized by category, such as birthday parties, baby announcements, and thank-you notes. Click the Show Stationery button in the upper-right corner of the compose window (refer to Figure 10-1 earlier in this chapter) to check out the possibilities. Clicking a stationery choice gives you a preview of what your message will look like, complete with whatever text you've already typed.

Although many stationery templates include lovely pictures, Apple doesn't expect you to use them in your mailings. These are merely premade drop zones for adding your own pictures. Click the Photo Browser button in the upper-right corner of the New Message window — it's adjacent to the stationery button — and drag a picture from Photo, Aperture, or some other location into the picture placeholder on the template. Double-clicking this new photo summons a zoom slider. You can also pan the image with a touchpad, letting you place the image just so.

You need not accept Apple's wording in any of these templates. If you're wishing a happy birthday to Janie instead of Jessica, just single-click the area with text and make the substitution. Your words stay true to the design.

TIP

Find a stationery pattern you really like? Drag it into the Favorites area to build a custom collection.

TECHNICAL STUFF

Because Mail templates conform to *HTML* (the language of the web), most people receiving your email will be able to view the stationery you intended. It doesn't matter whether they're on a PC or Mac. Mail also lets you use your own custom designs as templates.

Saving drafts

You're almost there. But what if you're waiting to insert an updated sales figure into a message? Or what if you decide it wouldn't be a bad idea to let off some steam before submitting your resignation (via the cold harsh world of email, no less)? Click the red gumball button in the upper-left corner of the Mail message. A window appears, providing options to Save, Don't Save, or Cancel. Click Save to save the message as a draft — and do whatever it takes to calm down. When you're ready to resume working on the message, demanding a raise instead, choose Mailbox⇨Go to Favorite Mailbox. Alternatively, press ⌘+4) which takes you to Drafts.

Attaching files

You can attach payloads to your emails. *Attachments* typically are word processing documents, but they can be any types of files: pictures, music, spreadsheets, videos, and more.

To send a file with your email, click the Attach button in the upper-right corner of your outgoing message. The Attach button has a picture of a paperclip on it. In the window that appears, select the file you have in mind from the appropriate folder on your storage drive.

TIP

Given the market dominance of that *other* operating system, it's a fair bet that you're sending attachments to a Windows user. Windows is particular about the files it can read. It wants to see the *file extension*, such as .doc (see Chapter 7). Because Apple wants to make nice with the rest of the computing public, all you need to do is select the Send Windows-Friendly Attachments check box before sending an attachment to a PC pal. It's in the aforementioned attachments window that appears. If you don't see the Windows-Friendly check box, click Options.

If you want to always send Windows-Friendly attachments, choose Mail⟹Edit⟹ Attachments⟹Send Windows-Friendly Attachments.

Windows users may receive two attachments when you send mail from a Mac. (And you coulda *sworn* you sent a single file.) One reads *TheNameoftheFileISent*; the other, .___*TheNameoftheFileISent*. Your recipients can safely ignore the latter.

Attaching large files

WARNING

You should clue recipients in ahead of time when you're planning on sending them large files, particularly high-resolution images and video. And by all means, refer to the attachment in the message you send. Here's why:

>> Many Windows viruses are spread through email attachments. Although you know the files are harmless, your Windows pals may be understandably skittish about opening a file without a clear explanation of what you're sending.

>> Sending oversize attachments can slow or even clog your recipient's email inbox. It can take him or her forever to download these files. Moreover, ISPs may impose restrictions on the amount of email storage that users can have in their inboxes or in the size of a file that can be transported. The company you work for may enforce its own limits. In fact, some employers prevent staffers from sending messages (or replying to yours) until they've freed space in their inboxes. If the attachment is too big, Mail lists the size in red and (if known) lets you know what the actual limit is. Mail won't send the message.

TIP

Sometimes you *must* send oversized attachments, perhaps presentations or videos. As part of Yosemite, Apple introduced a feature that has certainly helped yours truly dispatch attachments that in the past would have been painfully difficult to get to the intended recipient. The feature is called *Mail Drop* and the solution is as simple as, well, sending mail. When you attempt to send such a message, a dialog appears with the Mail Drop option. Click Use Mail Drop and Apple takes it from there.

Attachments sent via this method are uploaded to iCloud, where they're stored for 30 days. The files are scrambled or encrypted. And if you were signed into iCloud when you sent such a payload, you'll be pleased to learn that the attachment doesn't count against your iCloud storage allotment. If the person you're sending the attachment to is using Mail in OS X (Yosemite or later), the attachment shows up in the message just like any other. Everyone else gets a link to download the attachment along with an expiration date by which they better do so. Even Mail Drop has limits. The attachment size must not exceed 5GB. There's also a 1TB Mail Drop storage limit.

TIP

To get past an ISP's size restrictions, Mail also gives you the option to resize images. Click the tiny pop-up menu near the upper-right corner of the New Message window, which shows up along with the image you're sending (see Figure 10-3). You can send an image at its actual file size or shrink it to a smaller size. Medium and Large are other options. If your largest files reside on an accessible web page, your best bet may be to send a link to the folks you're allowing to download those files. You can also share photos and other sizable files in a cloud-based storage locker through the likes of Dropbox, Box, Google Drive, and Microsoft OneDrive, among numerous other services. If you regularly share photos with another person, consider taking advantage of the iCloud Photo Sharing feature, which I discuss in Chapter 14.

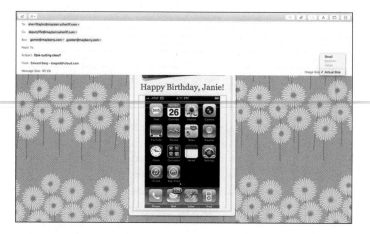

FIGURE 10-3: Changing the size of a photo before emailing it.

One more note about the attachments you intend to send out. To always position an attachment at the bottom of your message, choose Edit ⇨ Attachments ⇨ Always Insert Attachments at End of Message.

Spell checking

There's a certain informality to email. Rather than type a sentence that says, "How are you?", you might type "How r u?" But not always.

Spelling counts (or ought to) when you're corresponding with potential employers or, for that matter, with the person who's currently responsible for your paycheck. I know you won't want to be reprimanded if you send email with misspellings to your seventh-grade English teacher.

Fortunately, Apple provides assistance to the spelling-challenged among us.

WARNING

A spell checker is a basic feature; just don't put all your faith in it. You may have correctly spelled but misused a word. For example, you inadvertently used *through* in a sentence when you meant to say *threw,* an error that a spell checker won't catch.

To access the email spell checker, choose Mail⇨Preferences and then click Composing. From the Check Spelling pop-up menu, choose As I Type, When I Click Send, or Never.

Assuming that you ignored that last option, the Mail program underlines in red what it thinks are misspelled words, just as TextEdit and other word processors do. Right-click the suspect word and choose the properly spelled word from the contextual menu of suggested replacements.

TIP

If your spell checker keeps tripping over a word that is in fact typed correctly (your company name, for example), you can add that word to the spell checker dictionary. Control-click the word and choose Learn Spelling from the contextual menu. Your Mac should never make the same mistake again.

Signing off with a signature

You can personalize Mail with a signature plastered at the bottom of every outgoing message. Along with your name, a signature might include your snail-mail address, phone numbers, iMessage account name (see Chapter 11), and Twitter handle, as well as a pithy slogan.

To add your email John Hancock, choose Mail⇨Preferences. Click the Signatures tab and then click the Add (+) button. You can accept or type over the default signature that Apple suggests and choose whether to match the font already used in the message. You can assign different signatures to different email accounts.

Select Place Signature Above Quoted Text if that's your preference.

Managing the Flood of Incoming Mail

The flip side of sending email is sifting through the mess of messages that may come your way. You can spend hours trying to get through an email inbox, depending on your line of work.

The little red badge on the Mail icon on the dock indicates the number of unread messages demanding your attention.

New emails arrive as a matter of course through the Internet. You can click the Get Mail button on the Mail toolbar to hasten the process, as shown in my little tour of the Mail program in Figure 10-4. As an alternative, choose Mailbox⇨Get New Mail and then specify the mail account from which you want to receive missives. Or click Get All New Mail below the Mailbox menu or press the keyboard combination Shift+⌘+N. The message tally in the badge next to each Mail account rises until all the messages in the new load have been received.

The blue dot indicates an unread message

Get mail | Click to sort

FIGURE 10-4:
The drill on reading email.

TIP

If you click the Get Mail button and nothing happens, make sure that your account isn't offline. (If it is, the account name appears dimmed.) To remedy the situation, choose Mailbox⇨Take All Accounts Online. You can also take an individual account online or, for that matter, offline.

TIP

If that also fails to alleviate the problem, choose Window⇨Connection Doctor. Your Mac will verify that you're connected to the Internet and examine each email account to make sure that it's properly configured.

Single-click an incoming message to read it in the large pane adjacent to the list of incoming messages. Or double-click a given message to read it in its own window.

Choosing what to read

I'm no censor. I'd never tell you what you should or shouldn't read — online or off. So know that I have only your best interests at heart when I urge you to maintain a healthy dose of skepticism when it comes to tackling your inbox.

As you pore through said inbox, you'll probably notice mail from companies, online clubs, or websites that you may have expressed an interest in at one time or another. You may have subscribed to email newsletters on subjects ranging from ornithology to orthodontics. Most of the mail you get from these outfits is presumably A-OK with you.

I'll take it as a given that you're going to read all the emails you get from colleagues, friends, and family. Well, maybe over time, you'll come to ignore mail from Uncle Harry and Aunt Martha, especially if they insist on sending you lame joke lists. If your mother is now using email to hassle you about why you still aren't married, you have permission to ignore those emails, too.

That leaves email from just about everyone else, which likely falls into one of three buckets. These categories fit most people's definition of junk mail, or *spam:*

- » **They're trying to sell you something.** The "something" might be Viagra or Xanax. It might be a (supposedly) cheap mortgage. It might be a small-cap growth stock. It might be a Rolex. It probably means trouble.

- » **They're trying to scam you.** You have to ask yourself, why me? Of all the deserving people on the planet, how is it that you've been chosen by a private international banking firm to collect a small fortune left by a rich eccentric or the secret funds hidden by a deposed Third World diplomat? This, too, will probably get you in a pickle. (In Chapter 12, I discuss a special type of scam known as *phishing*.)

- » **They're sending you pornography.** It's out there. In a major way.

Replying to messages

A chunk of the mail that you receive presumably warrants some kind of response. To answer an email with an email of your own, click the Reply (left-pointing) arrow button on the toolbar. Or look inside the message, and roll your mouse over the line that borders the header information with the main body of the message so that Mail controls appear. Click the Reply (left-pointing) arrow.

In both scenarios, an already-addressed Reply message window appears, just waiting for you to type or dictate a response. After you've done so, whisk it along as you would any other email message.

TIP

If you want to respond to everyone who was part of the original message, click Reply All (double-left-pointing arrow) instead of Reply.

Organizing Mail by conversation

Mail lets you view messages by conversation with an attractive interface that conceals the repetitive text that would otherwise be visible in a string of separate messages.

TIP

You know that the feature is turned on when a check mark appears next to Organize by Conversation on the View menu.

When the Conversation feature is on, any of the missives that you receive that relate to an ongoing email exchange with the person (or persons) shows a number that indicates just how many of those messages are in this particular conversation, or *thread*. You see examples in Figure 10-5. Click the conversation to see the entire thread in the window to the right of the message list.

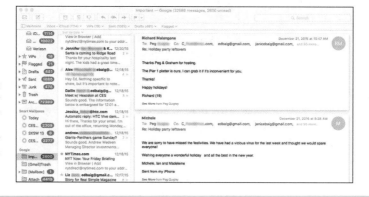

FIGURE 10-5: The number next to messages tells you how many messages are part of a conversation.

TIP

You can add a Conversation icon to the Mail toolbar to toggle back and forth between Conversation view and a view in which all the messages are expanded. To do so, choose View ⇨ Customize Toolbar.

Picking VIPs

Some mail, obviously, is too important to ignore — so important, in fact, that these senders are given special status. You have very important people in your life, so it goes without saying that you have very important senders whose messages are not to be missed. Only you know who these folks are — if not your boss, perhaps prospective clients and/or customers. I'm figuring that most of you will include your spouse, your kids, your parents, and maybe other members of your family.

In its infinite wisdom, Apple lets you turn these very important people into VIP Mail senders. You can choose up to 100 VIPs, in fact, and the process for awarding them this special designation is simple: In a Mail message, place the cursor to the right of a sender's name, click the downward-facing arrow, and select Add to VIPs. A star will appear next to the person's name, reminding you that he or she has earned VIP status.

From now on, or at least until you no longer consider the person worthy of the VIP designation, all mail from these folks lands in a special VIP Mail folder in the navigation pane (refer to Figure 10-4 earlier in this chapter). Mail also adds a mailbox for each VIP on the favorites bar so that you can look at all your VIPs individually or collectively. It's a great way to keep track of all the mail you've received from your supervisor, lest you forget some crucial task that he or she has asked you to complete.

To remove the VIP designation (say, after your supervisor has moved on), click the downward pointing arrow a second time, only this time choose Remove from VIPs. Or right-click (the alternative on a one-button mouse is Control-click) a VIP name in the Mail app sidebar and from the contextual menu click Remove from VIPs.

TIP

You can share iCloud contacts who are VIPs on one Mac with your other Macs running Mountain Lion, Mavericks, Yosemite, or El Capitan. Your iCloud VIPs turn up on the Mail apps on your iOS devices as well.

Opening mail from strangers

What was it your parents taught you about not talking to strangers? That's generally sound advice with email, too. As I hinted in the preceding section, cyberspace has a lot of misfits, creeps, and (I knew I'd have to throw in this phrase somewhere in the book) *bad apples.* They're up to no good. Because I don't want to cast aspersions on every unknown person who sends you email, go with your gut. Common sense applies.

WARNING

Even messages that arrive from people you know may not be completely clean, because sometimes, Mail accounts or contacts lists are hijacked by the bad guys. Though you can't always tell for sure, if something appears to be amiss when you receive a message from a supposed pal, proceed with caution.

You can find out a lot from the Subject line. If it refers to someone you know or what you do, I don't see the harm in opening the message.

If the greeting is generic — *Dear Wells Fargo Customer; Get Out of Debt Now* — I'd be a lot more cautious. Ditto if you don't see a subject line or if you see gross misspellings.

TIP

If a sender turns out to be a decent business prospect or your new best friend, you can always add him or her to your Contacts app by choosing one of the following alternatives:

>> Choose Message⇨Add Sender to Contacts.

>> Click to the right of a sender's name or address in the From line of a message and choose Add to Contacts from the contextual menu. (The alternative is Control-click.)

A few other handy shortcuts appear on this menu. As mentioned previously, you can add that person to the VIP list, copy the address, or send him or her a new mail message. You can also remove the person from the previous recipients list, and search for other messages in Mail from or to the person.

Junking the junk

If senders turn out to be bad news, you can sully their reputations — at least, on your own computer. Throw their mail into the junk pile. It's easy: Just click the Junk (thumbs-down) icon on the Message toolbar. The message will take on a light brown tint. Sometimes you'll see Messages that already carry that light brown hue; your Mail program is assuming that the given message is junk. It may not be, of course.

REMEMBER

Marking messages happens to be your way of training the Mail program about what you consider to be spam. Mail flags potentially objectionable messages by highlighting them with a brown tinge. Click Not Junk in the message if the junk label is inappropriate.

You can direct Mail on how to handle the junk. Choose Mail⇨Preferences and then click the Junk Mail tab. The screen shown in Figure 10-6 appears.

By default, the Mail program leaves junk mail in your inbox so that you get to be the final arbiter. If you want OS X to segregate suspect mail into its own mailbox, click the Move It to the Junk Mailbox option.

REMEMBER

As a matter of course, Mail exempts certain messages from spam filtering, including your VIPs. This typically also includes mail from senders who are in your Contacts app, as well as senders who've already received mail from you. Messages that use your full name are also exempt. In the Junk Mail section of Mail Preferences, remove the check mark next to any preferences you want to change.

TIP

Most reputable ISPs attempt to fight spam on their own. If you're satisfied with the job they're doing, leave the Trust Junk Mail Headers in Messages check box selected. Apple's Mail program will leverage your ISP's best efforts.

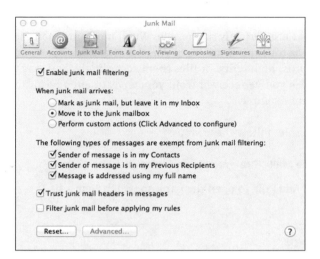

FIGURE 10-6:
The junkyard.

Avoiding spam

You can do your part to eliminate spam, too. Spammers are resourceful and can get your email address through various methods:

>> They employ automated software robots to guess at nearly every possible combination of addresses.

>> They watch what you're doing. Do you fill out online sweepstakes forms? There's a winner, all right: the spammer.

>> Do you hang out in chat rooms and Internet newsgroups? Is your account info visible in a social network? Bingo.

>> Do you post messages in a public forum? Gotcha again.

You can stop engaging in these online activities, of course, but then the Internet won't be nearly as much fun. I have a better idea. Set up a separate email account or an alias email to use in these out-in-the-open kinds of scenarios. (ISPs such as AOL let you set up myriad accounts or screen names, for example, and some services will let you set up aliases for your "real" accounts.) You'll still get spam there. Just don't bother using those accounts to send or receive email. Instead, treat your other account or accounts as the sacred ones you share with family, friends, and colleagues.

Setting the rules

As potent as Apple is at filtering spam, you can set up your own filters, or *rules*, for combating junk. You can set rules also to automatically reorganize the messages on hand that are perfectly acceptable. When incoming mail meets certain conditions, such as the subject matter or who sent the mail, the Mail program automatically forwards, highlights, or files them accordingly. You may want to redirect all the messages you've received from your investment advisor to a mailbox named Stocktips, for example.

To set up a rule, follow these steps:

1. **Choose Mail ⇨ Preferences and then click the Rules tab.**

2. **Select Add Rule to open the pane shown in Figure 10-7.**

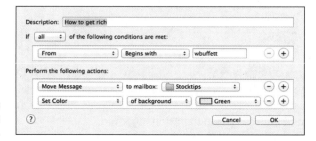

FIGURE 10-7: You have to establish rules.

3. **Choose parameters identifying which messages are affected by the rule.**

   To redirect email from your financial guru, for example, choose From from the first pop-up menu, Begins With from the second pop-up menu, and the name from the third pop-up menu. Click + to add parameters and – to remove them.

4. **Choose parameters specifying what happens to those messages.**

   You could highlight the messages in green and move them to the Stocktips mailbox, for example.

5. **When you finish entering parameters, click OK.**

Building Smart Mailboxes

In Chapter 6, you discover dynamic Smart Folders. Welcome to the email variation, *Smart Mailboxes.* Just as Smart Folders are constantly on the prowl for new items that match specific search criteria, Smart Mailboxes do the same. They're tightly integrated with Spotlight search.

You can set up Smart Mailboxes as a way to organize all mail pertaining to a specific project or all mail from a specific person. You may want to create a Smart Mailbox containing all correspondence with your boss for the most current fortnight, for example. Mail older than two weeks is replaced by the latest exchanges.

Incidentally, the messages you see in a Smart Mailbox are virtual; they still reside in their original locations. In that sense, they're similar to aliases, described in Chapter 7.

To create a Smart Mailbox, follow these steps:

1. **Choose Mailbox⇨New Smart Mailbox.**

2. **Use the pop-up menus and text fields to characterize the parameters of the mailbox (see Figure 10-8).**

The process is similar to the one you follow when creating a rule. To add criteria, click the + button. To remove a condition, click the – button.

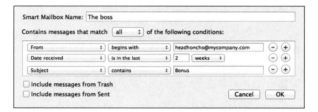

FIGURE 10-8:
The smart-
est mailbox
around.

3. **When you're finished, click OK.**

If you delete an email while in a Smart Mailbox, that message will also be deleted in its original location.

You can create a duplicate of a Smart Mailbox by holding down the Control key while you click the Smart Mailbox in the Mail sidebar. Then choose Duplicate Smart Mailbox, an option that also appears on the Mailbox menu. Why do this? One possibility: You want to create a new Smart Mailbox that uses only slightly different criteria from the mailbox you're duplicating.

Searching mail

With an assist from Spotlight, the Mac's fast and comprehensive search system, you can find specific email messages, or the contents of those messages, in a jiffy. And Mail search keeps improving through the most recent versions of OS X. For example, if you misspell a name or subject, the Mail app may recognize the mistake and serve up an appropriate suggestion or alternative. Here is how to search:

» To search within a message you have open onscreen, choose Edit⇨Find⇨ Find, and type the text you're looking for. You can perform a Find operation to find what you're looking for and (if you want) replace the word you find with another.

>> You can also search your email backlog. Just enter a search term in the search box at the upper-right portion of the Mail program screen. Choose All Mailboxes, Inbox, VIPs, Draft, Sent, or Flagged to determine how to display the results. You can use natural-language search queries along the lines of "Show me emails with attachments sent last week from my boss."

You can find messages without opening Mail. Spotlight, in my humble opinion, is the fastest and most efficient way to find wayward messages.

Opening attachments

You already know how to send attachments. But now the tide has shifted, and someone sends you one (or more). Attachments may appear with an icon in the body of the message or with a paper-clip icon in the message header area.

You have a few choices:

>> Drag the icon to the desktop or a Finder window.

>> Double-click the icon. The attachment should open in the program designed to handle it (such as Microsoft Word for a Word file or Preview for an image).

>> Click Save to save the file to a particular destination on your computer.

>> Click Quick Look to peek at the attachment without opening it. You can also choose File⇨Quick Look Attachments, or move the mouse pointer over the message header, click the Attachment icon, and then click Quick Look.

Normally, I tell people not to open attachments that they weren't expecting, even if they know the sender. Mac users can be a little more relaxed about this than their Windows cousins. While the times they are a-changin', the odds that the attachment will damage the Mac, even if it did carry some type of Windows virus, are low.

If you want to remove an attachment from an incoming message, choose Message⇨Remove Attachments.

Marking up attachments

Some attachments require a response from you. Maybe it's the contract to write a book such as this or a lease on an apartment you're renting.

Apple lets you annotate and fill in forms right from Mail. You can add substitute text, add shapes, and zoom in and circle portions of an image. You can even sign your name via the trackpad on your Mac, and insert said signature into an attached document or a PDF you are returning marked up to the sender.

Start by replying to a message, and then hover your cursor over the given attachment in the compose window. Click the Add Attachment button if the attachment isn't already embedded in your reply message. Click the caret that appears in a pop up menu and select Markup to summon the toolbar shown in Figure 10-9. From that toolbar, click the appropriate icon to sketch, draw shapes, add text, and so on. Click Done when you're satisfied and send the message on its merry way.

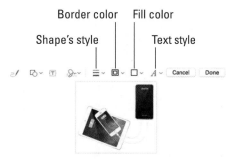

FIGURE 10-9:
You can mark up an attachment before returning it to sender.

If you don't see the popup menu, you may have to enable Markup. Go to System Preferences➪Extensions➪Actions and make sure that the Markups check box is selected.

WARNING

Markup works with PDF documents and images but not with certain other types of files, including Word documents.

Making the Most of Your Mail

Before leaving this chapter, I want to introduce other ways to get the most out of your email:

» **Become a swipe powerhouse.** With El Capitan, you can use your trackpad to swipe messages in your inbox for quick shortcuts, similar to the behavior on an iPhone or iPad. Swipe left to right to mark a message as unread (or read). Swipe in the opposite direction to trash a message. Meanwhile, if you're in full-screen mode while composing a message but you want to consult another message before proceeding, you can click outside the compose window, do what you have to do, and then click the draft to resume with your original message.

» **View a photo slideshow.** Picture attachments are afforded special treatment. In full-screen mode, by clicking Quick Look (under a drop-down menu when you click the attachments icon) and holding down the Option key at the same time, you can view attached images in a lovely full-screen slideshow. With onscreen controls, you can go back to the previous image, pause, advance to the next slide, and view an index of all pictures. You can also click to add pictures to your Photos library (see Chapter 14). When you're finished with the slideshow, press the Escape key on the keyboard to go back to the original email.

» **Pass it on.** Sometimes, you get stuff that is so rip-roaringly, hysterically funny (or, at the other extreme, so tragic and poignant) that you want to share it with everyone you know. To forward a message, click the right-pointing Forward arrow on the toolbar, or the one that appears out of nowhere when you roll the mouse by the line inside a message bordering the header with the body of the message. Enter the recipient's address in the New Message window that pops up. The entire previous email will go out intact, save for a couple of subtle additions: the Fwd: prefix in the Subject line and the phrase *Begin forwarded message* above the body of the message. You can add an introductory comment along the lines of "This made me laugh out loud."

» **Flag messages.** To call attention to messages you want to attend to later, place a little flag next to them. The easiest way to flag a message is to click the Flag icon on the toolbar. But you can also choose Message⇨ Flag or press Shift+⌘+L. Repeat Shift+⌘+L to remove the flag, choose Message⇨Flag⇨Clear Flag or click the Flag icon again. To help you determine the meaning of one flag compared with another, you can assign different colors to your flags.

» **Synchronize email.** If you have an iCloud account, you can synchronize all your rules, signatures, and other settings across all your OS X computers. You can also synchronize other Mail accounts.

» **Archive messages.** Mail that you'd like to stash somewhere but ultimately hold on to is worthy of special backup treatment. That's what archiving messages is all about. First, select the messages you want to archive. Next, choose Message⇨Archive. An archive mailbox is created for each account in which you have a message that you choose to archive. You can retrieve archived messages directly from that mailbox later.

» **Mark addresses that don't end with . . . .** Go to Mail Settings, click the Composing tab, and click Mark Addresses Not Ending with . . .. Enter the email address from your company (or wherever) that you do *not* want marked. From then on, when you're composing a message, all email addresses sent to or from that specified address will appear in black, while all other mail addresses will be shaded red. Why do this? The idea is that you can more easily identify mail dispatched to addresses outside your organization, alerting you to a potential security risk if you're exchanging, say, sensitive information.

>> **Use parental controls.** You can restrict who Junior can correspond with through email to only those addresses you've explicitly blessed. Choose ⌘ ⇨ System Preferences, and choose Parental Controls. Click the account you want to manage. You have to type your administrative password to make changes. Then click the People tab, and select the Limit Mail to Allowed Contacts check box. Click Manage and, at your discretion, enter the email addresses (and, for that matter, instant-messaging addresses) of anyone you'll let your kid communicate with. If you select the Send Requests To option, you'll receive an email plea asking for an okay to send messages to addresses not on your authorized list.

>> **Use data detectors.** A friend sends an invitation to a dinner party at a new restaurant. A travel agent emails the itinerary for your next business trip. Messages typically arrive with fragments of information you'd love to be able to act on. Mail in OS X makes it dirt-simple with *data detectors,* which can recognize appointments, addresses, phone numbers, and so on. When you move your cursor inside the body of a message next to data the program can detect, a tiny arrow signifying a pop-up menu appears. Click the arrow next to an airline departure, for example, and you can add the event to Calendar. Click next to an address, and Mail lets you create a new contact, add to an existing contact, or display an Apple map.

>> **Get rid of mail.** You can dispose of mail in several ways:

- Highlight a message and press Delete on the keyboard.

- Drag the message to the Trash.

- Click the Delete button on the toolbar.

The messages aren't permanently banished until you choose Mailbox ⇨ Erase Deleted Items. You can rid yourself of such messages in all your Mail accounts or designated accounts. Apple can automatically extinguish mail for good after one day, one week, or one month, or when you quit the Mail program. To set up this behavior, open Mail Preferences, click Accounts, choose an account, and select Mailbox Behaviors.

>> **Get notified.** You can receive alerts of new messages as they arrive or view the first few lines of a message in Notification Center, which on the Mac behaves much the same way that Notification Center functions on iOS devices such as the iPhone, iPad, and iPod touch. Refer to Chapter 3 for more details.

TIP

Do you frequently email reminders to yourself? I used to, at least before Apple added the handy Notes and Reminders apps. Details about how each program works are in Chapter 3.

Chapter 11

Schmoozing, Shopping, and Moving in Cyberspace

Folks routinely surf the web seeking specific types of information: headlines, stock quotes, vacation deals, weather, homework help, sports scores, technical support, you name it. But as much as anything, the Internet is about meeting and connecting with people. These people could be job prospects or would-be employers, or people who share your zeal for the Chicago Cubs, sushi, and Macintosh computers. Persuasion takes on a major role in cyberspace, too, as you get on your virtual high horse in various social media outlets and attempt to coax others around to your way of thinking.

Critics have often sneered, "These people need to get a life." But many *netizens* (citizens of the Internet) have rewarding lives online and offline, thank you very much. And on the Net, they're congregating in social communities with individuals of similar interests and passions.

I explore many of these avenues in this chapter.

Messaging with the Messages App

Messages (formerly iChat) is a core feature of OS X. You can use Messages to send and receive instant messages, or IMs. With IMs, conversations occur in real time, without the delays associated with email.

In addition, IM permits the kind of spontaneity that's not possible through email or even an old-fashioned phone call. Through a concept known as *presence*, you can tell not only whether the people you want to IM are currently online, but also whether they're willing to chat. Status indicators next to their names in a buddy list clue you in on their availability.

In truth, calling Messages an IM program really is selling it way short — kind of like telling somebody that Golden State Warriors star Stephen Curry knows how to make free throws. That's because the Messages app also incorporates text messaging, including a flavor unique to Apple devices (Macs and/or iOS devices) called iMessage.

Indeed, you can use iMessage to send unlimited text messages to pals with an iPhone, an iPad, an iPod touch, or another Mac, — in other words, products with an Apple pedigree.

But Messages works also with existing messaging accounts, including popular ones such as AOL's AIM, Jabber, Google Talk and Yahoo! And that opens up messaging to just anybody and almost any device.

What's more, you can do other tricks with Messages, including exchanging files, applying funky Photo Booth video effects and backdrops, or letting the person you're communicating with know your location.

In the following sections, you find out how to set up your messaging accounts and your buddy list and exchange text messages and files, talk via audioconferencing or videoconferencing, or even share your computer screen.

TIP

You can hold video chats via FaceTime, too, a separate app that I get to later in this chapter. You may find that FaceTime is easier to use than Messages, but the person you want to chat with must also have FaceTime, which is only available on relatively newer Apple computers and iOS devices. Also, FaceTime doesn't support conversations with more than two people the way the Messages does.

Getting started with the Messages app

Before we go much further, let's discuss how to set up your instant messaging account:

1. **Click the Messages icon on the dock to launch the app.**

2. **Choose Messages⇨Preferences.**

3. **Click the Accounts tab.**

4. **Click the + at the bottom of the window.**

   (Or click Add Account under the Messages menu.)

5. **Click the radio button for the account you want to add.**

   The main choices are:

   - Google

   - Yahoo!

   - AOL

   In a moment, I talk about *all* your options in a little more detail.

6. **After making your selection, click Continue and fill in the requisite account credentials.**

   If you choose Other Messages Account, you'll be asked to pick an account type from the drop down menu. Click Create when you've filled in the requested information.

The following summarizes the available options (not all of which appear in the drop-down choices under Other Messages Account):

>> **An existing AIM or AOL screen name and password:** As noted, Messages is tied in with AOL's popular IM program.

>> **A Jabber ID:** You can use a Jabber ID to exchange messages with cohorts who use the same Jabber servers. (Jabber is an open-standard chat system employed in many organizations.)

>> **A Google Talk or Yahoo! ID:** You can go to Google's and Yahoo!'s websites to sign up.

>> **An Apple ID:** You can use the iCloud.com ID that you got if you signed up for iCloud as your Apple ID. You also have an Apple ID if you signed up for an iTunes Store account. Or you can continue to use the mac.com ID or me.com ID you may have had under iCloud's predecessor services, known as .Mac (as in "dot Mac"), Mobile Me, and iTools. If you don't have an Apple ID, you can create one in Messages.

>> **A local network or classroom using Apple technology called Bonjour:** Bonjour is used for configuration-free networking throughout OS X. Through this built-in technology, Messages lets you see who on your local network is available to chat.

If you want to exploit video, you need a fast broadband Internet connection, plus a compatible camera. Apple's iSight or FaceTime camera (standard on most recent models) works well, but any digital camera or camcorder connected to your computer should do, including those you may connect through USB or FireWire.

Hey, buddy

Messages is useless without one more essential component: at least one other person with whom to schmooze.

TIP

Fortunately, when you sign into an instant messaging service, you usually have other folks to talk to, and longtime users of AOL's AIM service have probably built up a nice buddy list. Similarly, if you sign in with a Google Talk, or Yahoo! account, your buddy list may already be populated with names of people in those services.

The iMessage service lets you send and receive free and secure messages on your Mac, iPhone, iPad, and iPod touch with folks who have one or more of these devices. They'll either get your message on their mobile device or the next time they open Messages on their Macs. If, in return, someone sends you an iMessage, you'll get it on your Mac and any other iOS device you may have, with the caveat that it must be running iOS 5.0 or later (which by now it almost certainly does) and must have the same account type enabled. That is, you and your friend must have AIM enabled or iMessage enabled, and so on.

Through the Messages app you get many benefits:

>> You can send iMessages to other iOS devices and/or Macs through a phone number or email address. You can send regular text messages to non-Apple devices.

>> You can start an iMessage conversation on your Mac or some other Apple device and pick up where you left off on yet another device.

>> You can record and send audio clips.

>> You can eyeball photos and other attachments from a given conversation via a handy viewer.

>> Through read receipts, you can tell when your message has been seen by the recipient and when that person is composing a response.

>> You can share attachments of up to 100MB, including full high-definition videos and photos.

Take a look at the Messages window in Figure 11-1. Any ongoing conversations are listed down the left side of the screen, with the most recent on top. On the right side, you see the exchanges from your current conversation, including pictures that may have been part of your exchange.

To add new people to a message or conversation, click the New Message button (labeled in Figure 11-1) and then add a name, an email address or a phone number in the To field. Or, click the + all the way to the right of the To field, as shown in Figure 11-2, and choose a person from your Contacts app, your buddies, or any groups you've set up. Indeed, you can add multiple people to the conversation.

FaceTime Audio

Initiate FaceTime video call

Compose new message   Invite/Ask to share screen

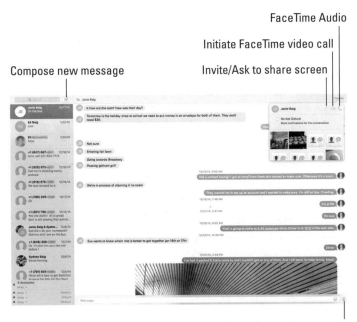

FIGURE 11-1: iMessage conversations look like this.

Record an audio message

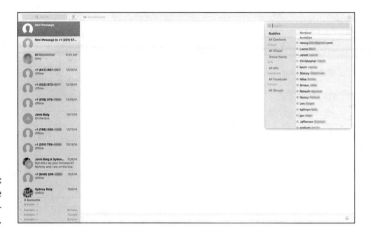

FIGURE 11-2:
Finding people
to communi-
cate with.

WARNING

If you are using iMessage to send a group message, everyone within the group must have a phone number or email address associated with iMessage. Folks with an iPhone (running iOS 8 software or later) can send a message to a group via the standard SMS texting protocol, even those who are not registered with iMessage.

Adding buddies and groups to your buddy list

Though you don't have to use the buddy list for all your friends and contacts, it can be helpful. To summon your list of buddies, choose Window➪Buddies or press ⌘ + 1 on the keyboard.

In your buddy list, you can add and organize your contacts:

>> **Add a new buddy to the list:** Click the + at the lower-left corner of the Buddies window and then choose Add Buddy from the resulting menu. In the window that appears, type your buddy's AIM, Yahoo!, Gmail, or Mac.com account, plus his or her real first and last names in the designated fields. You can also add the new buddy to a group.

Alternatively, choose an entry from your contacts by clicking the downward-pointing arrow in the lower-right corner of the Add Buddy window. The person's name turns up instantly in your buddy list.

TIP

>> **Add a group (perhaps your coworkers, soccer team, and so on):** After clicking the + at the upper-right corner of the field in which you want to address your message, which summons your contacts, click Group Name. You have to have already set up a group within Contacts on your Mac (or on another device via iCloud) for the group name to appear here.

Using the buddy list to chat

When you're available to chat as part of an IM conversation, you may see a buddy list that has a bunch of visual status cues. Your buddy may have included a mug shot, perhaps through Photo Booth. Or buddies may express themselves through small images called *buddy icons.* You can even animate these icons in OS X.

How you communicate depends on which of the icons at the bottom of the buddy list you end up clicking. Click the icon with the *A* to begin a text chat. Click the telephone-symbol icon to initiate a voice or audio chat. Click the movie-camera icon to connect through video. And click the icon with two rectangles to ask your chat partner whether he or she is willing to share his or her Mac screen.

Communicating online status

Mostly, you'll be able to tell whether your buddies are online at the moment and willing to give you the time of day. Here's how:

» A green circle to the left of a person's name means that he or she is ready and (presumably) willing to talk.

» A red circle means that the person is online but otherwise engaged. The person is considered to be Away.

» A yellow circle means that the person is idle and hasn't used the machine for a while. (The window tells you how long the person has been in this state.) Your buddy just hasn't bothered to change his or her status from Available to Away.

» If a name is dimmed, your buddy is offline or not authorized to communicate with you. That's typically the case when you first add a buddy via Google Talk or Jabber.

TIP

You can set your own status for everyone else to see, and you aren't limited to Available or Away. Click below your own name and choose Custom Available or Custom Away from the contextual menu. You can choose a custom message to appear next to a green or red circle, depending on your particular set of circumstances. Type any message you want, such as *Busy but can chat in a pinch* or *Back after lunch.*

Incidentally, if you've been absent from the computer for a while, the Mac kindly welcomes you back to the machine and asks whether you want to change your chat status from Away back to Available.

Chatting

To initiate an instant message, follow these steps:

1. **Double-click a name in the buddy list, which pops up whenever you open Messages.**

   Or highlight a name in the list and click the *A* icon.

   Alternatively, you can choose File⇨New Message and enter the name of the person with whom you'd like to chat, assuming that the person is among your buddies or contacts. If the person isn't in your buddy list or Contacts app, enter the person's email address or (in the case of an iPhone) their phone number in the To field of the Messages window.

2. **Type something in the bottom box.**

   Hey stranger will suffice for now.

   What you type instantly appears in a bubble in the upper portion of the window. In the View menu, you can make text bigger or smaller. Your contact of course can choose to ignore your message, just as you can ignore a message that comes the other way.

   If the person responds, what he or she has to say appears in its own bubble. And so on. If you look back at Figure 11-1, you'll see what a conversation looks like.

Adding emoticons

You can type your own smileys and emoticons or check out Apple's own collection. Click the emoticon icon at the right edge of the field in which you type your message. All sorts of choices are presented to you, ranging from a small picture of a bumblebee (for use, I suppose, when you really want to sting it to the person you are interacting with) to a confounded face (to let the other person know that he's making zero sense).

Saving an IM exchange

Now suppose that you're having an important IM exchange with your lawyer or accountant, or swapping tuna-casserole recipes with your best friend. You may want a record of your conversation that you can easily refer to later. To create a transcript of your session, choose Messages⇨Preferences, click the General tab of Messages Preferences, and then select the Save History When Conversations Are Closed check box (see Figure 11-3). You can find the appropriate transcript by opening Finder and searching for *"chat transcript"* under the Kind category when conducting a Spotlight search.

To wipe away the record, choose Edit⇨Clear Transcript.

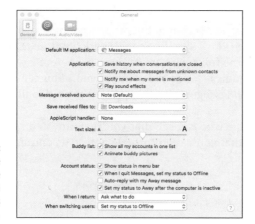

FIGURE 11-3:
Chatting the
way you like
it through
Messages
Preferences.

Exchanging files over IM

TIP

You can also use iMessages (or other text-chat services, such as AIM and Google Talk) to send files to your IM buddy or get a file in return. Not only is this method convenient, but also, unlike with email, it imposes no size restriction on the file you're sharing. (You can send only one file at a time, however.) Here are a few different ways you can send a file:

>> Select a name in your buddy list and then choose Buddies⇨Send File. Select the file you want to send.

>> Alternatively, drag a file to a buddy's name or into an open chat window.

>> If you're chatting with a bunch of folks at the same time, drag the file over the name of the person you want to send it to.

>> If you're in a video chat, drag a file to the upper half of the video chat window.

Participants in a chat have the option to accept or reject the incoming file.

Setting your Privacy preferences

Messages lets you block people and decide who can see you're online, but exactly how you can go about it varies by account. To find the available settings, follow these steps:

1. **Open Messages Preferences from the Messages menu.**

2. **Click the Accounts tab and choose the account in which you want to apply privacy settings.**

3. **Click the Privacy tab (if available) within that chosen account to see the settings.**

You'll see the Privacy tab in AOL but not in other accounts. In AOL, if a person gets on your nerves select the Block Specific People check box. Click Edit List, click the +, and add the names of the folks who are on your keep-'em-away list. (Just know that your would-be buddies can do the same to you.) You can also block specific addresses when using iMessages with an Apple ID or an iCloud account.

To proactively determine who can see that you're online and send you messages, choose a privacy level that you're comfortable with. The options are

>> Allow anyone.

>> Allow people in my buddy list.

>> Allow specific people. (If you make this choice, you have to type each person's AIM, .mac.com, iCloud.com, or .me.com address.)

>> Block everyone.

>> Block specific people. (Again, type the appropriate addresses.)

TIP

You can also arrange, inside Messages Preferences, to receive a notification whenever you get a message from unknown contacts. Or get a notification when your name is mentioned. Select the appropriate check boxes on the General tab to select these options.

TIP

Sometimes you'll want to take leave of a particular conversation, at least temporarily. If so, click the Details button (labeled in Figure 11-1), and select the Do Not Disturb check box to mute notifications for the given conversation.

Recording an audio message

Given the informal and short form nature of text messages, your words can sometimes get misunderstood. If you're concerned about that, you may want to consider recording an audio message so that the recipient can not only read what you have to say but hear how you say it. Click the microphone icon in the text field (consult Figure 11-1), and record your words. Click the red stop button when you've finished speaking. Click Send to send the message off, or click Cancel to re-record your message. The recipient will be able to play back the message inside the Messages conversation.

Seeing is believing; hearing, too

IMing and text chatting in general are kind of yesterday's news (though still darn useful). The 21st-century way of communicating is video phone calls. Apple provides two ways to accomplish this minor miracle: If you start a video chat via AIM

Jabber, Google Talk, or Bonjour, you'll go through Messages. If you start instead with a person using iMessage, you'll go through FaceTime, the separate app that first made its mark on the iPhone. I have more to say on FaceTime later in the chapter. (Never mind that a primitive version of this technology was exhibited at the 1964 New York World's Fair.)

Assuming that your camera and microphone are configured to your liking, you can take advantage of 21st-century innovations by clicking the video-camera icon in the buddy list or, for just an audio session, clicking the telephone icon. As usual, your IM partner has the option to accept or decline the invitation. If he or she accepts, you can gaze at each other full-screen. (Your image appears in a smaller window.)

By clicking the Effects button, you can replace the normal background with gorgeous or bizarre backdrops from Photo Booth, as highlighted in Chapter 5.

The quality generally is pretty good, though the picture may show some distortion, depending on your broadband connection.

Screen sharing

Now suppose that you and your buddy want to toil together on a website or some other project from far away. If you both have Macs dating back to Leopard (or newer), you can work on one screen or the other; just click back and forth to swap screens. This stunt works in AIM, Jabber, Google Talk, and Bonjour but notably not in iMessage or Yahoo!.

You can share the screen in a couple of ways. Choose Buddies ➪ Invite to Share My Screen with *name of person (or phone number)*, or choose Buddies ➪ Ask to Share *name of person's* Screen. Or after you've initiated a conversation, click Details in the Messages window and then click the Screen Share button (labeled in Figure 11-1). Then select Invite to Share My Screen or Ask to Share Screen."

If you're the one being asked, rest assured that you can politely decline or even block the user. But positive thoughts, here, folks, so I assume that you've given or received the green light. You and your buddy can both run amok on the shared desktop, even copying files by dragging them from one desktop to the other. Messages keeps an audio chat going so that you can let each other know what you're up to.

Not satisfied with what your chat buddy is telling you? Press Control+Escape to put an instant kibosh on the screen-sharing session or click the X to close.

If you're sharing the other person's screen, you'll notice your own Mac desktop in a tiny window.

WARNING

As you might imagine, this screen-sharing business can get a little too close to home, especially if you don't fully trust the person you're letting loose on your computer. Be especially leery if someone who's not in your buddy list comes calling with a screen-sharing request. You should also be careful before granting permission to someone from your Bonjour list. People aren't always who they say they are. You can also share your screen without giving control to the other person. The person can highlight areas on your screen by clicking but can't doctor or move the file.

Face Time for FaceTime

Suppose that you want to talk to a friend who has an iPhone 4 or later, iPod touch, or iPad 2 or later. Through FaceTime, you can gab and see them, too. FaceTime works from Mac to Mac as well. You need OS X version 10.6.6 or later and an Ethernet or Wi-Fi connection to the Internet. (People at the other end using an iPhone 4 or later, recent iPod touch, iPad 2 or later, or iPad mini can use a cellular connection as well, provided that the devices are running iOS 6 or later.)

You can use the iSight, or FaceTime camera that's standard on recent Macs. Or you can use an external camera hooked up to your Mac through FireWire, USB, or (via an adapter) Thunderbolt.

FaceTime does audio calls too. Anyone receiving such a call on a Mac must have OS X 10.9.2 or later.

Getting started with FaceTime

FaceTime is built into OS X.

The first time you use it, you have to sign in to FaceTime by using your Apple ID, which can be your iTunes Store account or another Apple account. If you'd rather use a new Apple ID, you can create one. You also have to enter an email address; callers will use that address to call you from their Macs or iOS devices.

If this is the first time you've used this email address for FaceTime, Apple sends an email to that address to verify the account. Click Verify Now and enter your Apple ID and password to complete FaceTime setup.

If you want to add another email account to associate with FaceTime, choose FaceTime ⇨ Preferences and click Add Another E-Mail in the FaceTime Preferences window. That way, people can reach you via more than one email account.

Making a FaceTime call

To initiate a FaceTime video call after you've signed in to the app, enter a name, an email address, or a phone number in the window shown in Figure 11-4. Or, click the + button or the Contacts button to summon your list of contacts. From there, do one of the following:

>> To make a FaceTime video call, click the video icon next to a person's name.

>> To make a FaceTime audio call or regular phone call, click the audio icon.

In Figure 11-4 you also see a log of all recent FaceTime audio or video calls that you've made or received, or the incoming ones you missed (which appear in red). Consider this Recents list a handy shortcut to calling one of these folks back.

FIGURE 11-4:
Choosing the person to FaceTime with.

You can check out what you look like in a window before making a FaceTime call. Powder your nose, straighten your tie, put on a happy face. After a call is under way, you can still see what you look like to the other person through a picture-in-picture window that you can drag around the video call window. To mute your voice, click the microphone icon (shown in Figure 11-5); you'll still be seen. Click the Full Screen button (also shown in Figure 11-5) to take over the full Mac screen; you'll still see a picture-in-picture window. The Mute, End Call, and Full Screen buttons disappear after a few seconds. To bring them back during a call, move your cursor over the FaceTime window.

If you failed to connect with a recipient through FaceTime, click the green Call Back button in the call window. Or tap to send a Message.

FIGURE 11-5:
A FaceTime call
in progress —
with daughter
Sydney.

Receiving a FaceTime call

FaceTime doesn't have to be open for you to receive a video call from a friend. The app can open automatically so that your Mac starts ringing and you see the caller's name (and maybe picture too) in the window, as shown in Figure 11-6. Click the green Accept button to answer the call or the red Decline button to reject it.

TIP

If you failed to reach someone, you can click the Call Back button that appears to try FaceTime with the person again later. (You see a badge next to the FaceTime icon on the dock showing the number of FaceTime calls you missed, if any.)

TIP

If you don't want to be disturbed by an incoming FaceTime call, open Face-Time Preferences from Mac's toolbar and turn off FaceTime. You can also turn FaceTime off from the FaceTime menu.

FIGURE 11-6:
Please take my call.

Doing more FaceTime tricks

You can do even more in FaceTime:

>> **Change orientation.** When you get a call from an iPhone or an iPod touch, the call window on your Mac rotates if the caller changes the orientation of his device. You're not about to rotate the Mac as you would one of those

handheld devices, but you can still change the orientation that the caller sees. Choose FaceTime➪Video and then choose either Use Portrait or Use Landscape. Or click the small picture-in-picture window and then click the Rotate icon. You can also rotate two fingers on the trackpad.

» **Resize the video call window.** You can make the video call window bigger by choosing Window➪Zoom. Choose the command again to revert to the standard-size window. As with any window, you can expand it by dragging a window edge, and you can go full-screen during a call.

» **Pause a call.** If you need to pause a video call, choose FaceTime➪Hide FaceTime or Window➪Minimize. Click the FaceTime icon on the dock to resume the call.

» **Add a caller to or update contacts.** In the Recents list, click the circled right arrow next to a caller's name or number. In the next screen, click Create or Update Contact, filling in or adding any missing contact information as needed.

» **Block caller.** Choose FaceTime Preferences, click the Blocked tab, and then select the Add + button to add addresses for callers you want to block.

» **Change how you are reached.** You can list any of the email accounts and phone numbers for FaceTime as the account that the people trying to reach you can use. To add an account, open FaceTime Preferences, and then click Add Email. You can also click to remove the check mark next to any accounts that you no longer want people to be able to use to get hold of you in FaceTime.

» **Change ringtone.** In FaceTime Preferences, click Ringtone and choose any alternative tones from the drop-down list.

TIP

Open Notifications settings in System Preferences to arrange alerts for FaceTime calls, and to determine whether and how you see FaceTime notifications in Notification Center.

TIP

If you're traveling in another country, you can arrange it so that any local calls made to iPhone users through FaceTime are using the proper native format for making that call. In FaceTime Preferences, click Apple ID, choose Change Location, and select the appropriate country or region.

Social Networking

Who do you know? Who do your friends know? Who do the friends of your friends know? What's on their minds? And how can you benefit from six (or many fewer) degrees of separation?

BLOGS

Blogs (short for *weblogs)* have become Internet phenomena, with thousands of new blogs popping up every day. The *blogosphere* has already been exploited by politicians, educational institutions, marketers, publicists, and traditional media outlets.

Some bloggers may dream of becoming journalistic superstars overnight, though only a few achieve such status. Many people in the mainstream media fret that bloggers lack editorial scrutiny and journalistic standards, but then again, many blogs have become highly respected media outlets in their own right. Still, most blogs are nothing more than personal journals meant to be read by a tight circle of friends and family. Bloggers share their musings, provide links to other content, and invite comments from others.

Destinations for creating and hosting a blog include Google's free Blogger.com service, WordPress (also free, with premium options), and TypePad (starting at around $9 a month).

Blogs and other news feeds are sometimes distributed through technology known as *RSS,* shorthand for *Really Simple Syndication.* You can receive RSS feeds through third-party apps, including RSS Bot, NewsBar, and Leaf RSS Reader, which are among the many news readers available in the Mac App Store (read on).

In Safari, you can also open the sidebar, click the Shared Links (@) button at the top, and then click the Subscriptions button at the bottom. From there, click Add Feed to add a feed from the web page you're visiting.

Those questions are just the tip of the iceberg in terms of what online social networks are all about. By leveraging your direct and indirect contacts, you may find a place to live, broker the deal of the century, or land a recording contract. That's the hope, anyway. I hate to be a glass-is-half-empty kind of guy, but none of these outcomes is guaranteed.

Still, social networking sites can help you network and help you be social. They may combine blogs, instant messaging, photo and video sharing, games, music, and a lot more.

Facebook

Facebook is the leading purveyor of social networking these days, with more than 1.5 billion members and counting. Yes, you read right: *billion* with a *b.* You can read news feeds from friends, play games, post pictures, opine on any topic left to your imagination, read what these other people are reading, and so much more.

Apple embraced Facebook in a major way starting with Mountain Lion, and that embrace has continued into the El Capitan era. Here are the ways you can integrate Facebook and your Mac:

» **Populate your contacts.** If you supply your Facebook account credentials to the Mac (do so in the Internet Accounts section of System Preferences), all your Facebook friends magically show up in your Mac Contacts app, complete with their Facebook profile pictures, email addresses, phone numbers, and whatever else they chose to share. (If you've already set up Contacts listings for these folks, the Facebook info is added to any other addresses and phone numbers you may have had for these pals.)

What's more, all this stuff is kept up to date. If a Facebook friend changes his phone number or image through the social network, for example, the change is automatically applied to his listing in the Mac's Contacts app. Like I said, it's magic.

» **Keep your Calendar up-to-date.** All your friends' birthdays (at least, those who share the day of their birth in Facebook) are listed in Calendar. You have no more excuses for not getting them a card or present.

» **Share items on Facebook directly from your Mac apps.** Facebook, of course, is listed on the Share menu that shows up in numerous OS X and third-party apps. You can post links from Safari to Facebook, as well as photos from Photos, Preview, Quick Look, and Photo Booth.

When you choose Share⬦Facebook, a so-called *share sheet* turns up, an example of which is shown in Figure 11-7. If you summon a share sheet to share a photo in Facebook, for example, you can choose which of your Facebook friends get to see the picture and in which Facebook album the photo is posted. At your discretion, you can also choose to make your location discoverable when sending the photo.

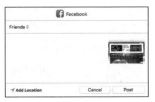

FIGURE 11-7:
You can post to Facebook throughout OS X.

LinkedIn and others

LinkedIn also gained most-favored nation-status in OS X. This highly popular business-oriented social network is integrated throughout El Capitan.

You can find other major social networks too, of course, including Google-owned Google+, and Google-owned YouTube, which has become a cultural phenomenon in its own right and is most representative of the video breed. But many other popular examples exist, even if they don't fit the classic definition of social networking. There's FaceBook-owned Instagram, Craigslist (global communities with free classifieds), Flickr (Yahoo!'s image-sharing site), Tumblr (also owned by Yahoo!), and Pinterest (pin images on a pinboard).

Speaking of social communications, read the next section for a Twitter-size explanation of Twitter.

Twitter

140 characters is all Twitter gets u. Built around *tweets,* a popular form of *micro blogging.* Author's followers can read and reply to tweets.

Tweets are all about the kind of brevity exhibited here, because you're indeed limited to 140 characters when you send one of these small bursts of information in real time on its merry way. I'm sorry to say that a space counts as one of those precious few characters.

You don't have to tweet to get a lot out of Twitter. By following what other people have to say or share, you can get a quick handle on news (often before it's reported in conventional media outlets), ideas, opinions, and what's trending around the world. By clicking the links that are often included with tweets (the links are often condensed to save character space), you can take a much deeper dive into what a person is trying to say or show through photos, videos, and conversations. You can reply to tweets, *retweet* them (often accompanied by your own wry comments — kept brief, of course), and send someone a direct message.

When you're ready to write your own messages, you may want to mention other folks in your tweet, just to widen the number of people who are likely to see what you have to say; the people who follow the folks you mention will be exposed to your own tweet. It's a good way to collect followers. You do that by using a Twitter username preceded by the @ sign.

As it did with Facebook, Apple elevated Twitter's presence throughout OS X.

Go to System Preferences➪Internet Accounts, and enter your Twitter credentials. From then on, you can tweet from the Share menu, via tweet sheets, which are similar to the share sheets in Facebook.

Ever mindful of the strict 140-character limit, Apple counts down the number of characters for you as you compose your tweet. You can add your location to a tweet as well.

If any of your followers mentions you in one of his or her own tweets, or if someone sends you a direct message in Twitter, you'll be notified in Notification Center, unless you modify the setting in System Preferences under Notifications.

If you want to spread the word about an app in the Mac App Store, you can click the app's Buy button and then choose Share on Twitter from the resulting menu. You can also share the app on Facebook, copy the link or tell a friend via email.

TIP

And by all means, follow me on Twitter @edbaig.

Buying Stuff Online: The Mac App Store

Grandpa, what was it like when people shopped in stores?

I doubt you'll hear such a question any time soon. But more and more, people are purchasing products online, and those products aren't just books, music, and software. Increasingly, folks go to the Net to shop for big-ticket items: backyard swing sets for the kiddies, high-definition televisions, even automobiles. Not to mention the groceries. Electronic commerce (*e-commerce*) is alive and kicking, with Amazon.com and eBay.com at the top of the virtual heap.

Speaking of commerce, I've already mentioned the Mac App Store, modeled after the App Store for the iPhone, iPod, iPod touch, and iPad. These days, the Mac App Store is Apple's preferred way to sell you software, including the El Capitan upgrade itself, which you don't get through a sale; it's free, after all. What's more, you can install El Capitan on any other Macs you own that meet the system requirements.

OS X upgrades are delivered through the Mac App Store, as are updates for any other software you buy through the joint.

When you enter the Mac App Store by clicking its icon on the dock, you're welcomed by a screen that looks like Figure 11-8. I say *looks like* because the content of the store is ever-changing.

Armed with your Apple ID, you're ready to search for Mac apps, purchase and download the ones you like, and (if you're so inclined) write reviews to let others know what you think of those apps.

If you already have an iTunes Store account, you can use it to make purchases from the Mac App Store.

REMEMBER

FIGURE 11-8:
Lots of rich apps are available in the Mac App Store.

Finding apps

You can browse the stores in numerous ways. Your main choices are as follows:

>> **Featured:** Apps that are featured are the new apps that Apple, for one reason or another, thinks merit attention. On the Featured page, you see ad banners that rotate with new offerings. Apple sometimes lumps apps together in collections to get you to consider programs that you might not otherwise stumble upon.

>> **Top Charts:** Here's where you'll find the top paid apps (those requiring you to part with real loot), the top free apps, and the top-grossing apps.

>> **Categories:** As its name suggests, you can find apps here by category. Numerous categories were available to pore through as of this writing. Ready? Here goes: Business, Developer Tools, Education, Entertainment, Finance, Games, Graphics & Design, Health & Fitness, Lifestyle, Medical, Music, News, Photography, Productivity, Reference, Social Networking, Sports, Travel, Utilities, Video, Weather. Did I miss any? Did Apple?

>> **Purchased:** As the name suggests, these are apps you've bought, either on this Mac or another machine.

>> **Updates:** Here's where you can download updates to any of the apps on your machine, including OS X itself.

If you already know the name of the app you're looking for (or think you do), enter it in the search box in the upper-right corner of the Mac App Store window.

Figuring out whether an app is worth it

You can get an awful lot of information about an app to help you make an informed purchasing decision. Figure 11-9 shows the landing page for Quicken. Near the top, on the left side, you see the app's price: $74.99. Move down the page, and you see pictures of the app and get some information on its category, version number, size, languages, and seller (Intuit).

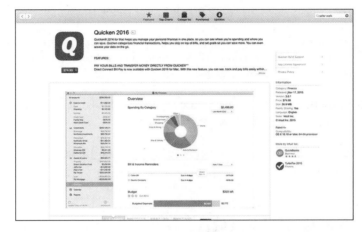

FIGURE 11-9: Read all about an app to see whether it's worth your time and money.

You also see the app's rating, which is based on whether it contains violence, offensive language, suggestive themes, and so on. Quicken carries a 4+ rating, meaning that it contains no objectionable material. The other ratings guidelines are listed as 9+, 12+, or 17+. Purchases can be shared with other members of your clan through Family Sharing.

Scroll down some more to see customer ratings and reviews by people just like you, sorted as you want by most helpful, most favorable, most critical, or most recent. Feel free to add your own two cents after playing around with some apps.

Making a purchase

When you're sold on an app, click the app price to buy it. (Or click the word *Get* if the app is free. If you've previously purchased the app, you'll see the word *Open* instead.) You have to be signed in to the Mac App Store with your store account or Apple ID to complete the purchase. The first time you try to fetch an app from a new computer, you must present your credit-card number and billing credentials.

After you're past all that and the download commences, you see a progress indicator in Launchpad and Finder that lets you know when you can start playing with the new program.

If you received an iTunes gift card (and aren't you lucky?), click Redeem in the Quick Links section of the Featured, Top Charts, and Categories pages to credit your store account or to fetch the specific app associated with the gift code.

Some apps — frequently games, but other types of apps as well — give you the option to purchase add-on features after the fact. These features are known as *in-app purchases,* and when you agree to the transaction, they typically unlock features you wouldn't otherwise be able to get to. When you make an in-app purchase, you're again asked to provide your Apple ID and password.

If and when you grow weary of an app, you can easily uninstall it. In Launchpad, hold down an app's icon until all the icons on the screen start to jiggle. Click the X Delete button on the app you want to get rid of.

None of this seems foreign to any readers of this book who own an iPhone or iPad. Removing an app on those devices is similar.

You can always reinstall an app by clicking the Install button for the app in the Purchased list.

Read All About It: iBooks

Apple also sells its version of e-books (electronic books) for Mac users, as well as for folks with an iPhone, iPad, or iPod touch. In the Apple lexicon, an e-book is an iBook, and you can buy such books from the iBooks Store on your Mac, which you launch from inside the iBooks app.

Best sellers, classics, and textbooks are for sale (or, in some cases, are free!) and finding something pleasurable to read is easy and enjoyable.

Finding something to read

In many ways, the layout of the iBook Store is similar to that of the Mac App Store. Just as you have numerous ways to find suitable apps, so it goes with books.

Apple will surface certain books in the Featured section of the store, or you can consult Top Charts (top paid and top free books), *The New York Times* best-seller list (fiction and nonfiction), select titles from various categories (biographies and memoirs, mysteries and thrillers, travel and adventure, and so on), and find books by writers who appear in a Top Authors list.

A RESEARCHER'S TOOLBOX

Imagine that you could alter or update the *Encylopedia Britannica* or *World Book Encyclopedia* at will. Now you have some idea of what Wikipedia (www.wikipedia.org) is all about. It's billed as being a free encyclopedia that *anyone* can edit. At the very least, entries are timely, and Wikipedia covers a broader topic spectrum than a print encyclopedia could ever handle. Moreover, the collaborative global perspective may provide insights that are lacking in other reference material.

I know what you're thinking: There's a flip side to all this. What if I'm mischievous? What if I'm biased? What if I'm a misinformed know-it-all? Why couldn't I change the text to read that the South won the Civil War or Dewey beat Truman? Yes, it can and does happen, because the very essence of a wiki allows anyone who has an Internet connection to mess with any of the references. In most instances, blatant vandalism and dubious submissions are corrected by the collective efforts of honest writers and editors around the world.

But open-sourced wiki entries are organic and never quite finished, and mistakes are introduced, overtly or subtly, consciously or otherwise. One side of an argument may be presented more eloquently than another. You almost always find room for interpretation and debate. Wikipedia is a remarkably useful online resource, provided that you recognize its limitations and don't treat everything you come across as gospel.

You also find links for free books, books that have been made into movies, and more. Some titles have special multimedia features, including interactive pictures and videos.

When you land on a title that sparks your interest, you can get all sorts of information to help you reach an informed decision about whether the book is ultimately worth your time and money. Figure 11-10 shows a representative listing: the Details page for the Stephen King novel *Doctor Sleep.* The page offers a description of the book, publisher information, an excerpt from a *Publishers Weekly* review, the number of pages, and more.

Click the Ratings and Reviews link to read critiques by fellow bookworms or to compose your own review. Click Related to view other titles by King and to see some of the books that readers who bought this particular book also bought. Even better, you can click Get Sample to download a sample of the book before buying it.

If you do decide to purchase it, click the Buy Book button, which also lists the price: $12.99, in the case of *Doctor Sleep.* You have to enter your Apple ID and password to complete the transaction.

FIGURE 11-10:
Gaining insight
into *Doctor
Sleep* before
deciding to
buy it.

TIP

Incidentally, the titles you buy from the iBooks Store on your other devices are stored in iCloud, which means that you can download them to your Mac. There's a caveat, though: The computer must be authorized. Open iBooks, choose Store⇨Authorize This Computer. Be aware that you can authorize five machines, so if you bump up against the maximum number, you must deauthorize one of your other computers first. The Deauthorize This Computer option also appears under the Store menu.

Reading a book

The books you buy through the iBooks Store land in your iBooks library, shown in Figure 11-11. The book cover thumbnails representing iBooks you've downloaded as a sample show a Sample label in the upper-right corner. The books that reside on iCloud and haven't been downloaded to this particular Mac display a cloud icon in the upper-right corner of their thumbnails.

You can group thumbnails by collection (Books, PDFs, Kids), by author (with the author names appearing in a panel down the left side of the library window), or by category. If you prefer, you can display a list of your books without revealing any thumbnails.

While the iBooks app can organize your PDFs, if you click to read a PDF, it'll open in Preview, Adobe Reader, or some other designated program.

The beauty of reading iBooks on the Mac as opposed to, say, reading them on your smartphone or tablet is the extra screen real estate at your disposal. You might put the space to good use by keeping multiple books open in multiple windows — useful for a student doing research.

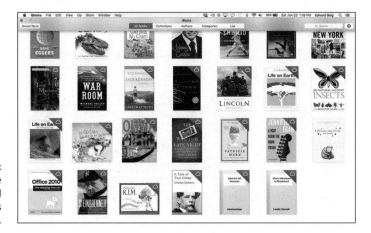

When you're ready to read a title, double-click its thumbnail. You can advance a page or go back to a previous page within an open book in one of three ways:

>> Use the arrow keys on your keyboard.

>> Move the mouse pointer to the right or left edge of the page and then click the onscreen arrow that appears.

>> Use the left or right swipe gesture on your mouse or trackpad.

Here are some other iBooks tricks:

>> **Summon the table of contents.** Click the Table of Contents button (labeled in Figure 11-12). Be aware that the button may look a little bit different, depending on the book.

>> **Bookmark a page.** Click the triangle next to the Bookmark button (also labeled in Figure 11-12). If a page is bookmarked, the bookmark icon on the upper-right corner of the book turns red. Click the triangle again to delete the bookmark.

>> **Change the font, font size, or theme.** Click the icon that has small and large As, and choose a font from the list that appears: Athelas, Charter, Georgia, Iowan, Palatino, Seravek, San Francisco, or Times New Roman. You also have three themes or backgrounds to choose among: white, sepia, and a night theme that turns the background black.

>> **Highlight a passage.** Select some text, and pick a color from the list that appears. Highlighted text appears in a pane on the left side of the screen.

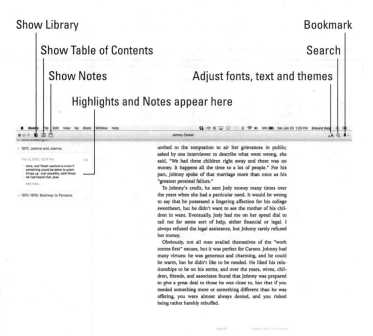

Show Library

Show Table of Contents

Show Notes

Highlights and Notes appear here

Bookmark

Search

Adjust fonts, text and themes

FIGURE 11-12:
You can't do
all this with a
paper book.

>> **Add a note.** Select some text. Upon doing so a card pointing to the high-lighted text shows an Add Note option. Click Add Note and a blank stickie-style note appears in the left or right margin of the book. Type your note inside the blank stickie. To remove the note (and highlight) click the selected text again, and click Remove Note or if you prefer Remove Highlight & Note.

>> **View a definition.** Don't know what a word you come across means? Not a problem. Double-click the word in question, and your Mac kindly provides a dictionary definition. Bonus: You might also see a thesaurus listing.

>> **Search.** Find a word, character, phrase, or page number. Type your search query, and click any appropriate result.

>> **Have a book read aloud.** To have the Mac read to you (or your child), click the speaker button. (The speak-aloud option is available only for certain titles and not shown in Figure 11-12.)

TIP

If you start reading an iBook on your Mac (or, for that matter, on any of your other devices), you can resume reading from where you left off on another machine, provided both devices have Internet access and you've signed into them with the same Apple ID. There's no reason to bookmark the last page you were reading.

Mapping Your Way Around

The Maps app is handy whether you need help finding your way around an unfamiliar place or are wondering whether there's a better route to avoid traffic. In some metropolitan areas, including New York City as shown in Figure 11-13, you can call upon public transportation directions too.

Inside the app, you can exploit a local-search feature to find restaurants, shops, and landmarks in the vicinity, with ratings from Yelp, pictures, and reviews. You can get turn-by-turn driving directions to wherever it is you want to go, as well as walking directions and, as mentioned, transit directions (in select areas), which are sometimes accompanied by timely weather or other alerts. And you can send directions from your Mac to your iPhone or iPad, which pipe in with voice navigation.

The Maps app is integrated throughout OS X, meaning that you can summon maps inside your Contacts, Calendar, Mail, Messages, Notes, and Reminders apps or share via Facebook, Twitter or AirDrop. Hover your cursor over an address in Contacts, for example, and you see a tiny indicator that resembles a magnifying glass; click it to summon the location inside Maps.

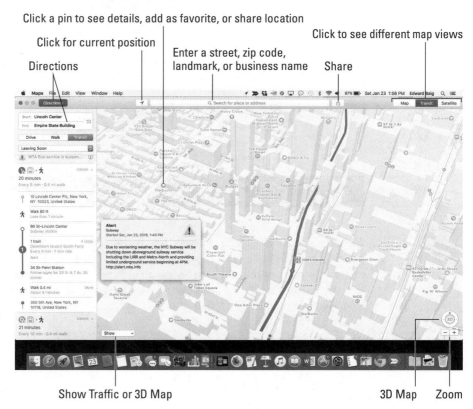

Click a pin to see details, add as favorite, or share location

Click for current position

Directions

Enter a street, zip code, landmark, or business name

Share

Click to see different map views

FIGURE 11-13:
Viewing buildings and landmarks in midtown Manhattan.

Show Traffic or 3D Map

3D Map   Zoom

Apple's Maps boasts splendid graphics, and in select cities, you can display a photorealistic 3D Flyover view of the area. Zoom in by using multitouch gestures on the Mac's trackpad (if you have one) or Magic Mouse or Magic Mouse 2.

Figure 11-13 shows close-up depictions of buildings, hotels, and landmarks in midtown Manhattan. When you click the different view tabs at the top, you can see a hybrid of this view and satellite imagery or just the satellite view.

If you click a pin on the map representing a restaurant or hotel, you see an information card similar to the one shown in Figure 11-14. The card reveals all kind of helpful stuff, including the phone number of the place, Yelp reviews, pictures, and directions. You can add the place to your Contacts app or choose it as a favorite. And click the Share button to send it to your iPhone or iPad, or to share it in numerous other ways.

FIGURE 11-14: Feeling hungry? The Maps app can give you the lowdown.

Meantime, click the traffic button (under the Show button in Figure 11-14) to see whether you'll get to your destination quickly or whether traffic has slowed to a snarl. Orange dots that turn up on a map indicate a slowdown along the route. Red dots mean that traffic is stop-and-go, and given a choice, maybe you should be a no-go.

Showing Your Game Face

You don't have to be connected to the Internet to play games on your Mac, of course. But when you *are* connected, you can best exploit Game Center, another feature borrowed from the iPhone and iPad. Through Game Center, you can play online games with friends locally and around the world.

After signing in to Game Center with your Apple ID and password, you can choose whether you want to go with a public profile or hide behind a nickname when you show up on leaderboards and multiplayer games. Top available Game Center games are listed on the Game Center screen, which is visible in Figure 11-15.

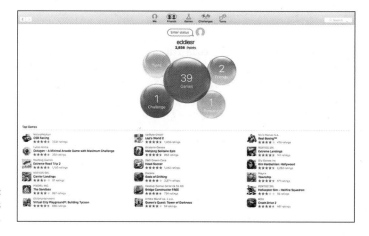

FIGURE 11-15:
I'm always ready to play.

In Game Center, you can click the balloons to access different areas:

>> **Friends:** Click the Friends tab to see not only a list of your friends' names, but also the games you have in common (see Figure 11-16).

>> **Games:** Click Games to see the games you have on your Mac and on your iOS devices. If you don't have any games, click Find Games in the App Store to be transported there directly.

>> **Challenges:** Click Challenges to view any competitive challenges to play a specific game against another person. If you want to challenge the person, click his scores or achievements.

>> **Requests:** If you receive any friend requests, they turn up when you click the Requests tab.

>> **Turns:** If you're involved in a turn-based multiplayer game, it may be time for your move.

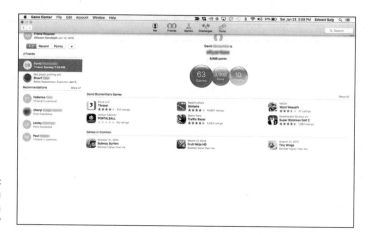

FIGURE 11-16:
Would you
like to play a
game?

You can also arrange to receive Game Center notifications in the Notifications
pane of System Preferences. And through parental controls, you can restrict your
kid from joining multiplayer games.

Playing games on the Internet is a hoot. Playing on the Internet in general is a
hoot, too.

Chapter 12

Mounting a Defense Strategy

O S X has generally been immune from the swarm of viruses that have plagued Windows computers through the years. Folks traditionally have needed to call a security specialist for their Macs about as often as you've summoned the Maytag repairman.

But times change. Heck, Whirlpool bought Maytag. So when it comes to computers nowadays, you can't take anything for granted — even if you own a Mac.

The Truth about Internet Security

Some people suggest that OS X isn't as bulletproof as was once believed. Way back in May 2006, the McAfee Avert Labs security threat research firm issued a report claiming that the Mac is just as vulnerable to targeted *malware* (*malicious* soft*ware*) attacks as other operating systems. Although the volume of threats is low, no invisible cloak is protecting Apple's products.

More recently, none other than Apple co-founder Steve Wozniak let on that he created Mac viruses back in the day but destroyed the code before it could ever spread.

And Macs have been the target of so-called KeRanger *ransomware*, software that effectively locks up important files on your computer until you agree to pay the ransom, which was reportedly one bitcoin, or about $400.

The good news is that OS X works under-the-hood to keep your system safe in several ways. A feature called *Gatekeeper* can help protect you from inadvertently downloading malicious software when you fetch a program outside the Mac App Store. Mavericks expanded on the concept of *sandboxing*, which ensures that the apps on your machine do what they're meant to do — and, perhaps more important, don't do what they're not meant to do. In other words, apps are effectively isolated from the rest of your system, from other apps they have no business interacting with, and from data that best remains separate.

Meanwhile, Apple reviews the apps that you do buy through the Mac App Store ahead of time. If any apps do turn out to include malware, they're removed. Apple also ensures that the developers who sell software through the place register with the company first. But Mac loyalists shouldn't get complacent, either. For starters, you should install the security updates that show up on your Mac. You'll be notified of updates that are available inside the Mac App Store. And you should load software on your computer only when it's from companies and websites you trust.

One other crucial point: Sensible security starts with you. That means backing up all your important digital jewels — a process that's a whole lot simpler with a feature that would make H.G. Wells beam. It also means paying heed to any OS X updates that Apple delivers periodically. But before I delve into the OS X version of Time Machine, I'll examine a very real threat that has more in common with Wells' *The War of the Worlds*.

Spies in our midst

Viruses are menacing programs created for the sole purpose of wreaking havoc on a computer or network. They spread when you download suspect software, visit shady websites, or pass around infected discs.

Computer *malware* takes many forms: viruses, Trojans, worms, and so on. And Windows users are all too familiar with *spyware*, which is the type of code that surreptitiously shows up on your computer to track your behavior and secretly report it to third parties.

Spyware typically differs from traditional computer malware, which may try to shut down your computer (or some of its programs). Authors of spyware aren't necessarily out to shut you down. Rather, they quietly attempt to monitor your behavior so that they can benefit at your expense:

>> At the lesser extremes, your computer is served pop-up ads that companies hope will eventually lead to a purchase. This type of spyware is known as *adware.*

>> At its most severe, spyware can place your personal information in the hands of a not-so-nice person. Under those circumstances, you could get totally ripped off. Indeed, the most malicious of spyware programs, called *keyloggers* or *snoopware,* can capture every keystroke you enter, whether you're holding court in a public chat room or typing a password.

Gone phishing

Dear Citibank Member,

As part of our security measures, we regularly screen activity in the Citibank system. We recently contacted you after noticing an issue on your account. We requested information from you for the following reasons:

We have reason to believe that your account was accessed by a third party. Because protecting the security of your account is our primary concern, we have limited access to sensitive Citibank account features. We understand that this may be an inconvenience but please understand that this temporary limitation is for your protection.

This is a third and final reminder to log in to Citibank as soon as possible.

Once you log in, you will be provided with steps to restore your account access. We appreciate your understanding as we work to ensure account safety.

Sincerely,

Citibank Account Review Department

The text of the preceding emailed letter sounds legitimate enough. But the only thing real about it is that this is an actual excerpt lifted from a common Internet fraud known as a *phishing* attack.

Identity thieves, masquerading as Citibank, PayPal, or other financial or Internet companies, try to dupe you into clicking phony links to verify personal or account information. You're asked for home addresses, passwords, Social Security numbers, credit card numbers, bank account information, and so on. To lend authenticity to these appeals, the spoof emails often are dressed up with real company logos and addresses, plus a forged company name in the From line (such as From: support@ebay.com).

Phishing may take the form of falsified company newsletters, or you may see bogus requests for you to reconfirm personal data.

TIP

So how do you know when you're being hoodwinked? Obvious giveaways included in some fake emails are misspellings, rotten grammar, and repeated words or sentences. No company that's on the level is going to ask you to reconfirm data that's been lost. And reputable companies usually refer to you by your real first and last names and business affiliations, rather than as *Dear Member* or *Dear PayPal Customer.*

If you have doubts that a communication is legit, open a new browser window and type the real company name yourself (such as www.ebay.com or www.paypal.com). Or pick up the phone and call. Your gut instincts concerning phony mail are probably on the mark.

WARNING

Bottom line: *Never* click links embedded in suspicious emails. When you hover the cursor over a link such as www.paypal.com, you see the true web address pop up — one that leads somewhere else entirely (perhaps to Kazakhstan or some other former Soviet republic). A similar online fraud called *pharming* also involves the use of fake websites, only this time, traffic is redirected from a legitimate bank or other destination to a bogus website that looks virtually identical. If you smell a rat, proceed gingerly. Don't share personal or sensitive information unless you're convinced that the site is legit.

Firewalls

More than likely, if you're connecting to the Internet through a network router (see Chapter 17), you're protected by a shield called a *firewall*. But OS X also has a software firewall, which you can use to block unwanted web traffic. Here's how to access it:

1. **Choose ú ⇨ System Preferences.**

2. **Click Security & Privacy.**

3. **Click the Firewall tab and then select Turn On Firewall.**

   You have to click the lock icon and enter your name (which may already be filled in) and password to make changes. When the firewall is off, all incoming connections to the computer are permitted. When it's on, all unauthorized applications, programs, and services are blocked.

If you click the Firewall Options button, you'll be able to modify the firewall settings, shown in Figure 12-1.

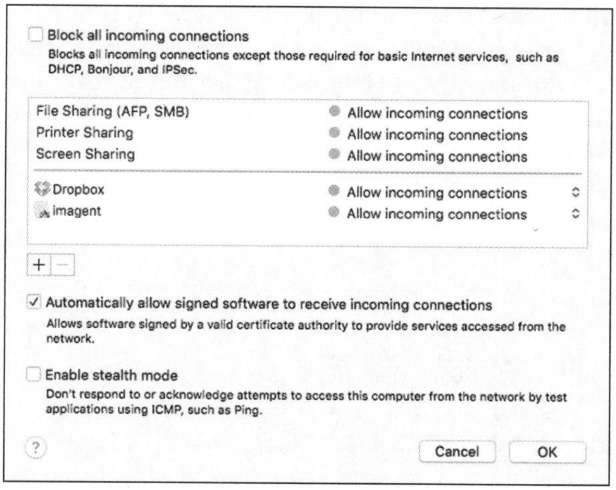

FIGURE 12-1:
Making the
connections —
or not.

You can use your Firewall Options settings to block all incoming connections except those that are needed for basic Internet services. You can also add or remove applications so that their connections can or can't come through. You can select the option to allow *signed software* — programs that are securely validated — to receive incoming connections.

You can also operate the computer in stealth mode so that any uninvited traffic receives no acknowledgment or response from the Mac. Malicious hackers won't even know that a machine is there to attack. And you can help safeguard your machine by selecting various options in the Sharing pane of System Preferences. I touch on sharing in Chapter 17.

FileVault

If your computer houses truly hush-hush information — your company's financial books, say, rather than Aunt Minnie's secret noodle-pudding recipe — you can scramble, or *encrypt*, the data in your Home folder (and only your Home folder) by using an OS X feature known as *FileVault.* You know your secrets are protected should thieves get their grubby paws on your machine.

TECHNICAL STUFF

By the time this book was written, FileVault was up to FileVault 2. It automatically applies the level of encryption employed by Uncle Sam. It's what nerds refer to as XTS-AES-128 (for Advanced Encryption Standard with 128-bit keys). And let me tell you, it's *really* secure. I recall Apple claiming that it would take a machine approximately 149 trillion years to crack the code. Even if Apple is off by a few billion years, your system is pretty safe.

The FileVault window shown in Figure 12-2 turns up when you choose Security & Privacy in System Preferences and select the FileVault tab. Each user must enter his or her password. Apple automatically generates a *recovery key* that you can use to unlock the vault. You can store this key with Apple, which asks you to answer security questions (such as "What street did you live on when you were 9 years old?") to verify your identity. It's also stored in iCloud when FireVault is turned on, making it easier to recover.

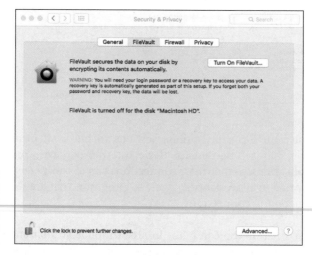

FIGURE 12-2: Keeping your computer secure in System Preferences.

As an administrator, you can also set up a safety net *master password recovery key* for your system, which you can use to unlock FileVault. This computerwide password can be used to bail out authorized users on your system who forget their passwords. And it might be a lifesaver if you run a small business through your Mac and have to let a wayward employee go. You'll be able to recover any data left behind in that person's account.

WARNING

Heed Apple's warning: If you forget your login password and recovery key or master password, your scrambled data may as well be toast. But you can store your recovery key with Apple. If you need to recover it, Apple asks for *precise* answers to the three questions you provided. Apple may limit the number of times you can attempt to give the proper responses.

If FileVault is turned on and you're not logged in to the machine, other people with whom you normally share folders on the computer won't be able to access those folders. It's worth mentioning that FileVault can exact an extreme performance hit on home directories with, say, Photos or iTunes libraries; it can take a long time to decrypt files when you log in and scramble them again when you log out.

Password Management: The Key to Keychains

Have you stopped to think how many passwords are in your computing life? You probably have so many that you use the same ones over and over, though security experts think that's not such a keen practice.

The pun police will get on me for saying this, but Apple has the key to managing your passwords, account numbers, and other confidential info: a feature known as keychain. A *keychain* can store passwords for programs, email accounts, websites, and more.

Moreover, through iCloud you can exploit the aptly named iCloud Keychain feature, which lets you keep such passwords in sync across other Macs and iOS devices. Visit System Preferences⇨iCloud and makes sure the Keychain box is selected. Click Options to set up an iCloud security code, which allows you to approve new devices, and enter the phone number for which you'd like to receive a text (SMS) that verifies your identity when you use such a code. If you don't choose to set up an iCloud security code, your keychain data will be stored locally on your Mac.

Meantime, you might create keychains for different purposes (one for online shopping, say) by opening Keychain Access in the Utilities folder inside the Applications folder. Your keychain password is initially the same as your login password, and for many users, that's the way it stays. To add keychain passwords, choose File⇨New Password Item or click the + at the bottom of the Keychain Access window. Fill in the account name, keychain item, and password. Apple lets you know whether you've chosen a wimpy password or one that's (relatively) bulletproof.

If you ever forget any of the passwords you've used on your Mac (including web passwords), here's how to go about recovering it:

1. **Open Keychain Access, and click either All Items or Passwords in the pane on the left.**

2. **In the larger pane to the right, double-click the item that has the password that you want to recover.**

   A window opens.

3. **Make sure that the Attributes tab in that window is highlighted (as it is by default), and select the Show Password check box.**

4. **When prompted, enter the username and password that you use to log in to the Mac, or the password you set up to log in to Keychain.**

   The Mac reveals the password you're trying to recover, displaying it in the field adjacent to the Show Password check box.

TIP

Try this simple alternative to recover a web password: Open Safari, choose Safari⇨Preferences, click the Passwords tab, and select the Show Passwords check box. When you're prompted, enter your Mac username and password. When you do so, all your web passwords are revealed.

Logging In and Logging Out

If you work in an office or other environment where anyone can peek at the monitor to see what you've been up to, log out of your account when you finish doing what you're doing. But if you'd rather not bother logging out, or if you don't think you'll remember to do so, go to the Security & Privacy pane of System Preferences, click General, and select the Require Password After Sleep or Screen Saver Begins option. You get to choose a time frame (immediately, 5 seconds, 1 minute, 5 minutes, 15 minutes, 1 hour, 4 hours, or 8 hours).

Another decision: Choose whether to show messages when the screen is locked, perhaps supplying a phone number or an email address that someone can use if they find your computer. (Read more on finding a lost Mac later in this chapter.)

You can also select the Log Out after x Minutes of Inactivity option by clicking the Advanced button in the lower-right corner of the window and choosing just how many minutes of inactivity that should be.

You also may want to select the Disable Automatic Login option on the General tab of the Security & Privacy pane. If you're really distrustful, click the Advanced button on the Security & Privacy pane and select the Require Administrator Password to Access Locked Preferences check box.

Restricting App Downloads

Apple has gone to the nth degree to make sure that the apps available for purchase and download in the Mac App Store are safe. But this store isn't the only place where you can go for apps. Take note of the Allow Apps Downloaded From options in the General section of the Security & Privacy pane of System Preferences. You can either

>> Select an option to allow only apps from the Mac App Store.

>> Select an option that allows you to get apps from the Mac App Store *and* identified developers.

>> Select an option that lets you get apps from anywhere.

If you go this final route, it's possible that malware will come with your downloaded apps.

Hiding Your Mac's Whereabouts

Some software that you run on your Mac benefits from knowing where your computer is located. If the Safari browser knows where your Mac is, for example, it can take advantage of geolocation-capable sites that can help you find close-by ATMs, coffeehouses, and pizza joints. Of course, Safari Suggestions and Spotlight Suggestions are hamstrung when the Mac has no clue as to where it is. What's more, by being aware of its whereabouts, a Mac can set the proper time zone for your machine.

AirPort on the Mac can determine its whereabouts by picking up signals from Wi-Fi networks (assuming that the machine is connected to the Internet). The collected location data isn't supposed to identify you personally.

Still, if this wigs you out, deselect the Enable Location Services check box on the Privacy tab of the Security & Privacy pane in System Preferences to stop providing such information to various applications. Apps that want to use your Mac's location are also listed, so deselect any of the programs that could theoretically benefit from knowing your whereabouts if you feel uncomfortable. If an app has requested permission to tap into your location within the past 24 hours, you see a tiny Stealth-airplane-looking icon that indicates as much.

TIP

You can still forbid a website from using your current location on a case-by-case basis, even if you don't choose to disable Location Services. When you come upon a site that wants to know your location coordinates, you typically see a dialog asking for permission on the fly. Click Don't Allow to deny permission or Allow to grant it.

Securing Your Privacy

Preventing an app from knowing your location is one way to safeguard your privacy, but consider other options. Once again, click the Privacy tab of the Security & Privacy pane in System Preferences. The left side of the window lists certain apps and tools; on the right are additional apps that can take advantage of those apps and tools. You can give permission to such apps by selecting the check boxes next to their name. Deselect the check boxes if you have a problem with those apps using your contacts.

On the left side of the screen, you see a Diagnostics & Usage list. Apple hopes that you'll agree to share information automatically from time to time — information about how your Mac is working and how you use it. This information is collected anonymously, but if you're not comfortable with the practice either, just say no by deselecting the Send Diagnostic & Usage Data to Apple check box, as well as the Share Crash Data with App Developers box.

Find My Mac

I know that you care a great deal about your computer. But like everyone else, you're busy and distracted from time to time, and however unlikely, you might leave a running Mac notebook in the back of a taxi. (C'mon, like you're going to have a running desktop in a cab, much less leave it there.) Worse, your Mac might be stolen.

The Find My Mac feature (a variant of Find My iPhone on Apple's prized smartphone) increases the odds that you'll get the lost machine back. Make sure that the feature is selected in iCloud Preferences (under System Preferences). Then, if your machine ever does go AWOL, just sign in to iCloud from any web browser on a PC or other Mac, or from the Find My iPhone app on an iPhone or iPad. Then click Find My iPhone. Yes, that's what it's called, even though you're on a search mission for your Mac.

In a web browser, you see a map like the one shown in Figure 12-3. Each of the green droplets on the map indicates the location of one of your devices — at least, its location as close as Apple can pinpoint it. Click the drop-down arrow at the top center of the screen to see a list of all devices that you've set up to work with Find My iPhone (or Mac and so on). With luck, the computer you're looking for won't be offline. If Find My iPhone finds your Mac, click the Mac in the list, which summons the window shown in the top-right corner of Figure 12-3.

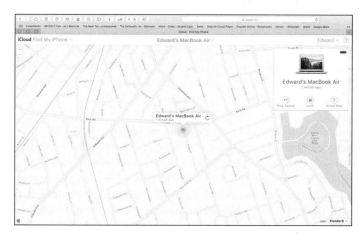

FIGURE 12-3:
Locating a lost
or stolen Mac.

But now what are you going to do? How do you alert the Good Samaritan (or crook) who has your machine that you want it back? Your first option is to sound an alarm on your missing Mac by clicking Play Sound in the window shown in Figure 12-3. But this feature is useful only if the missing Mac is in your house. (The feature was designed for such scenarios as an iPhone getting concealed under the couch cushions.) An alarm is useless if the person who hears it doesn't know how to get in touch with you to return it.

Instead, click Lock in that window to lock the machine so that the person who has your Mac can't look at your private or sensitive information. Using the keypad that appears, enter a six-digit passcode (one that you can easily remember) to unlock the computer if and when you do get it back. (You have to confirm the passcode by entering it a second time.) After you do that, you're given space to type an optional message that appears on the Mac's lock screen — a message that you hope will persuade the person who has your computer to return it. Offering a reward isn't out of the question (unless you're dealing with a thief, who's unlikely to cooperate anyway). Click the Lock button when you've finished typing the message. You receive a confirmation email.

CHAPTER 12 **Mounting a Defense Strategy**   231

If you come to the conclusion that the machine was indeed stolen or that the person who now has it has no intention of giving it back, click Erase Mac in Find My iPhone (refer to Figure 12-3) to wipe the contents and settings on the computer. Given that this is a major step, Apple requires you to enter your Apple ID before proceeding. Erasing the Mac can take up to a full day to complete.

You have several compelling reasons for hanging out in the iCloud, and the potential to retrieve a lost Mac is right up there with the best of them.

Entering a Time Machine

The feature that generated most of the excitement when Apple announced Leopard in 2007 was Time Machine — and rightfully so. Here, finally, was a relatively effortless way to back up everything on your system. Time Machine lets you gracefully float back in time to retrieve a file that was lost, damaged, or subsequently changed. Why, it's almost science fiction.

To exploit Time Machine, you need to supply a big-enough extra drive to store what's on your computer. Time Machine pretty much takes over from there. It automatically keeps backups every hour on the hour for the past 24 hours, as well as daily backups for the past month. Beyond that, Time Machine goes weekly, at least until the backup drive is packed to the rafters. When you have no more room on the backup drive, Time Machine starts deleting old backups.

In Time Machine Preferences, you can choose to be notified after these old backups are removed. (This is a darn good reason why you ought to devote an empty drive to your Time Machine backup.) If you're using Time Machine to back up a laptop, you can determine whether backups should continue while you're using the machine on battery power.

Setting up Time Machine

Plug in that new secondary hard drive or solid-state drive (SSD), and your Mac asks whether you want to use it for a Time Machine backup, as shown in Figure 12-4. You won't regret saying yes, and that's really all you need to do unless you want to customize which files are backed up. If you're not sure, you can click Decide Later.

FIGURE 12-4:
Are you ready for time travel?

The Mac dutifully begins copying everything on the computer, including system files. This first copy job is likely to take a while, especially if your Mac is stuffed with files. (I recommend letting the computer do its thing while you're asleep.) Subsequent backups are a lot quicker, because by then, the Mac copies only what's changed, such as a manuscript you edited.

The results are worth it, because you can go back in time to see what a file or folder looked like on the day it was backed up, using Quick Look if you want a quick preview. Suppose that you're looking at the batch of photos that make up the Last Import folder in Photos (see Chapter 14). When you go back in time with Time Machine, you see how the Last Import folder changed on different dates. In other words, the remarkable thing about Time Machine is that it captures multiple copies of your digital belongings.

TIP

Although Time Machine is initially set up for automatic hourly backups, you can arrange an immediate backup. Click and hold the Time Machine icon on the dock, and choose Back Up Now from the menu that pops up.

I suspect that most of you will choose to back up the full contents of your computer. The process is simple, and if you have the storage capacity, why not? But if your secondary hard drive is crammed, or if you have stuff you want to keep private, you can omit certain items from being copied. Open Time Machine Preferences and click Options. Then click + in the resulting Exclude These Items from Backups window to add the files, folders, and drives that you want to exclude, or just drag said items to the same window.

You can also turn off Time Machine in Time Machine Preferences by sliding the Off–On switch to the left. Frankly, you won't find many instances in which you'd want to flip off the switch, but the option is there nonetheless.

Going back in time

Time travel is way cool. I'm betting that you'll hunt for files from a moment in time just because Apple makes this historical journey such a visually intoxicating experience. Click the Time Machine dock icon, and your current desktop slides out of view. You and whichever Finder-like window was active or front-most at the time you clicked the icon are now floating in space, as shown in Figure 12-5. So if you know that the particular item you're looking for used to reside in a given folder, open that window before embarking on your journey. Or enter its name in the search box in the Finder window.

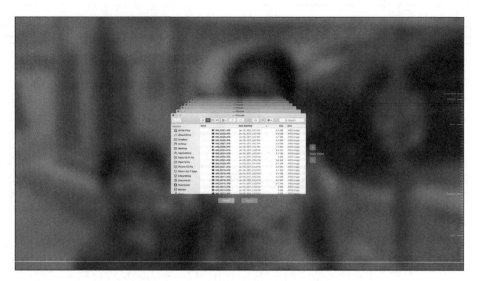

FIGURE 12-5:
Time Machine
is on your side.

Now you can venture across the sands of time to discover the lost or altered file. Say that you unintentionally wiped out a critical document several weeks ago and now hope to recover it. Use the timeline along the right edge of the screen or the navigational arrows toward the lower-right corner to go back to the time of the deed. When you click, the windows fly forward or backward for a second or two until landing on the day you chose.

If your search-and-rescue mission doesn't immediately uncover the lost file, try typing its name again in the Finder search box. You're searching for the file on that particular date. When you encounter the wayward file, highlight it and click Restore. It's transported to the present, with Time Machine conveniently dropping the file in its original location. Click Cancel to return to the present.

TIP

If the main hard drive or SSD on your Mac bites the dust, you can use Time Machine to restore your entire computer:

» On an older computer that came with an OS X Install or Restore DVD, and of course the requisite optical drive, insert the disk, and select Restore from Time Machine. If you have a USB install drive, insert that USB drive. You'll have an option to choose the date from which you want to restore your system.

» On the many machines that don't have an optical drive, connect a backup drive and start your Mac from the recovery system by pressing ⌘+R at startup. Then select Restore from Time Machine Backup.

You can also use Time Machine to transfer important settings, applications, and files to another Mac. Open Migration Assistant (in the Utilities folder inside the

Applications folder), and choose From a Time Machine Backup when you're asked how you'd like to transfer your information.

Time Machine is unquestionably a great feature, but you still may want to consider backing up your data in the cloud — typically, through third-party services such as Carbonite and Mozy. How come? If your Mac and the drive you're using for Time Machine are stolen or damaged, your data is still protected on the Internet. But these services are slow and potentially (depending on how much you're actually backing up) pricey.

Take some comfort as well that some of your digital jewels are backed up in cyberspace through iCloud.

A nice complement to Time Machine is a *clone* backup on yet another external drive. Try such programs as SuperDuper! (www.shirt-pocket.com/SuperDuper) and Carbon Copy Cloner (www.bombich.com). Having a clone gives you a fuss-free way to boot up after a disaster.

A couple of additional Time Machine security notes:

>> If you chose to encrypt files in FileVault (as described earlier), the files remain encrypted as part of your Time Machine backup.

>> If you have a Time Capsule and are running Mountain Lion or later, you can also store encrypted backups there.

So even in Time Machine, you need a password to get at Aunt Minnie's pudding recipe. What can possibly be more secure than that?

Getting an iLife

4

Chapter 13

Living in an iTunes Nation

The demographers may have missed it, but a major population explosion took place during the aughts. Everywhere you looked, vast colonies of tiny white earbuds proliferated. They were spotted on subways and on the street, on airplanes, buses, and college and corporate campuses.

Those signature white earbuds (eventually EarPods) were initially connected to iPods and later to their close Apple kin, iPhones. There's every chance that you're reading a Macintosh book because of them. Although iPods and iPhones are meant to work with iTunes software on Windows machines as well as on Macs running OS X, your first infatuation with the Mac may well have occurred in an Apple Store, when you ostensibly went to check out the darling of all portable music players, if not later, on Apple's prized smartphone.

You also may be thinking that if Apple hit such a home run with the iPod, iPhone, and iPad tablet, perhaps Steve Jobs and crew knew something about making darn impressive computers too. (Naturally, you'd be right.)

So although this book is first and foremost a computer book, forgive this momentary homage to these other Apple devices.

iTunes: The Great Mac Jukebox

As stand-alone devices, iPods, iPhones, and iPads may have signified star power, but they always had to share (and, truth be told, probably relinquish) top billing to the maestro behind Apple's musical ensemble: the iTunes software.

iTunes is one of those melodious programs that music enthusiasts (and everyone else) get just for owning a Mac. But iTunes isn't just about music; these days, it's also about organizing and consuming TV shows, movies, podcasts, and more.

Tuning in to the iTunes interface

To open iTunes, click its dock icon, which resembles a musical note resting in a circle. When you do so, you're asked whether you want to share information about your music collection with Apple. The benefits to you: Apple may be able to uncover missing album covers, let you get images of favorite artists, and help you discover new music.

If you already have music (or other content) on your Mac, iTunes can scan your machine for media. Otherwise, you can go to the iTunes Store to start building a collection anew.

You'll visit the store soon enough. For now, check out Figure 13-1, which is an example of one of the iTunes views after you've built up a library. You're looking at Songs view, because Songs is displayed in the drop-down menu near the upper-right corner of the screen. In Figure 13-2, later in this section, you see the Albums view. Other choices in this drop down, at least when the My Music tab is selected, are Artists, Composers, and Genres.

Now look at those tabs near the top of the screen, from left to right: My Music, Playlists, For You, New, Radio, Connect, and iTunes Store. You'll read about each of these in this chapter.

Please note though that Apple frequently changes the iTunes layout, so what you see in Figure 13-1 may look somewhat different on your own computer.

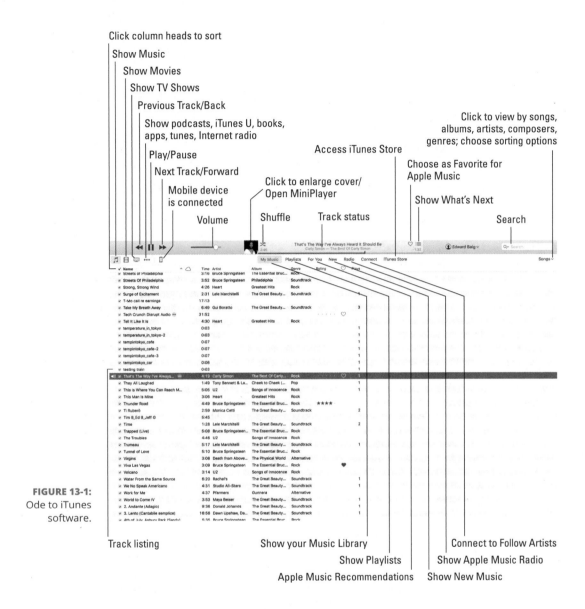

Click column heads to sort
Show Music
Show Movies
Show TV Shows
Previous Track/Back
Show podcasts, iTunes U, books, apps, tunes, Internet radio
Play/Pause
Next Track/Forward
Mobile device is connected
Volume

Click to enlarge cover/ Open MiniPlayer
Shuffle
Track status

Access iTunes Store

Click to view by songs, albums, artists, composers, genres; choose sorting options

Choose as Favorite for Apple Music
Show What's Next

Search

FIGURE 13-1:
Ode to iTunes software.

Track listing

Show your Music Library
Show Playlists
Apple Music Recommendations

Connect to Follow Artists
Show Apple Music Radio
Show New Music

Controlling the controls

The following list highlights some of the key controls and features of iTunes:

>> **Back/Forward and Previous/Next Track:** The double arrows pointing to the left and right are your Back and Forward buttons, respectively. Place the cursor above these buttons and hold down the mouse button to rewind or fast-forward through a song. If you click these arrows instead, you advance

or retreat to the next or previous track. It's worth noting that you go back to the previous track only if you're at the beginning of a track; otherwise, iTunes rewinds to the beginning of the current track.

>> **Play/Pause:** Click the single arrow pointing to the right to play a song. When a song is playing, the button changes to two vertical bars. Click again to pause the music. Alternatively, press the spacebar to play or pause.

>> **Volume:** Dragging this slider increases or decreases the volume, relative to your system volume settings.

>> **AirPlay:** This control lets you alter the volume and change which speakers you're listening through — those on your Mac, for example, or those on your Apple TV or some other AirPlay–capable speakers. You can play music on your computer and an AirPlay-capable device separately or simultaneously. (The AirPlay icon is not visible in Figure 13-1).

>> **Cover art:** Whenever possible, iTunes depicts the album cover of the material you're listening to. In the Songs view, shown in Figure 13-1, click the cover art to the left of the Now Playing pane to display the album cover in its own separate window. Roll the cursor over the album image to bring up Play/Pause and Volume controls inside the album window. You also see, below the album cover, a list of the music that's up next in your current listening rotation. Click the X in the upper corner of this window to return to the previous view.

>> **Albums view:** Apple's handsome Albums view interface uses album covers, too, but you approach it somewhat differently. Back in iTunes 11, Apple added a feature called *Expanded View* that displays all the songs in an album that you're listening to, and does it in a most elegant way. Apple matches the dominant color scheme of the album cover, as it does in Figure 13-2 with the Carly Simon cover.

>> **Shuffle:** When the symbol in this little button is highlighted (it turns blue), tracks play in random order. Be prepared for anything. There's no telling when Eminem will follow The Wiggles.

>> **Repeat:** Click once to repeat all the songs in the library or playlist you're currently listening to. Click twice so that the number *1* appears on the button. Only the current track repeats. If you don't see the Repeat icon, click Controls⇨Repeat⇨All.

>> **Equalizer:** If you've ever tweaked the treble and bass controls on a stereo, you'll appreciate the equalizer. It allows you to adjust sound frequencies to match the genre of a song, the speakers on your system, or the ambiance of the room in which you're listening. Choose Window⇨Equalizer to display the Equalizer window. You can adjust the equalizer manually by dragging the sliders or choose among more than 20 presets (such as Bass Booster, Bass Reducer, Flat, Hip-Hop, and Lounge). To bring up those presets, click the pop-up menu in the window.

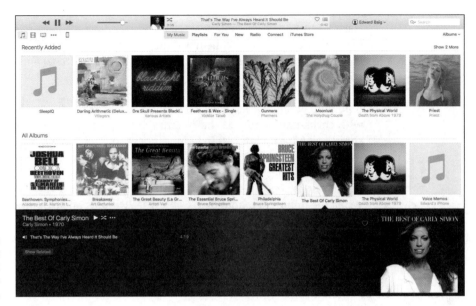

FIGURE 13-2:
In Albums
view, you
can admire
cover art.

>> **Visual effects:** If you were conscious during the '60s, you'll welcome these funky psychedelic light animations and 3D effects that dance to the beat of whatever's playing. And if you're the offspring of a Baby Boomer, you'll arrive at this amazing realization: Maybe Mom and Dad were pretty groovy in their heyday. You can drum up your visual serenade by pressing ⌘+T or by choosing View⇨Show Visualizer. You can also use the View menu to choose the types of visualizer effects you want.

Managing Your Music

So exactly how does music make its way into iTunes? And exactly what becomes of the songs after you 'em? I thought you'd never ask.

Ripping audio CDs

A remarkable thing happens moments after you insert the vast majority of music CDs into your Mac — assuming, of course, that the Mac has an internal optical drive or an accessory that you've connected via USB. (The newest models lack the built-in drive.) Typically, iTunes opens, and the contents of the disc — song titles, artist name, length, album name, and genre — are recognized and copied for iTunes to access. The software fetches this licensed information from a massive online database run by a company called Gracenote.

Here's another remarkable feat: Next time, you won't have to keep inserting said CD into the computer to hear its music. That's because you can rip (copy) the contents to the Mac's hard drive or solid-state drive (SSD) and then stash the disc somewhere else.

A pop-up window asks whether you'd like to import the CD. Agree, and all songs with check marks next to their names are copied; be sure to click to deselect any songs you have no interest in before proceeding. In some instances, you copy a CD by clicking Import CD. An icon for the CD you just inserted also appears near the upper-left corner of iTunes, adjacent to icons for Music and Video

TIP

While the import is taking place, you'll see Options and CD Info buttons. Here, you can find out a little more about the disc at hand, assuming that Gracenote knows such details as the year the album was produced, the composer, the genre, and so on. You can add to or change the names and facts if you know better. You can get track names (if need be), and submit CD track names to Gracenote too (if not already known).

As iTunes goes about its business, a gear icon spins next to the song being ripped; the gear turns into a green circle and gains a check mark after the song has been copied. You can monitor the progress of your imports by peeking at the top display shown in Figure 13-3. It shows you how much time remains before a particular track is captured and the speed at which the CD is being ripped.

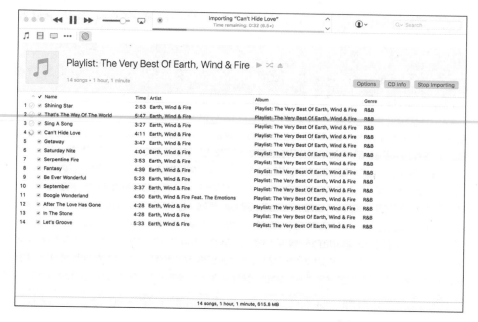

FIGURE 13-3:
Ripping a CD.

Incidentally, you may be able to listen to the CD while ripping a disc, and you can certainly do other work at the same time. When iTunes has completed its mission, remove the CD by pressing Eject (if your keyboard has a dedicated Eject key), pressing the keyboard combination ⌘+E, or clicking the little eject symbol next to the name of the CD you copied in Finder. Copied songs are stored in the iTunes library by default. (If that doesn't seem to be happening, open iTunes Preferences, click the Advanced tab, and make sure that the check box titled Copy Files to iTunes Media Folder When Adding to Library is selected.)

TIP

If you weren't connected to the Internet and couldn't grab song names when you copied a disc, you can add that info at a later date. With a CD inserted, click Options near the upper-right corner of the iTunes display (to the left of the CD Info button), and choose Get Track Names from the list that appears. You can also click Submit CD Track Names to send CD information to Gracenote.

In the meantime, if you want to edit a song or artist information, select the song in question, choose File⇨Get Info, and type your changes. Look around the Get Info window. You'll see places for song lyrics (if known), a place to add artwork, and more.

Importing other ditties

Songs previously downloaded from the Internet can be imported into iTunes with relative ease. The assumption is that you obtained those music files legally. If you didn't, placing them inside iTunes will blow up your computer. (That's not really the case, but I urge you to play by the rules just the same. People's livelihoods depend on it.)

To import audio files from other applications or your desktop, choose File⇨Add to Library and then select the file. Or drag the music into the library, into a playlist (more coming), or onto the iTunes dock icon.

Adding music from iCloud

Later in this chapter, I tell you how to go about buying music from the iTunes Store or streaming it via Apple Music. If you're using iCloud, any songs you purchase from iTunes on a different Mac, Windows PC, or iOS device are available to you on the Mac you're using (and on all those other devices, too). You don't need to sync anything. You're exploiting a feature called *iTunes in the Cloud.*

It's up to you whether you want to turn on automatic downloads to bring those purchases to your Mac. On one hand, you can't beat the convenience. But be wary if your hard drive, SSD, or other storage is limited.

To turn on automatic downloads, choose iTunes⇨Preferences⇨Store. Select the types of content you want to download automatically: music, apps, and/or books. If your computer has been turned off, and you want to see whether any ditties haven't landed yet, choose Store⇨Check for Available Downloads.

iTunes Match

You probably didn't get all your music from iTunes. You may have ripped CDs. You may have purchased music from another online service. And (sorry, but I have to acknowledge the possibility) you may have obtained it through a file-sharing service whose legal status — I don't pretend to be a lawyer — is dubious.

That's where a premium iCloud feature called *iTunes Match* fills the bill. The service stores up to 25,000 of your tracks in the cloud, no matter how it was obtained (in most cases), and makes it accessible on up to ten devices and computers, including any of the Macs you own that have iCloud access — that is, as long as they're running Lion or a later version of OS X.

What's more, matched songs that are available in the iTunes Store — again, where you actually obtained them doesn't matter — are made available at what is considered to be iTunes Plus quality or, in techie terms, 256 kilobits per second. If the song isn't available in the iTunes Store (and you'd be hard-pressed to find mainstream material that isn't), you'll be able to listen in its original audio quality, which may not be quite as good as if that song were available in the iTunes Store.

Apple charges $24.99 a year for iTunes Match, but if you're a big fan of music (as I am) and boast a sizable music collection, the fee is well worth it. A bonus of subscribing: iTunes Radio, of which I have more to say later in this chapter, is ad-free.

If you're subscribing to iTunes Match on a Mac for the first time, choose @ Store⇨iTunes Match and click the Subscribe for $24.99 button. You'll have to enter your Apple ID and password.

To turn on iTunes Match on another Mac after you're a subscriber, visit iTunes Preferences, tap the General tab, and make sure the iCloud Music Library option is selected.

WARNING

Don't forget to sign in with an Apple ID that's identical to the credentials you used on the first computer you used to set up iTunes Match.

A small cloud icon appears next to any music that's stored in the cloud, as opposed to on your computer. Click the cloud to download the song to your computer so that you can play it when you're offline. You can also stream that song without having to download it — provided, of course, that you have Internet connectivity.

REMEMBER

iTunes Match isn't available in all countries.

Creating playlists

You listen to music under a variety of circumstances, such as entertaining at a dinner party, soothing a crying baby, setting a romantic mood, or drowning in your sorrows after a painful breakup. In the last situation, you wouldn't want to hear Barbra Streisand belting out "Happy Days Are Here Again," even if the song is otherwise a staple of your iTunes library. With a playlist, you can organize material around a particular theme or mood.

You have several ways to create a new playlist in iTunes. The following steps highlight the simplest way and point you to other options in the explanatory text below each step:

1. **Click the Playlists tab.**

2. **Click the + button in the lower-left corner of the iTunes window.**

3. **Choose New Playlist (or New Smart Playlist or New Playlist Folder) from the menu that appears.**

   If you're a fan of the menu bar, you can also choose File⇨New⇨Playlist. Or you keyboard shortcut fans can press ⌘+N. (The new Smart Playlist or New Playlist Folder options are also available.)

   However you issue the New Playlist command in iTunes, a new playlist panel appears in the main iTunes window.

4. **Click the title of your new playlist and give it a name.**

   Apple inelegantly calls your new playlist. . .well, *playlist,* but of course you're meant to change it to a more appropriate descriptor, such as Jazz Crooners, Dance Mix, Corny Songs, or whatever.

5. **Drag songs or albums to the panel to add them to your playlist.**

   Apple kindly lets you know how many songs reside in the newly named playlist and how long it will take you to listen to the whole bunch.

   You might also like to add songs to your playlist as follows:

   - In the Songs view (refer to Figure 13-1 earlier in this chapter), select a song and drag it to the left. Suddenly, out of nowhere, your list of playlists appears. Drag the song into the appropriate playlist.

   - You can also hover the cursor over a song so that three circled dots appear next to the song title. Click Add to Playlist from the resulting menu, and then select the playlist for your song.

TIP

REMEMBER

- If you're adding multiple songs to the playlist, hold down the ⌘ or Shift key to select a bunch of tracks. You can drag the whole batch over in one swoop. Or select a bunch of songs and choose File⇨New⇨Playlist from Selection.

If a song that you're adding to a playlist is stored in iCloud, a copy automatically downloads to your computer.

In addition to adding songs to your playlist, you can edit your playlist as follows:

>> **Change the order of songs in the playlist:** You can sort your new playlist by name, time, artist, genre, rating, and plays, if not the order in which you added songs to the playlist, by clicking the column heading that corresponds to the criteria by which you want to sort the list. You can also change the playlist order by dragging songs one on top of another.

>> **Delete songs:** To delete a song from a playlist, highlight it and press Delete. Don't worry; the original track remains in your library. Songs in playlists never really leave the library; the playlist merely functions as a pointer to those files. For the same reason, a particular song can show up in as many playlists as you want without consuming any additional space on your storage drive.

When playlists get smart

Putting together a playlist can be fun. But it can also take considerable time and effort. Using *Smart Playlists*, you can have iTunes do the heavy lifting on your behalf, based on specific conditions you establish up front: how fast a song is based on beats per minute (BPM), the type of music, a song's rating, and so on. You can also limit the playlist to a specific length, in terms of minutes or number of songs.

Here's how to create a Smart Playlist:

1. **When you click the + on the Playlists tab to create a playlist, you have the option to choose New Smart Playlist. Or you can choose File⇨New⇨Smart Playlist.**

2. **In the dialog that appears, click Add (the + icon) associated with a pop-up menu to choose the parameters on which you're basing the Smart Playlist from that menu.**

   Click the – button for a menu that lets you remove a condition. You can also set up the Smart Playlist so that all the criteria you list must be met or any of the criteria can be met. Click + or – to add or remove a rule.

A Smart Playlist is identified in the iTunes sidebar or Source list (as it is commonly referred to) by a gear icon to the left of its name.

Take a look at the Smart Playlist shown in Figure 13-4. It has iTunes looking for all songs with *Love* in the title that you haven't heard in a couple of months or haven't heard more than 14 times. The song must have been encoded with a bit rate between 128 and 256 Kbps. The overall length of the playlist can't exceed two hours. If you want iTunes to alter the Smart Playlist as songs are added or removed, select the Live Updating check box.

FIGURE 13-4:
Finding the love in a Smart Playlist.

You can edit the criteria that make up a Smart Playlist by clicking the Playlists tab, right-clicking (Control-clicking) the playlist name in the sidebar, clicking Edit Smart Playlist from the resulting menu. From there, change or select the underlying criteria that will define the rejiggered Smart Playlists.

Figure 13-5 shows the result of this melodious love collection.

FIGURE 13-5:
Love is here to stay in this playlist.

When playlists get even smarter

In a nutshell, Genius playlists promise to create an instant playlist of songs from your library that (in theory) mesh well with the given song you are listening to. (Maybe not *instant* because it can take a bit of time to configure itself the first time it's turned on.)

There are four ways to turn iTunes into a Genius working on your behalf:

>> First is to create the aforementioned Genius playlist.

>> Alternatively, if you don't want to go with a Genius playlist right off the bat but want Apple to start playing songs that go great with whatever you're currently listening to, you can call on a Genius shuffle feature.

>> A third option is to create a Genius Mix, with songs selected from a chosen genre; iTunes plays like a commercial-free radio station (more on that later in this chapter).

>> Yet another choice is to click Genius Suggestions from the menu summoned after clicking the three circled dots. You'll see a list of songs that fit Apple's Genius criteria. You can click any of the songs to play them, or from this menu click either Start Genius or Save as Playlist.

Here's another way to create a Genius playlist:

1. **Choose Store⇨Turn on (or Update) Genius.**

2. **Hover the cursor over the track you'd like to use to generate the playlist and Control+click until the three circled dots appears.**

3. **From the menu that appears, choose Create Genius Playlist.**

Figure 13-6 shows a Genius playlist created from the seed song "A Song for You," by Donny Hathaway. You can save a Genius playlist and refresh it if you don't like the results. And you can limit the collection to 25, 50, 75, or 100 songs by clicking the arrow next to the number of songs in the current list. (Look for the arrow below the Based On heading in the upper-left corner of the playlist window.)

To help craft the playlists, Apple anonymously compares data you share from your iTunes library with anonymous data from countless other users, so you'll have to opt in to start a Genius playlist. To do so, you can click Start Genius under the iTunes Store menu while a song is playing, or select a seed song for the Genius Playlist. To select a seed song, click its title in your music library, click the right arrow that appears, and choose Start Genius.

FIGURE 13-6:
This playlist is
pure Genius.

Genius Mixes

Sometimes, you want the Genius inside iTunes to continuously play songs in your library that go great together, as though you were listening to commercial-free radio. That's what the concept of a *Genius Mix* is. iTunes segregates songs into Genius Mix categories, putting, say, a Classical Mix together, or a British Invasion or a Soundtracks Mix. The mix is based, of course, on the music that's already in your library. Figure 13-7 shows some of the Genius Mixes iTunes created on my behalf.

To get started with Genius Mixes, click the Playlists tab, and then click Genius Mix in the sidebar or Source list. Move the pointer over the Genius Mix you want to start playing and then click the play arrow that appears.

Meantime, if you can't decide what to play yourself, you might choose the Genius Shuffle option. It presents itself under the iTunes Control menu or when you press and hold down the Option key and the Genius Shuffle icon near the upper-left corner of the iTunes window that appears. Apple will instantly play songs it thinks sound swell together.

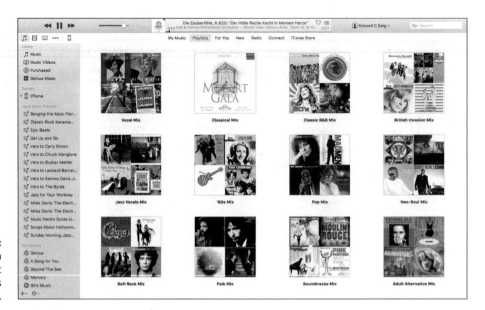

FIGURE 13-7:
Putting a
mix of music
together is
pure Genius.

Up Next

When you listen to music on broadcast radio, there's an element of unpredictability. You rarely, if ever, know what the disk jockey (DJ) is going to throw at you next — not that there's anything wrong with that. Indeed, you may be one of those folks who loves surprises, which is not only why you frequently listen to radio, but also aren't shy about turning on the shuffle feature during playback. (A bit later in this chapter, I talk about Internet radio, as well as Apple's own Apple Music radio service.)

But then there are the rest of you, the people who don't leave anything to chance. If this describes you, you'll almost certainly appreciate the Up Next feature. Up Next is all about letting you know what the next song in your listening queue is, followed by the song after that, the one after that, and so on. You can peek at the list by clicking the Up Next icon to the right of the song that's playing. (It's labeled in Figure 13-1 earlier in this chapter.) With your Up Next list displayed, here's what you can do:

>> If you see a song in that list that you want to play immediately, click its name in the list.

>> If you see a song in the list that you don't want to play at all, roll the mouse pointer over the track and click the circled X to remove it from the queue.

>> When you move the mouse pointer over the list, you probably notice the by-now-familiar circled three-dot icon. Click that arrow, and you see several additional options.

- Click Play Next to have the given track jump to the top of the Up Next list.

- You can also start Genius from here or seek Genius Suggestions or add the song to an existing playlist or start a custom station.

- You can go directly to the album, song, or artist in your library.

- You can show the track in the iTunes Store, which is useful for discovering and buying other music by the artist or similar music.

TIP

>> In the Up Next list, you find a tiny icon that resembles a clock. (It's just to the left of the Clear button that clears the Up Next list.) If you click the little clock icon, the Up Next list morphs into the Previously Played list, providing a summary of what you've been listening to of late. It's a good, quick way to replay a song you can't get enough of.

MiniPlayer

A lot of times, you listen to music in the background while working on other stuff. But you still want to be able to control what you're listening to — and see the Up Next list. The MiniPlayer lets you control and see what you're listening to in a smaller window that doesn't hog a lot of room on the screen. Even so, the version of the MiniPlayer added with iTunes 11 includes the Up Next button. And if you want to listen to something specific, you can search your entire music collection via a search box that appears in the MiniPlayer when you mouse over the album cover art and click the magnifying glass. Click the MiniPlayer button (refer to Figure 13-1 earlier in this chapter) to shrink iTunes.

TIP

In MiniPlayer itself, you can choose to show enlarged artwork (album cover) or go with a smaller thumbnail. And if you want to keep MiniPlayer in the foreground on your desktop, visit iTunes Preferences, click Advanced, and select Keep Mini-Player on Top of All Other Windows.

TIP

Go in the opposite direction and make iTunes take over most if not the entire screen again by clicking the Mini Player button a second time.

Loading tunes onto a portable device

Transferring your songs, playlists, and — as you'll see — videos, audiobooks, and podcasts to an iPod, iPhone, or other portable device is as simple as connecting the device to your Mac through USB or (with a really old iPod and older Mac)

FireWire, depending on the model. And the model you have also determines your syncing options. If you have an iPod Classic, iPod Nano, or iPod Shuffle, you'll have to sync through iTunes. You can sync with iTunes if you have an iPod touch, iPhone, or iPad as well, but you can also download items to those devices directly via the iTunes Store available on those devices. If you use Apple Music or subscribe to iTunes Match, you cannot sync music to your iOS device, though you can sync movies, apps, and books.

For the purposes of this discussion, let's assume that you can sync your device. Each time you connect, the device automatically mirrors any changes to your songs and playlists in iTunes — that is, unless you select Manually Manage Music and Videos on the Summary tab in the iTunes window when the device is connected. In such a scenario, you can drag items to your device. Wireless syncing options are available through Wi-Fi on the iPhone or iPad.

A connected iPod, iPad, or iPhone shows up in the upper-left corner of the iTunes window (refer to Figure 13-1). Click the little Eject icon next to the name of your device before disconnecting it from your Mac. Or click the tab with your device name to summon a page that shows your backup and sync options, including backing up to your Mac.

If you want, you can take advantage of the AutoFill feature to have iTunes randomly fill your device with a selection of songs. Hey, it's your music, so you should trust the software to fill the device with stuff you like. The downside is you're cutting down on the available space you might use for other media, including pictures and videos.

Burning audio CDs

I'll be brief because optical CD or DVD burners are no longer standard issue on the Mac, so you'll most likely have to supply an external USB accessory. Of course, you'll also have to supply a blank recordable CD or DVD. Knowing how to create a playlist is a handy precursor to burning or creating your own CD that can be played in virtually any standard compact disc player.

REMEMBER

As you choose the tracks to burn onto the disc, be mindful of the lengths of those tracks; regular CDs have room for about 74 or 80 minutes of music, or approximately 20 songs. You'll also get to choose the gap between songs (from 0 to 5 seconds; 2 seconds is the default.) Keeping the gap at 0 means that with CDs of live performances, for example, there's no annoying second or so of silence between songs.

Tuning In to Internet Radio

Listening to your own CDs and digital tracks is terrific. Presumably, a lot of thought went into amassing your collection. But at times, nothing beats the serendipity of radio: not knowing what's coming next, hearing a nugget you haven't heard in decades, or hearing a new jewel for the first time.

You don't have to leave your Mac to revel in the radio experience. In iTunes, both the Internet tab and the Radio tab at the top give you plenty of options.

When you click the Internet tab, you have access to a heck of a lot more radio stations than you'll find on AM, FM, or even subscription-based satellite radio. These stations are *streaming Internet radio* stations, and you can choose among hundreds of them. Some of them are AM or FM stations from around the country. Some are Internet-only stations.

Apple categorizes these by genre, as shown in Figure 13-8. Click the triangle next to a category name to see all the station options in that genre. Double-click to tune in to a particular station. The station starts playing in a few seconds, mercifully minus the static of regular radio. If you don't see the Internet tab, click the three dots at the upper left, click Edit, and select the Internet Radio check box.

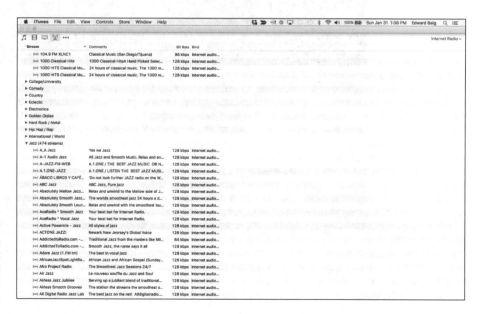

FIGURE 13-8: You won't find all these stations on AM or FM.

TIP

Pay attention to the *bit rate.* The higher the bit-rate number, the better a station sounds, though you're at the mercy of your Internet connection. (If you don't see the bit rate, choose View ⇨ View Options ⇨ Show Columns ⇨ Bit Rate.) You can also choose to view Comments and Kind if those options aren't already selected.

You can include Internet radio stations in a playlist. You must be connected to the Internet to hear them, of course.

Apple Music

Streaming Internet radio stations have their place and are great. But Apple (like many of its industry rivals) curates its own streaming radio stations for your listening pleasure. The result is the radio portion of the Apple Music service, which you can get to by clicking the Radio tab in iTunes. You'll land in an environment like the one shown in Figure 13-9.

FIGURE 13-9: Customize Apple Music to choose the kind of music you want to hear.

As part of Apple Music, anyone using a Mac (or for that matter portable devices from Apple and Android) can tap into deejay-hosted Beats 1, a global 24-by-7 radio station broadcast live from studios in Los Angeles, New York, and London.

The other Apple Music radio stations, and the benefits that come with them, are reserved for people who subscribe to Apple Music. The cost is $9.99 a month for an individual or $14.99 a month for a family membership that covers up to six people. If you aren't sure Apple Music is for you — and I'll be the first to tell you that although I like it, other fine music subscription services are out there, including one of my favorites, Spotify — sample it for three months under a free trial.

Apple Music membership benefits include a bunch of genre-focused curated Apple Music radio stations. And if you hear music from these stations that tickles your fancy, click the heart (refer to Figure 13-1) to train the service into serving up more songs just like it.

You can also click the three dots next to the song title (when you hover the cursor over it) for other drop-down menu choices. For example, you can add the song to your My Music collection, of which I'll have more to say shortly. You can add the song to a playlist or an iTunes wish list. You can share the song or station (via email, Twitter, Facebook, and Messages), or jump to the particular artist or album to explore other music from that performer. And you can use the song in question as the seed song that blossoms into its own custom radio station.

And if your opinion of the song is less harmonious, you can also tell Apple Music to "Never Play This Song."

Songs with explicit lyrics are shown with a tiny *E* next to their title to ward off you (or perhaps your kids).

TIP

Speaking of material that you or your children may not want to hear, if you are turned off by vulgar words or other potentially sensitive or scatological lyrics, head to iTunes Preferences, click the Restrictions tab, and place a check mark next to the Restrict: Music with Explicit Content option.

The various tabs at the top of your iTunes display hint at other sections of Apple Music. Click New to peek at Hot Tracks, Hit Songs, and other new music that Apple wants to bring to your attention.

Click For You for recommended playlists and albums that the Apple Music editors think you'll like, based on your current collection and the songs you choose to buy or designate as favorites. The For You section is frequently updated to keep the material fresh.

Click Connect to follow certain artists and learn about new releases and tours, view candid photos, and even watch some video. You can read what fans of the artist have to say about the performer and contribute your own comments.

You've probably figured out by now that the My Music tab leads to your own iTunes music collection or library. If you subscribe to Apple Music, you can add the music you hear streaming on the radio to your collection. As a subscriber, you can also stream any song in the vast Apple Music collection that you want to hear and add that song to My Music too.

WARNING

Of course, there is a great big catch here: If you no longer subscribe to Apple Music, you won't be able to play back any of the music that you don't outright own. Which leads me to the next section on finding and buying music.

Finding Music (and More) Online

iTunes serves as a gateway to a delightful emporium for music lovers. The iTunes Store is where hunting for songs is a pleasure for all but the most tone-deaf users. Don't believe me? How else to explain the billions of downloads since Apple opened the place? To enter the store, click the iTunes Store button in the upper-right corner of the iTunes window.

Sadly, you won't find every song on your wish list, because some performers or the music labels that control the artists' catalogs foolhardily remain digital hold-outs. They have yet to put their records up for sale in cyberspace. Fortunately, the roster of digital holdouts is shorter and shorter. Even The Beatles, once the poster children for the playing-hard-to-get, eventually relented. The complete Fab Four catalog is available these days in iTunes.

Now that I have that rant off my chest, I'll put a positive spin on buying music online compared with doing so in the physical world. For one thing, your neigh-borhood record store isn't going to carry the more than 43 million and counting DRM-free (Digital Rights Management) tracks available in the iTunes Store. And sadly, many of those physical stores have disappeared, in large part because of the popularity of cyberpurchases. Moreover, every tune in the iTunes joint is always in stock.

REMEMBER

Shopping online for music affords you other privileges. Most notably, you have the opportunity to cherry-pick favorite tracks from an album without having to buy the entire compilation. Note, however, that some record labels require that some tracks be purchased only as part of a full-blown album.

What's more, you can sample all the tracks for up to 90 seconds without any obligation to buy. (And if you subscribe to Apple Music, you can listen to the entire song as often as you like.) Most of the songs that you wanted to buy used to cost 99¢ a pop, but the most popular material these days more typically fetches $1.29 a track. On the other hand, you can find bargain selections for as little as 69¢, and even some freebies as you'll discover later in this chapter. Then you have the matter of instant gratification. You can start listening to the music you buy inside iTunes mere seconds after making a purchase, as you see later in the chapter.

Seeking online music recommendations

In a real-life music store, you might find an adolescent clerk willing to recommend an album or artist. (Although why is it you have a sneaking suspicion this kid doesn't speak the same language you do, much less enjoy the same repertoire?) If you get really lucky, you may come across a Julliard graduate moonlighting between gigs. But more often than not, you're browsing the shelves on your own — not that that's a bad thing; I love spending time in record stores.

But face it, we all need a little counsel now and then. You'll find plenty of it in the iTunes Store from Apple as well as from people like you who happen to adore music. To get started, click the iTunes Store tab near the top of the screen.

The front page of the place is like the window of a physical record store. You see colorful album-cover thumbnails, promotions for particular artists, and more.

Store pages are laid out with new and noteworthy releases, Hot Tracks, and lists of top songs, albums, music videos, and more. You may see a few exclusives and other recommendations presented in the main genre you choose from the Music pop-up menu.

Apple frequently changes the layout and features of the iTunes Store. So don't be surprised if what you see differs from the way it's described in this book.

Figure 13-10 shows the front page of the store when you haven't selected a specific genre.

Now suppose that you click the banner for Sia's *This Is Acting.* You're transported to a page like the one shown in Figure 13-11. In this initial view — the Songs tab — you see a list of songs in the compilation. Click any of these songs to hear a 90-second sample. Click the Ratings and Reviews tab to see ratings and reviews provided by fans just like you. You can contribute your own rating (based on a five-star system) and write a review by clicking . . . well, Write a Review. Doesn't some small part of you want to be a critic?

Now click the Related tab. Here's where you see the top albums and songs by Sia, as well as other related records that listeners bought. You also see top albums in the genre most people would associate Sia with: pop.

FIGURE 13-10:
Browsing classic selections in the iTunes Store.

FIGURE 13-11:
You can get individual songs on Sia's *This Is Acting* for $1.29 a pop or pay $9.99 for the whole album.

A quick aside on rating music: You can rate the songs in your own library on a five-star scale. Click the song you want to rate. Under the rating column (refer to Figure 13-1), click the appropriate number of stars or drag your cursor to add or remove stars. Alternatively, Control+ click a song and then choose. You can rate an album too; if you do so, all the individual songs that make up the album will carry the same rating as the album itself (unless you individually change the rating for a given song).

The search for great music continues

I've already mentioned some of the ways you may stumble upon terrific music. Check out the following list for other methods, keeping in mind that the quest can be deeply addictive:

>> **Search:** A great starting point in your exploration is to search for artists or song titles by entering the name in the Search Store box near the upper-right corner of the screen. As you type characters, iTunes displays possible matches.

>> **Top Songs/Top Albums:** If you happen upon an album page but aren't familiar with the performer's music, consult the Top Songs/Top Albums list (on the Related tab) and click a song to hear your 90-second sample. You can also sample Top Ringtones (for your iPhone), if that option is available.

>> **Listeners Also Bought:** If you're impressed by what you hear by a given artist, you may also be attracted to other music purchased by fans of the artist's work.

TIP

You used to be able to hobnob with the stars — well, not exactly hobnob. But an eclectic cast of the rich and famous — Liv Tyler, Madonna, Mike Myers, William Shatner, Kim Cattrall, Bill Maher, Billy Bob Thornton, Carole King, B.B. King, Nicole Kidman, Russell Crowe, Jennifer Garner, Taye Diggs, Jackie Chan, Smokey Robinson, RuPaul, Andrew Lloyd Webber, Kanye West, Sting, Al Franken, LeBron James, Lance Armstrong, Tim McGraw, Bill Cosby, Rev. Al Green, and many more — put together lists of their favorite works. The artists usually provided brief descriptions of why they chose certain songs. Regrettably, purchasing songs from these celebrity playlists isn't an automatic ticket to stardom. Even worse, Apple no longer provides celebrity playlists as a regular feature (though, as mentioned, some artists serve as DJs in iTunes Radio). But because of the nature of cyberspace, you can still find links to the celebrity playlists floating out there. Check out `https://itunes.apple.com/WebObjects/MZStore.woa/wa/viewCelebritiesSeeAll?cc=us` to find some of the songs favored by artists whom you admire.

When you're ready to buy

So now that you have all these recommendations, you're ready to spend some money. First, though, you have to set up an account with Apple (assuming that you haven't already done so) or use an existing AOL account. Here's how:

1. **Open iTunes, and choose Store▷Create Apple ID.**

You won't see Create Apple ID on the menu if you already have an account.

2. **In the sign-in window, click Continue.**

3. **Fill in the requested name, password, payment details, and other info.**

   The rest is easy.

4. **Find a song that you want to buy, and click the dollar amount of the song — typically, $1.29.**

   You may have to fill in the account credentials again, depending on how recently you entered such information.

   To make sure that you really mean it, Apple serves up the warning dialog shown in Figure 13-12, unless you click the Don't Ask Me about Buying check box.

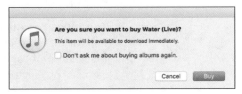

5. **Click Buy to complete the transaction.**

   FIGURE 13-12:
   We're happy to take your money, but. . .

   In a matter of seconds (usually), the song is downloaded to the aptly named Purchased playlist.

If you've cherry-picked the songs you've bought from select albums, Apple sometimes lets you buy the rest of the titles on the album at a reduced cost. There's a six-month limit to take advantage of this Complete My Album feature, from the time you first downloaded a song from an eligible album. You see some of your Complete My Album options on the iTunes Music storefront.

TIP

If you click Account under Quick Links (on the right side of the page), you'll be taken to an Account Information page. If you select Manage next to Alert Me "Based on Purchases," Apple sends you an email letting you know when artists whose music you've bought in the past have added new music to the Music Store. To do so, select Send Me Email Alert About Artists I've Previously Downloaded. You can also request Genius alerts based on your library content. While perusing the Quick Links list, take note of your other choices. Among them is a My Wish List section that lets you save items from the iTunes Store (and App Store) that you may want to purchase later. More ways to get you to part with your money.

Allowances and gifts

If you've bought one too many lame sweaters or neckties over the years as 11th-hour birthday gifts, iTunes may be your salvation. Click Send iTunes Gifts in the Quick Links list to buy something truly valuable. iTunes gift certificates can be issued in amounts of $10, $15, $25, $50, $100, or some other amount you designate.

You can email the certificate or print it. You can even give a specific song, TV show, movie, video, or audiobook, or create a custom playlist for that lucky person. You can also order iTunes gift cards from your Mac, though you'll find such cards for sale at numerous physical retailers.

The whole gift shebang takes only a minute or so. It sure beats battling the crowds at the mall.

If you select Allowances instead Send iTunes Gifts, you can set up a regular monthly allowance (in $10 intervals, up to $50) that gets topped off automatically on the first of the month. In the iTunes Gifts window, select Set Up an Allowance. If all goes well, Junior will learn a thing or two about fiscal responsibility. Unused balances are saved until your kid makes another purchase. Should your son or daughter abuse any privileges, of course, you can pull the plug on his or her iTunes allowance at any time by heading over to the Account Information page.

You can gift an entire album inside the iTunes Store. On the Album page, click the arrow next to the album's Buy button and choose Gift This Album from the pop-up menu.

Note your other choices in this menu: You can add the album to a wish list, tell a friend about it, copy the link, or share it on Facebook and/or Twitter.

To redeem a certificate you've received, click Redeem in the Quick Links list, and enter the redeem code on your gift card or certificate. You must enter your Apple ID and password to proceed.

Sharing music with other computers

If your Mac is part of a local computer network (see Chapter 18), you can share the music in your library with other machines running iTunes version 4.5 or later, sometimes as a stream, sometimes by actually transferring the track to the device that you are using. In iTunes Preferences, click the Sharing tab, and select the Share My Library on My Local Network option. You can share the entire library or selected playlists. For added security, you can require users of other computers to enter a password. iTunes must remain open on your machine for other computers to access your music.

If you want to update play counts in your iTunes library when you play music on other computers in your network, or on an iPod, iPhone, or iPad, select the Home Sharing Computers and Devices Update Play Counts check box.

iTunes: More Than Just Music

It was inevitable that the iTunes Music Store would become just the iTunes Store because, as you know by now, you can purchase a lot more than just music and then share it on an iPod, iPhone, or iPad.

Reading books

You can read electronic books on your Mac through the iBooks Store (see Chapter 11) as well as various third-party apps, notably Amazon, whose Kindle for the Mac app is free. (Most of the books aren't free, of course.) Click the Books tab in the iTunes Store to check out the numerous iBook choices Apple makes available, as well as audiobooks (see the next section).

Listening to audiobooks

You can fetch the iTunes equivalent of books on tape and play them on your Mac, covering a wide range of authors from Ernest Hemingway to James Patterson. You can sample 30-second previews as well, but the truth is, audiobooks tend to go on for hours, compared with 3 or 4 minutes for your average song, so a 30-second preview probably won't give you more than just the barest hint of how the book reads. Prices vary, too. A 22-minute audio of Stephen Colbert's remarks at the White House Correspondents' Dinner costs $2.95; an 8½ -hour audio version of "Papa" Hemingway's *A Farewell to Arms* goes for $23.95. To find audiobooks, click the Books tab.

TIP

Mac owners who buy audiobooks from the popular Audible.com service (owned by Amazon.com) can download books directly into iTunes.

Capturing podcasts

Podcasts are another form of Internet radio but are very different from the radio I describe earlier in this chapter. For one thing, many podcasts go beyond "mere" radio by incorporating video. Moreover, podcasts are downloadable files you can listen to at your leisure.

As you'll see after choosing the Podcasts option inside iTunes, podcasts cover a broad range of topics (business, politics, sports, TV and film, technology, and so on) and are served up by experienced broadcasters, mainstream media outlets (NPR, *USA TODAY, The Wall Street Journal),* as well as ordinary Joes and Josephines.

Most podcasts are free to download and often commercial-free. You can fetch individual episodes by clicking Free or subscribe to podcasts that arrive on a regular basis by clicking Subscribe. As with audiobooks, you can click to hear (or watch) a sample.

You can find the podcasts you've downloaded by choosing Podcasts from the Library pop-up menu.

Catching up on *Mad Men* and *Game of Thrones*

Quick story. I'd never seen the hit series *Lost* before downloading the pilot episode to iTunes (and then to an iPod). I was instantly hooked. I immediately understood the power of iTunes/iPod video.

Lost was among the first handful of TV shows that Apple made available on iTunes. The number of programs quickly mushroomed to incorporate everything from *Downton Abbey* to *Homeland*. Music videos and short films are also available.

Videos and TV shows inside iTunes typically cost $1.99 to $2.99 apiece; high-definition shows fetch the higher price. You can sample 30-second previews and also subscribe to a season for a given series.

REMEMBER

You can drag movie or video files you create yourself or obtain from other sources into iTunes.

TECHNICAL STUFF

Before you can transfer some videos to an iPod, iPhone, iPad tablet, or Apple TV set-top box, you may have to convert the videos to a format those devices recognize. Select the video; choose File➪Create New Version; and then choose Create iPod or iPhone Version, Create iPad or Apple TV Version, or Create AAC Version.

Buying and renting movies

Apple started not only selling motion pictures through iTunes, but also renting them. Newer films typically cost $14.99 to purchase or $3.99 to rent in standard definition, or $19.99 to purchase or $4.99 to rent in HD. Rented movies come with restrictions. You have 30 days to start watching, but only 24 hours to finish after you've begun playing them.

Movies and TV shows that you purchase inside iTunes are typically saddled by DRM restrictions that let you play them back on only up to five "authorized" computers.

Through iTunes, you can view the trailer and read plot summaries, credits, and customer reviews.

You can watch a movie on your computer, of course, and watching a flick on a Mac laptop is a great substitute for the dreadful film the airline might choose to show you. But when you're staying put, you probably want to watch on the widescreen TV in your home theater. Apple sells the aforementioned Apple TV box ($69 for the older model; $149 or $199 for the newer version), which connects to a high-definition TV (with an available HDMI port) and wirelessly communicates with your iTunes library to show movies, pictures, and videos and play music through the television.

App Store

If you have an iPhone, iPod touch, or iPad, you can access a gaggle of nifty programs for those devices, covering games, news, productivity, social networking, and a whole bunch more. Apple had something north of 1.5 million apps as this book went to press, with the vast majority priced at less than $10 and many free. Although you can access the App Store wirelessly on an iPad, iPhone, or iPod touch, you can also get there directly via iTunes.

Fetching apps from the App Store for your portable devices is very similar to buying Mac apps in the Mac App Store, discussed in greater detail in Chapter 11.

iTunes U

Bet you thought iTunes was all about fun and games. Hey, learning is fun, too. You can take in a lecture on the Roman Empire by a professor at the University of California–Berkeley or find out about green chemistry from Yale. iTunes offers thousands of educational audio and video files from top colleges, museums, and other global organizations. K–12 classes are available, too. Tuition is free, and better still, you get no surprise quizzes. Click the iTunes U tab in the iTunes Store to enter the Ivy-covered virtual lecture halls of your computer.

Chapter 14

Taking a Photos Close-Up

Disruptive technology is a concept that has been floating around for more than a decade. Loosely defined, it describes how a once-dominant technology gets elbowed aside and is eventually displaced by something new. The expression was coined by Harvard Business School Professor Clayton M. Christensen, and those Ivy educators are pretty darn smart. Disruptive technology is just what happened in the world of photography, where digital cameras dramatically overtook the film side of the picture-taking biz. (You remember film, right?) Ever capable cameras are built into virtually every mass-market cellphone you can buy.

With the OS X Photos app, Apple brings its own special smarts to digital photography. Photos, which replaced the longtime iPhoto program as the go-to photography software on your Mac, is part digital shoebox, part processing lab, part touch-up artist, and more. It lets you import, organize, view, edit, and share your masterpieces with an adoring public (or, at the very least, family and friends). And if you use the Photos app on an iPhone, you already have a head start on how to use the app on your Mac because both apps use a similar organizational structure. (For those who remain loyal to iPhoto, the program still lurks in the background on older Macs.)

Getting Pictures into the Computer

Taking pictures with most digital cameras is a snap. Taking *good* digital pictures is another matter entirely and beyond the — pun alert — focus of this book. After you press your digital camera's shutter button, images end up on small (and usually removable) memory cards. Even as the price of memory declines, the capacity of these cards rises. You can now capture many hundreds of pictures on relatively inexpensive and reusable cards.

In the past, it was a challenge to get digital images onto your computer, where the real fun begins. Photos and iCloud drastically simplify the process, as does the fact that most Macs now have slots for SD (Secure Digital) memory cards.

Connecting a digital camera or iOS mobile device

In some cases, you run a direct connection from the digital camera (or iPhone, iPad, or iPod touch) to the Mac by connecting the USB cable supplied with the camera. Once that happens, follow these steps:

1. **Turn on the camera.**

2. **Launch the Photos app, assuming it isn't already open, and click Import.**

   You can arrange for Photos to always open when you connect this particular camera by selecting the Open Photos for This Device check box, next to the device name in the upper-left corner of the Photos screen. If you want to delete the photos from the device after you import them, select the Delete Items after Import check box.

3. **Choose one of the following options, as shown in Figure 14-1:**

   a. *Click Import All New Photos to do just that.*

   b. *Click only the photos you want to import to select them and then click Import Selected.*

If everything went down as it should and Photos was called into action, skip to the next section. If you ran into a problem, you can try the following:

TIP

>> Check to make sure that your camera is turned on and you have a fresh set of batteries.

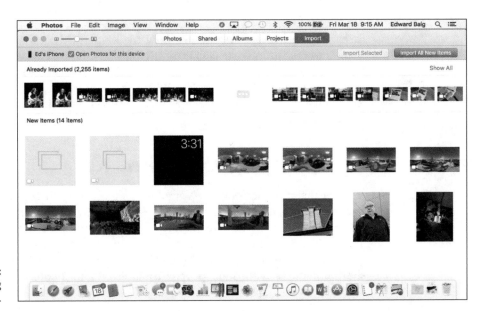

FIGURE 14-1:
Importing
pictures.

>> Because every camera is different, consult the instructions that came with your model to make sure that it's in the proper setting for importing pictures (usually, Play mode). Don't you just hate when that happens? You want an answer now, and here I am directing you to some manual that was likely translated into English from another language. Translated poorly, I might add.

Importing images from other sources

Not all the pictures in your Photos library arrive by direct transfer from your digital camera. Some reach the Mac by a third-party phone, the web, email, CDs or DVDs, flash drives, or memory card readers. And most of the more recent Mac models, as mentioned, have SD card slots to handle Secure Digital–type memory cards. Other pictures may already reside somewhere else on your hard drive.

In the case of a third-party phone, you can copy photo files from that device to your Mac's internal disk and then either drag the files from Finder to the Photos windows, drag the files to the Photos icon on the dock, or in Photos, choose File⇨Import. Again, you can copy all or just some of the photos on your mobile device.

WARNING

Do not eject your camera or third-party device while the photos are being imported.

When you insert a memory card into your Mac, the computer may treat that card as though it were the camera, and fire up Photos. The difference is that instead of using an actual camera name, Photos identifies the card as No Name (and in some cases actually will identify the card by the name of the camera in which those images were captured, such as EOS_Digital.)

Photos is compatible with JPEG, TIFF (the most common image file formats), RAW (a photo-enthusiast format available on pretty much all dSLR cameras), and other formats.

Demystifying iCloud images

None of the aforementioned ways to get pictures on your Mac is terribly taxing. But then, doing next to nothing to have pictures arrive on your computer is even easier, and you'll do next to nothing to take advantage of iCloud Photo Library and My Photo Stream. The distinction between the two can be confusing. To really throw you, there's also something called iCloud Photo Sharing, which is about sharing pictures with other people. I address iCloud Photo Sharing later in the chapter.

With My Photo Stream, your most recently imported pictures are uploaded automatically to iCloud, where they can then find their way to your iOS devices and your Mac. Such photos (and videos too) are stored for 30 days. (iCloud Photo Library doesn't share this 30-day limitation.)

You do have to ensure that you're all signed up with iCloud. After you do so, if you take pictures via an iOS-capable device such as your iPhone, iPad, or iPod touch, those pictures land more or less immediately on your other iOS devices as well as on your Mac. Photo Stream works on Windows PCs, too. But if you import pictures from a digital camera or SD memory card, those images can also make it into Photo Stream.

Even better, because many Macs have reasonably generous storage capacities (depending on the model), you can keep a master set of your pictures on your home computer. But there are limits to the number of pictures you can upload to My Photo Stream: 1000 per hour, 10,000 per day, or 25,000 per month. The photos uploaded to My Photo Stream do not count against any iCloud storage limits. To make sure that Photo Stream is sending the photos on your iPhone, iPad, or iPod touch to your Mac's hard drive (or SSD), connect the device to Wi-Fi at least once during a 30-day period or save images to your Camera Roll.

Only JPEG, PNG, TIFF, and RAW photographic file formats can be uploaded to Photo Stream. Video doesn't work. However, you can upload video to the iCloud Photo Library.

On the Mac, Photo Stream works with Photos, of course, as well as with the since retired Apple program called Aperture.

To ensure that My Photo Stream is turned on in Photos, visit Photos Preferences, tap the iCloud icon, choose Options, and from there select (if it isn't already selected) the My Photo Stream check box. Then click Done. You can start out in System Preferences as well. Click iCloud, select Photos, and then select Options.

Downloaded photos appear in the Photos app on your iOS devices and in the My Photo Stream Album view in Photos on your Mac.

You won't see the My Photo Stream album if you select the iCloud Photo Library check box in iCloud or in Photos Preferences. That's because iCloud Photo Library stores all your photos across your Mac and other devices in the appropriately titled All Photos album.

All your photos live in iCloud. But as Figure 14-2 shows, you can choose to download the originals to your Mac, in full resolution. The advantage: You can display the images in their full splendor even when you're offline. Of course, the flip side is that those pictures will take up more room on your hard drive or SSD.

You can choose to Optimize Mac Storage, which means full-resolution pictures (and videos) remain in iCloud and the originals are kept on your Mac only if it has ample space. The iCloud Photos app lets you upload JPEGs that are less than 16GB.

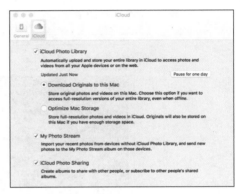

FIGURE 14-2:
Choose how you want to store your iCloud photos.

Of course, you may not want to keep every last picture. Later in the chapter, I tell you how to remove photos from iCloud Photo Library.

But for now, look at the organizational principles at work in Photos.

Finding and Organizing Images

Right from the outset, Photos helps you organize pics (and videos) so that you can easily find the ones you want to view later. At the very top of the Photos screen, you'll see four tabs: Photos, Shared, Albums, and Projects. A fifth tab, Imports, appears only when a digital camera or other device is connected to your Mac (as is the case in Figure 14-1).

You'll start exploring ways to get at your photos in the first of these tabs, Photos, which has three main views: *Moments, Collections* and *Years.* This organizational path will be familiar if you use the Photos app on an iPhone or an iPad.

As you might imagine, pictures categorized by years (see Figure 14-3) are just that, all the images captured in a given year. Scroll up or down to move from year to year. You can rapidly skim through an entire year's worth of images by holding down the mouse button and running your cursor across the mini-thumbnails that represent all the pictures in that year. As you skim past, each thumbnail momentarily gets a bit larger. When you release the mouse button, the last picture you landed on opens. One other thing to note about this yearly grouping is that you'll see headings with the name of the country or countries in which the pictures with a given year were taken, assuming the location was known.

FIGURE 14-3:
In Year view, see all the pictures in a given year.

The collections category (see Figure 14-4) is a subset within a year, maybe all the pictures you took vacationing with the family in Paris. Group headings may still reveal the country or countries where the pictures were taken, but now the location descriptor might be more specific, displaying a city or landmark, for example, and a date range (such as Aug 11-14, 2013).

Within that grouping is yet another subset called moments, as shown in Figure 14-5. These might be the pictures you took while touring the Eiffel Tower. You'll again see the heading/location data if known, with the descriptor perhaps even more specific.

Photos you shared or others shared with you

Create albums, smart albums, books, calendars, cards, slideshows, and prints

Photos by location and date

Photo albums

Change among Years, Collections and Moments views

Share options

Books, calendars, cards

Search

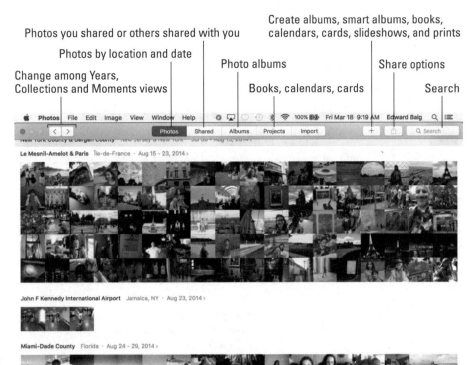

FIGURE 14-4: Collections view displays a subset of pictures in a particular year.

Slide to resize thumbnails

This thumbnail represents a video

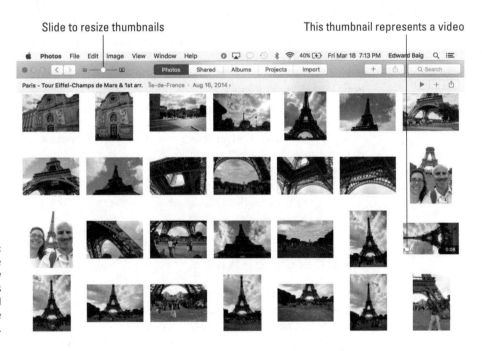

FIGURE 14-5: Use the Moments view for pictures taken around the same time and place.

Use the arrows on the upper-left corner of the display to move from years to collections to moments and back. You can also pinch in or out on your trackpad to change these views.

Seeing everything in Photos view

You already know that your entire image collection shows up in a grid of *thumbnails*, or miniature pictures, the size of which varies by the Years, Collections, and Moments views. If you're having trouble making out the thumbnails, try these tricks:

>> **Adjust the thumbnail size:** In the Moments view, drag the zoom slider (adjacent to the arrows near the upper-left corner of the screen) and watch how the thumbnails grow. Cool, huh? Now drag the zoom slider to the left to make the pictures shrink. You can peek at many more pictures in the viewing area that way.

>> **Double-click a photo to make it larger.** You can do this from any main view. Double-click again to return to the thumbnail view; regardless of where you started, doing so places you in the Moments view.

TIP

Movie thumbnails appear with a little camcorder icon and the duration of the clip. Clicking a movie thumbnail starts playing the movie in the same window in which you just viewed still images. If you move your cursor over a movie thumbnail, you'll actually see the video come alive in that thumbnail (though at that point you won't hear any audio). The same goes for a Live Photos image taken with the iPhone 6s or 6s Plus (or later).

Your iCloud Photo Library and the number of pictures you store on your Mac can mushroom fast. If all Apple did was drop all those pictures into one large digital dumping ground, of course, you'd have a heck of a time finding that oh-so-precious shot of your proud kid getting her elementary-school diploma. So how do you uncover the very images you want to admire over and over? Well, you already know through the Years, Collections, and Moments views how to zero in on pictures from a particular time or place, which can be a huge timesaver as you pore through potentially thousands of images. But you can also click the tabs at the top of the Photos app to get to your pictures in other ways.

Choosing albums

Under the Albums tab (see Figure 14-6), you'll find, well, albums and events. There are all sorts of albums, ranging from standard album you create yourself — I'll show you how shortly — to special albums known as Smart Albums.

FIGURE 14-6:
Albums view.

Apple also kindly lumps like-minded images into special albums on your behalf. There's a Last Import album, which houses the latest batch of pictures you brought on board, and albums for pictures that you designated as favorites by clicking a heart symbol. And you'll find an album for all your videos. And there's a fun one I'll get to called Faces.

You'll also find albums containing images you imported from your iOS devices, including slo-mo videos, time-lapse videos, photo bursts, selfies, and screen-shots. You might also see iPhoto Events (from the old iPhoto program).

Meantime, there's the Recently Deleted album, which is the last resting place for the pictures that won't survive your critical eye. And there is an album for photos that are in your library but hidden.

In Figure 14-6, the albums you created are in the middle of the display, below the My Albums heading. The special albums from Apple are at or near the top of the screen.

Displaying the sidebar

Another way to view your photos, albums, and special projects is to summon the sidebar, a panel that runs down the left side of the display. (The sidebar was known as the source list in iPhotos.) To make the sidebar appear, choose View⇨Show Sidebar or press ⌘+Option+S.

Using the Search field

One of the easy shortcuts for finding specific pictures on your Mac is to use the Search field in Photos. You can type a word, phrase, title, description, keyword, or date to search for photos. Highlight the match that meets your search criteria.

TECHNICAL STUFF

Photos captures more than just photos when picture files are transferred. Through captured *metadata,* the program usually knows the make and model of the camera used to take the image; the date and time the picture was taken and imported; the size in *pixels,* or picture elements; the aperture setting of the camera; whether a flash was used; and more. Such data is factored into searches.

Facing everyone in Faces view

How awesome would it be to locate photos based on who's in them? Your wish is Apple's command. The magical Faces feature is based on facial detection and recognition technologies. The feature is off by a few whiskers here and there: Photos may fail to recognize a face or falsely match a name with a face. Still, you can't help but walk away impressed, even if Faces isn't quite up to *CSI* standards.

When you first open Photos, the program scans your library in the background to find facial matches. It also scans faces when you import new photos.

Here's how to connect names to faces in this view:

1. **Click the Faces album in the Albums view, or click Faces under the Albums view in the sidebar.**

   When you first get started, you'll see people's mugs in individual circles.

2. **Double-click one of the faces in a circle to get started.**

3. **Type the name of the person.**

   Apple displays pictures with the person whose face it thinks it recognized. The face is circled inside the image.

4. **Examine each photo to confirm that Apple correctly matched a face — a check mark should already be in place.**

   a. *If Apple did get it right, click Add and Continue.*

   b. *If Apple didn't get it right, click the photo to remove the check mark(s) and click Add and Continue.*

5. **Repeat Step 4 for each photo that Apple has added.**

6. **When you want to stop reviewing facial suggestions, click Finish Later, and then click Done.**

   The Faces feature in Photos gets smarter as you go along and correctly IDs more pictures.

In the Faces view shown in Figure 14-7, every person whose face you've identified appears in their own circle. If you click the Photos tab in the Faces view, you see all the underlying photos of that person that are represented here. Click the Faces tab in the Faces view to go back to seeing the person's mug in the circle.

FIGURE 14-7:
A Faces
face-off.

TIP

If you see suggested faces at the bottom of the screen for a person who has already been identified, drag one or more faces at the bottom onto their circle in the upper portion of the screen.

Identifying faces in other ways

A second way to add new faces is to click the Info (i) button on the toolbar. Doing so summons the *Information pane*, shown in Figure 14-8, which is a great source of information about an image, from the camera used to the location in which the pic was snapped.

Examine the picture. If you see an Unnamed label below a face, just type the person's name — again, if known. If no label appears, click the circled + in the Information pane. Drag the circle that appears over an undetected face, grabbing the corners to make the circle larger or smaller as needed. The position and size of the circle determines the way the circled images look on the Faces page. Click to name the person.

FIGURE 14-8:
Using the Infor-
mation pane to
identify a face.

Fixing matches that have gone awry

REMEMBER

As I mention at the beginning of this section, Faces sometimes misjudges who's in your photos. Here a few common mistakes you may come to, um . . . recognize:

>> **The photo bomber:** Photos sometimes shows a face of someone who's in the background of a crowded scene, such as a picnic or a ballgame.

>> **The 2D celebrity:** Photos can mistake the face of a picture within a picture for a real person if, for example, someone you know is posing in front of a movie poster.

>> **The dark, sideways glance:** Perhaps the image is poorly lit or blurry. Maybe the angle is off or the mug shot is too small.

>> **The hipster turned preppy:** Maybe you had a beard and glasses in one picture and were clean-shaven and wearing contact lenses in another.

>> **The time machine:** Maybe you have a picture of your kid when she was 2 years old, but now, a few years later, she looks completely different.

If you're concerned that Photos may mismatch other names, you can remove a name from a face. How?

Double-click a snapshot, click the wrong name, and type the correct name. Sometimes Photos will ask you who the person is, as in "Is This Edward Baig?" Click the check mark to indicate that it is *moi* or the x to say "nope."

You can also remove a person from the Faces album. Merely click a face and press Delete on the keyboard. Click Undo Ignore This Face in the Edit menu (or press ⌘+Z) You can also hide Face names, by selecting the Hide Face Names option in the View menu.

Mapping photos in Places view

Many of today's cameras (and virtually every state-of-the-art camera phone) are so clever that they can detect where they are — and, by proxy, where the shooter is — when a picture is snapped. So it stands to reason that if your camera knows where a picture was taken, Photos can exploit location information for your benefit. Photos that have been geotagged partly rely on the Global Positioning System (GPS) coordinates that your camera captures along with the image.

Remember that the headings in the Years, Collections and Moments views include location information, if known. Clicking the header inside Photos effectively morphs it into the Maps app, as shown in Figure 14-9. Overlaid on top of the maps are thumbnails that represent the photos taken in the areas shown on the map. The number on the corner of the thumbnail tells you how many pictures were taken in the area. If you click the thumbnail, you can view those very pictures.

FIGURE 14-9: The Places feature maps your Photos library.

Here's a quick look at what you can do in this view:

>> You can reveal more of a map by dragging. Double-click or (via trackpad) pinch to zoom in on an area. Or click + or – to zoom in or out, respectively.

>> You can even switch the look of the map to a satellite view, a standard map view, or a hybrid of the two. Just click the corresponding button in the upper right.

TIP

Even if you hadn't clicked a place, you can check out a photo's location on a map. Click the Info (i) button to open the Information pane, and you can see where the picture was taken on a small map adjacent to the actual photograph, with a red pushpin pointing to the right spot.

Don't fret if your camera can't capture location data. You can type your own location information and be as general (such as Chicago) or as specific (Grandma's house) as you like. Just type the more specific location name in the Assign a Location section of the Information pane.

You can also add animated maps to slideshows and maps to photo books (discussed later in this chapter).

REMEMBER

If Photos doesn't seem to be capturing location data, open System Preferences, make sure the Enable Location Services setting (found on the Privacy tab in Security & Privacy) is selected for Photos.

Meantime, in Photos Preferences, if you select the Metadata: Include Location Information for Published Items option, any location information captured with your pictures is included if you share those images via email or on an online photo site such as Flickr. Deselect this item if you don't want to include such information when you share your pictures in cyberspace.

Assigning keywords

Keywords may be the keys to finding pictures in the future. *Keywords* are labels, or tags, applied to a set of photos. Open the Information pane and add a keyword in the section provided. As you type, Photos suggests words you've used before. Apple provides some keywords right off the bat: Favorite, Family, Kids, Vacation,

FIGURE 14-10:
The key to keywords.

and Birthday. You can find them in the Keyword Manager, shown in Figure 14-10, which is found under the Window menu in Photos.

In Keyword Manager, you can add, remove, and rename keywords as well as create shortcuts (FA for Family, say). You can drag keywords to the top of Keyword

Manager to create a quick-pick list. And of course you can add multiple keywords to an image, perhaps Kids and Birthday. Once keywords are in place for a photo, you can search for them in the Photos search box.

Placing your work in albums

In the film age, really organized people took the time to methodically place prints in old-fashioned picture albums. I admire people like that because I lack this particular organizing gene.

Fortunately, Photos equivalent of placing pictures in albums is much simpler. The process is similar to creating playlists in iTunes (see Chapter 13). You can place all the pictures from your weekend in Philadelphia (as shown in Figure 14-11) in one album, pictures of the high-school reunion in another, and so on. Here's the drill:

1. **Select the photos you want to add to an album.**

2. **Choose File⇨New Album, or press ⌘+N, or click + in the toolbar.**

3. **Choose New Album from the pop-up menu.**

4. **Type a name for your new album, and then click OK.**

   You can use Hawaii Honeymoon, Dance Recital, or whatever. You'll see the number of items being added to your album.

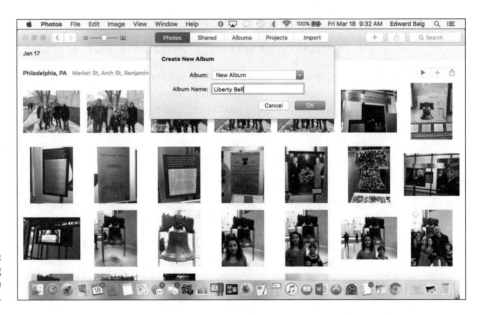

FIGURE 14-11:
Adding pictures to an album.

A quick word about how to select the pictures that will populate your album:

>> Drag entire events or individual photos onto the album name or icon in the Source list.

>> To select a batch of photos to drag over, hold down the ⌘ key while clicking the pictures you want to include.

>> To select adjoining photos, hold down the Shift key and click the arrow buttons.

>> To select all the photos between two photos, hold down Shift and click the first image; then hold Shift and click the last image.

TIP

Although photos are lumped into albums, the pictures actually remain in the Photos library. The images inside albums are merely pointers to the original files. So you can place the same picture in multiple albums. You can also remove pictures from an album without fear that the images will be deep-sixed from the Photos library.

TIP

After you create a bunch of albums, you can group them into a folder. Choose File➪New Folder, give the folder a name (such as Vacations), and drag all the relevant albums into the folder. When you select the newly created folder, you see all the pictures stored in all the albums contained in that folder. Folders turn up in the sidebar if it is in view. Otherwise, you'll see folders among your list of albums in the Album view.

Creating a Smart Album for photos

Just as you can create Smart Playlists in iTunes, you can sire Smart Albums in Photos based on specific criteria, such as keywords, photos you've rated highly, pictures taken with a particular camera, or the shutter speed. To create a Smart Album, follow these steps:

1. **Choose File➪New Smart Album.**

2. **In the dialog that appears, type a name, just as you do for a regular album.**

3. **Select the conditions that must be met for pictures to be included in the Smart Album.**

Click the + button to add criteria or the – button to remove criteria. As new pictures are imported into your library, those that match these conditions are added to the Smart Album automatically.

In Figure 14-12, I've set up a Smart Album seeking pictures taken without a flash at the beach since early 2012. The pictures in the album had to be taken with one of two designated camera models, in this case a Canon or a Sony. I guess my criteria were too taxing, because not one photo in this particular collection matched up.

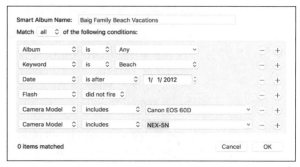

FIGURE 14-12:
A very smart Smart Album.

Enjoying a Split view

I already showed you how to make the sidebar appear or disappear. If the sidebar isn't visible and you're examining an individual photo in a Moments view in its own window, you can use the area to the left of the window, the place otherwise occupied by the sidebar, to view thumbnails of other photos. Apple calls this the *Split view*, and you can get there by clicking the Split View button, which is labeled in Figure 14-13. You'll see this button only when you've clicked a photo to open it. You can scroll through the thumbnails to see more photos than are visible on any one screen.

FIGURE 14-13:
Through Split view, you can admire one picture while glancing at others.

Enjoying Full Screen view

Truly gorgeous images, or at least pictures you hope to make truly gorgeous after you edit them (more on that later), may deserve the full-screen treatment. To make that happen, select a photo, and choose View⇨Enter Full Screen. To exit full screen, choose View⇨Exit Full Screen, or press Esc. You can also click the green Full-Screen droplet.

If you'd like to always show the Photos toolbar when you are in Full Screen mode, choose View⇨Always Show Toolbar in Full Screen. A checkmark confirms your selection. Choose View⇨Always Show Toolbar in Full Screen again to remove the check mark.

Something to hide

I'd like to believe that every picture I shoot is museum-quality. Truth is, I shoot my share of duds, which can be easily discarded. But then I find those tweeners — pictures that I don't want to showcase but I'm not ready to get rid of. You're about to encounter the Photos equivalent of shoving something into the closet or under the bed.

After selecting the photo or photos you want to hide, click Image⇨Hide *x* items, where *x* is the number of photos you want to conceal. An alternative method is to press ⌘+L.

Hidden photos will be hidden from Moments, Collections, and Years views. Want to find them again? They hang out in a Hidden album, found in the Albums view. Of course you may want to hide the Hidden album itself. To do so, click View⇨Hide Hidden Photo Album. To make it come back, click View⇨Show Hidden Photo Album.

To have pictures climb out of their foxhole, open the Hidden album, select the photos that are about to return to your good graces, and go to Image⇨Unhide *x* Photos. You can also press ⌘+L to unhide designated photos.

Touching Up Your Photos

Here's a dirty little secret: The drop-dead-gorgeous models gracing the covers of magazines don't really look like that. (Well, maybe some do, but work with me here.) The unsung heroes are the touch-up artists who remove a flaw from a picture here and a blemish there. We should all be so lucky to be able to put our own mugs in the best light. And lucky we are for having Photos on the Mac.

Photos is by no means a photo-editing superstar along the lines of Adobe's Photoshop. But for the mainstream snapshooter, Photos comes with several handy editing tools for removing red eye or applying special effects. Take a look at the various editing controls to the right of the picture shown in Figure 14-14. Let's take these one by one.

Enhancing an image

When you click the Enhance button, Photos automatically takes a stab at improving your picture by adjusting what photographers refer to as *white balance*, basically casting the proper color on the faces in a pic. If you don't like the results of this one-click automatic fix, click the Revert to Original button that shows up. If you are satisfied, click Done.

Rotating an image

Sometimes, the picture that turns up in the photo library is oriented incorrectly because of the way you rotated the camera when shooting the original. To fix the orientation in Photos, select the image, click the Edit button, and then click Rotate. The image rotates counterclockwise by 90 degrees. Keep clicking until the picture is oriented properly. Press the Option key while clicking to make the picture flip the other way.

Cropping an image

Cropping means snipping away at the periphery of an image so that you can get up close and personal with the subject at hand while removing traces of that yo-yo in the background who's sticking out his tongue. You have several ways to crop an image after clicking the Crop button. Check out Figure 14-14 to get a look:

>> **Automatic cropping:** Click the Auto button at the bottom-right corner of the screen.

>> **Manual cropping:** Choose the cropping area by dragging the corner of the selection rectangle to resize it.

>> **Specific Dimensions:** Click Aspect, and choose an appropriate *aspect ratio:* 16:9, 8:10, 5:7, 4:3, 3:5, or 3:2. You can also choose your own custom aspect ratio, or go with a square or a freeform selection. If you get messed up, revert to the original.

>> **Flip things around:** Click Flip to flip the image horizontally; click @@ option+Flip to flip vertically. It's kind of fun to see what a picture looks like when the person standing to the right of another is suddenly to the left.

>> **Straighten:** Does the photo look crooked? Or maybe you just can't come to terms with the fact that the leaning tower of Pisa is actually *leaning.* Rotate the tilt wheel to adjust the angle of the picture.

Apple supplies a safety valve: Click Reset to start over. Click Done to save your changes.

TIP

In helping you crop an image, Apple applies a compositional principle known as the *Rule of Thirds,* a popular guideline in photography and painting. The cropping area you drag around is divided into nine equal parts like a tic-tac-toe grid, (this is not shown in Figure 14-15). The thought is that if you place key elements of the picture in focal points where the lines intersect, you generally end up with a more interesting photo.

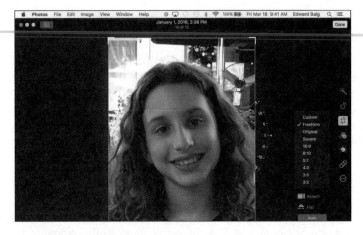

FIGURE 14-15:
Holy crop.

TIP

If you want to crop an image (or apply other edits) *and* keep the original, choose Image ⇨ Duplicate x Photo or Duplicate x Photo from Original. You can use the duplicate to do your cropping.

Applying filters

The beauty of photo software is that you can edit and doctor up images to make them look sillier, funkier, or prettier, or even go from color to black and white. So it goes with the eight filters that you can apply to any of your photos by clicking the Edit button and then clicking Filters. Your eight choices go by the names Mono, Tonal, Noir, Fade, Chrome, Process, Transfer, and Instant. Click any of these to instantly see the effect. Once again, if satisfied, click Done; if not, click either Revert to Original or None, which removes any of the other filters you applied.

Adjusting adjustments

By clicking Adjustments, you can tweak various Light, Color, and Black & White settings in your pictures. Drag the respective sliders for each of these settings. As you do, you'll immediately see the effect on your pictures. Click the drop-down arrows to fine-tune these elements further. Figure 14-16, shows you some of the choices you can make. For example, under Light, you can drag sliders to adjust exposure, highlights, shadows, brightness, contrast, and black point.

FIGURE 14-16:
Getting
adjusted.

Repairing blemishes

What do you do when that otherwise-immaculate portrait is ruined by a small stain on your sweater or by the sudden appearance on your face of the zit that ate Cincinnati?

Click Retouch to turn on Photo's high-tech spot remover or software airbrush. Drag the slider to select a brush size. Drag the size slider until the circle you'll use to pinpoint the spot that needs retouching is big enough to cover the area. Then click and hold down the mouse button as you brush over a freckle, blotch, or pimple. Photos paints over these spots, using surrounding colors. Use short strokes to avoid smearing an image and making the picture appear even more ghoulish. Alternatively, click while pressing the Option key to choose the source area. Click Done when you're finished.

Retouching larger images is easier than doing smaller ones, making full-screen mode all the more valuable when you're editing thusly. Still (I hate to be the one to tell you this), getting rid of minor defects won't win you a modeling contract.

Reducing red-eye

Flash photography often results in *red-eye,* which makes your subject appear to be auditioning for the lead role in *Rosemary's Baby: All Grown Up.* Fortunately, Photos, like Visine, can get the red out. The operation is so devilishly simple that you can select an Auto option and that mere act may do the trick. Otherwise, click a reddened pupil and drag the red-eye slider to match the red area's size. Click Done to complete the exorcism. Incidentally, the Red-eye fix tool will show up next to only pictures that could theoretically benefit from the appearance of such a tool. To make sure it is always available when you click Edit, choose View ↔ Always Show Red-eye Control so that a check mark appears.

Extensions

The Photos app on your Mac graciously invites some third-party apps to work inside Photos, letting you add editing capabilities or perhaps go further than Apple lets you in applying magic to your pictures. To take advantage of this feature, click Extensions and choose among any of the other photos apps on your computer that appear on the list. To add apps to the list, click More, which brings you to the Extensions portion of System Preferences.

Admiring and Sharing Pictures

Until now, I've been speaking of organizing and doctoring images. Enough of that. It's time to sit back and admire your handiwork — and show off your Ansel Adams skills to everyone else.

Creating slideshows

If you're of a certain generation, you may remember having to sit still while your parents pulled out the Kodak Carousel slide projector. ("There we are in front of the Grand Canyon. There we are in front of the Grand Canyon — *from a slightly different angle.*")

The 21st-century slideshow, in care of a Mac, brings a lot more pizzazz. Your pictures can have a soundtrack from your iTunes library. You can slowly pan across photos while zooming in and out and employing the Ken Burns Effect, named after the documentary filmmaker.

The quickest way to begin a slideshow inside Moments or Collections is to drag your cursor next to the heading for a group of photos, assuming that it is the batch of photos (and for that matter, video clips) that you want to include in the slideshow. Click the right-pointing arrow shown in Figure 14-16. You'll hear music Apple has matched up with the selected theme (the theme highlighted in blue that also carries a check mark). If you're satisfied with that theme and musical accompaniment, go on and click Play Slideshow to let the show begin. To change the theme, click any of the options from the list shown, noting that you can preview the theme in the small thumbnail. Theme choices are Ken Burns, Origami, Photo Edges, Reflections, Vintage Prints, Classic, and Magazine. By all means, try them all.

Meantime, click the Music tab to change the musical selection. You can even choose a song from your iTunes library. Press the Escape key to stop playing the slideshow.

Instant slideshows like this are great, but you may want to put more time and effort into the photos and videos to include in your slideshow. On such an occasion, you'll want to create a slideshow project. Follow these steps, using Figure 14-17 as reference point.

1. **Choose the photos (and videos) you want to have in your show.**

2. **Click the + in the toolbar and choose Slideshow.**

   You will find yourself now working in the Projects tab.

3. **In the Slideshow pop-up menu, choose New Slideshow.**

   If you've already created any slideshows, you could select any of those from the pop-up menu here to add pictures or make other changes.

4. **Type a name for your slideshow and click OK.**

5. **If you're happy with the order in which photos appear, leave them be; if you want to change the order, drag the thumbnails at the bottom of the screen.**

   You can add photos by clicking the + to right of the thumbnails.

FIGURE 14-17:
Slideshow
settings.

6. **Click the Themes and Music buttons on the right side to make your selections.**

   Your choices are the same as when you created an instant slideshow.

7. **Click the Duration button and drag the custom slider to determine how long the slideshow plays.**

   You can fit the slideshow to play as long as the music plays, provided the audio track is long enough the fit the slideshow.

8. **Select the Transition check box and choose a transition type to choose the transitions between slides.**

   You'll find this setting after clicking the Duration button. Your transition options are Dissolve, Push, Reveal, Move In, Uncover, and Cover. You can also choose the direction that the slides move in by clicking the up, down, right, or left arrow. If you want slides to fit the screen, select the Scale Photos to Fit Screen check box.

9. **Click the Preview button at the bottom left to make sure the slideshow meets your approval.**

10. **Click Play to begin the slideshow.**

TIP

You can add pictures to or remove pictures from a slideshow. To add pictures, select the picture(s) that you want to include in your slideshow, click the + button on the toolbar, choose Slideshow from the pop-up menu, and choose the appropriate slideshow.

To remove pictures from a slideshow, select the slideshow, click the doomed photo(s) in the photo browser at the bottom of the window, and press Delete.

You can export your slideshow to share it with others. Click the Export button on the upper right, choose an appropriate format (standard definition 480p or high definition 720p or 1080p) and fill in the other requested fields. You can also export it to iTunes, and from there you can share it with another device.

Sharing pictures

You can share pictures in a number of ways. Start by clicking the Share button in the toolbar and check out all your choices, which will vary depending on the apps on your Mac. Some of your sharing choices are Mail, AirDrop, Twitter, Facebook, Flickr, Notes, Messages, and iCloud Photo Sharing.

If you choose Mail, the picture will be embedded in your outgoing message and you get to the choose the appropriate image size, among small, medium, large or actual size. For more on Mail, read Chapter 10.

Booking them

You don't have many guarantees in life, but one of them is that bound coffee-table photo books of the family make splendid presents. Apple makes it a breeze to design these professionally printed books. And when the grandparents see what *you* produced, don't be shocked if they ask how come you're not working in the publishing business.

In Photos, you choose the size and design of these books and the batch of photos to be included. Images are sent over the Internet to a printing plant, which binds and ships the book on your behalf.

The resulting books are gorgeous keepsakes. As of this writing, you could choose among Square hardcover books ($39.99 for 10-by-10-inch books; $24.99 for 8-by-8-inch books), Classic hardcover books (13-by-10-inch for $49.99; 11-by-8 ½-inch books for $29.99), or Softcover books (8-by-8-inch books for $14.99; 8-by-6-inch books for $9.99). Additional pages are priced differently, depending (of course) on the size of the book.

To make a photo book, first select the photos you want to include in your book. Then in the toolbar, click the + button, and then click Book from the menu that appears.

Click a book format and choose a theme (Travel Shots, Photo Essay, Journal, Monograph, and so on.). You can have Photos auto-fill the pages with the photos that you've chosen or manually drag photos from the photo browser at the bottom of the screen onto the page. You can also add text and maps, move pages around, change colors, and more. Your book project is available under the Project tab. When you're satisfied and ready to buy, click Buy Book in the upper-right corner of the screen. You can preview your book design by rotating through a carousel and choosing a new theme. Photos automatically lays out the pictures in the book for you. You can customize the layout, text, and fonts in your book.

Cards and calendars

Once again, after choosing pictures, your mission starts when you click the + button and choose either Card or Calendar from the resulting menu. You can choose various sizes, with a card costing as little as 99¢ and 12-month calendars fetching $19.99. You need to enter your Apple ID and password to process the order.

You can design customized greeting cards, letterpress cards, and calendars (up to 24 months) by choosing a theme (some with text), a start date, and whether to add national holidays (from about four dozen countries). You can also import your Calendars, as well as all the birthdays from your Contacts app.

TIP

Click the Projects view to see your books, cards, and slideshows.

Ordering prints

If you don't want to print pictures on your own, you can order professional prints the old-fashioned way. Select your photo, click + in the toolbar and then click Prints and choose your printing options. As an alternative, choose File ⇨ Order Prints. Each 4-inch print costs 12¢. A 20-by-30-inch blow-up poster costs $17.99. Prices for in-between sizes vary.

You can continue to print with your own printer, of course. Choose File ⇨ Print. Select a print size and aspect ratio before proceeding with the print job.

iCloud Photo Sharing

What if your first child was born recently, and you want to share images of the adorable infant with *everyone?* It's not practical to invite everyone over to your house to view albums (unless they're all willing to take turns changing diapers). And emailing the pictures to your entire extended family isn't practical, given your lack of sleep.

A better alternative may be iCloud Photo Sharing. Put simply, you create an album and invite family, friends — really anybody you choose — to view it, which they can do from another Mac, a PC, or an iOS device. Here's how to proceed on your Mac:

>> Open System Preferences, click iCloud, and select Photos. From there, click Options, and select the Photo Sharing check box. A quickie reminder: Turn on iCloud Photo Sharing on any other device you intend to use it with.

>> This being a Mac, you have an alternative route for getting there. Open Photos Preferences, click the iCloud tab, and then select the iCloud Photo Sharing check box there as well.

Now that you're all set up, here's how to proceed:

1. **Choose the album, or batch of photos you want to share.**

   There is a sharing limit of 5000 photos and videos combined.

2. **Click the Share button. In the drop-down menu, click iCloud Photo Sharing, and then click + New Shared Album.**

   From this window, you can also add photos to already created Shared Albums.

3. **In the Shared Album Name field, type a name for the photo stream —** My Adorable Kids **or whatever seems apropos at the time.**

4. **In the Invite People field, type the email addresses or the phone number they used in iMessages.**

   You can also click the circled + to add names from your contacts, as shown in Figure 14-18.

5. **Click Create to proceed or click Cancel if you change your mind.**

   Everyone you've invited receives an email and a notification to subscribe to the stream. The friends you're inviting can subscribe to the new shared album. They must have an iCloud account to accept.

FIGURE 14-18: Choose and manage the people with whom you'd like to share photos.

You can continue to manage the shared album after creating it. Click the Shared tab in Photos, choose the album in question, and then click the icon near the top of the screen that looks like a head in a small circle. (You can see this icon in Figure 14-18.) From there, you can invite (or remove) people, select a Subscribers Can Post box, which lets the people you invite add their photos and videos, or select a Public Website check box to let anyone view your shared album on iCloud. com. It's a good idea to also select the Notifications box to see when your subscribers like, comment on, or add pics to the album.

It's quite possible that somewhere down the road, you'll decide to change your shared album. Here's how:

>> **To delete photos from a shared album,** click Shared in the toolbar, choose the specific album in which the doomed photos exist, select the photos marked for deletion, and either press Delete on the keyboard or chose Image⇨Delete from Shared Album. The photos automatically disappear from everybody's stream.

>> **To remove a subscriber,** again click Shared, select the shared album in question, and click the People button on the toolbar. In the window, you see all the people who subscribe to the album. Select each person you're going to drop from the stream, and click the down arrow next to the person's name and choose Remove Subscribers from the resulting menu.

TIP

>> **To add new subscribers,** type the invitee's email address or iMessage phone number in the window just mentioned. He or she receives an email invitation to subscribe.

>> **To take down the public photo stream,** uncheck the Public Website box and the shared stream will be removed from the web.

TIP

Remember to click the Shared tab to monitor any activity involving pics that you share with others and that others share with you.

Chapter 15

iMovie and GarageBand: The Show Must Go On

Hooray for Hollywood. Hooray for iMovie. And hooray for GarageBand too. The former provides the video editing and other software tools you need to satisfy your *auteur* ambitions. The latter might help you realize your dream of becoming a rock star.

I'll get to GarageBand later in the chapter. But first, iMovie.

Lights, camera, action!

Indeed, when your movie is in the can, you can share it with the awaiting public through a gaggle of options.

> *"I'd like to thank all the people who made this award possible. The wonderful cast and crew, my loving family, my agent. And a special thanks to the late Steve Jobs. . ."*

Of course, even if your filmmaking aspirations are of a more modest nature — producing slick highlights of Johnny's or Gillian's soccer games, rather than anything with genuine box-office appeal — iMovie is still a keen companion for your inner director and producer.

Apple has reinvented iMovie a couple of times over the years — and frankly, not always for the better, some will say. Still, I suspect that most novice moviemakers, as well as some more advanced shooters, will be very satisfied with the current version of iMovie as this book went to press, version 10.1.1 to be specific.

Touring the iMovie Interface

Take a gander at the iMovie 10 screen, shown in Figure 15-1. In this one example, you'll get a quick sense of how you might view, organize, and edit video.

FIGURE 15-1:
You oughta be
in pictures.

The Media tab is highlighted in the view shown in Figure 15-1, and that's where we'll start our tour. For now, though, let me mention that the Projects tab is indeed where you can find and open the movies and trailers that you're working on. In the Theater section, you can watch a high-quality version of your finished movies, trailers, and clips.

The upper-left side of the interface is where raw and finished content is segregated into libraries (Photos library, events, projects, and any movies you created). Click the Show list button in the upper-left corner of the iMovie display if the list isn't visible. (Click Hide the Libraries to make it go away.)

Adjacent to the Libraries list is the browser, where you can get a better look at whatever library is highlighted in the list. The viewer pane to its right lets you view videos in progress (and finished material) in a larger window. In some views, though not the one shown in Figure 15-1, the timeline takes up most of the bottom half of the screen. It's the area where you assemble your clips and do a lot of the editing work, often by exploiting the timeline.

Back to 15-1: Your tour continues along the upper edge of the screen, which is where you find a simplified toolbar. From left to right, its buttons let you create movies and movie trailers (the +), import video (the downward pointing arrows), switch among the Media, Projects, and Theater tabs, and share your work.

Just below that toolbar is another toolbar, sometimes referred to as the *adjustments bar,* with icons that you explore as you go through this chapter. For now, I want to mention that some of these icons or buttons let you crop scenes, alter the color and sound, apply special effects, and more.

With that general overview over, let's get on with it. Places, everyone. Ready? Action!

Shooting Your Oscar Winner

Legendary filmmaker Alfred Hitchcock is said to have asked, "What is drama but life with the dull bits cut out?" So before sitting in front of the Mac, you have to go out and capture some of that life on video. Trimming the dull stuff and converting your raw footage to worthy home cinema comes later.

Alas, I can't train you to become Hitchcock or Orson Welles or Steven Spielberg. Heck, if I could do that, I'd be sipping martinis in Cannes right about now (or at least authoring *Filmmaking For Dummies).* But I do know enough to send you off to Oz with the right gear. And that gear pretty much consists of a digital camcorder, a digital still camera that doubles as a video camera (just about all do these days), or, more than likely, just a smartphone with a built-in video camera.

iMovie can exploit only video footage in digital form, ruling out older *analog* camcorders that handled a variety of media: VHS tapes, VHS-C, 8mm, and Hi8. Most of you have phones that take excellent video, including in the 4K video format that iMovie can handle. The most common type of digital camcorder once made use of matchbook-size, 60-minute *MiniDV* tapes. Tape may not be fully extinct yet, but it's getting there.

In any case, iMovie supports a wide range of cameras. If you have any doubt about whether yours is supported, consult the list at `https://support.apple.com/en-us/HT204202`.

When you purchase a camcorder, make sure that you also get the proper USB or FireWire cable to connect to your Mac, if not a cable that's compatible with the latest Thunderbolt ports.

From Here to Eternity: Camcorder to iMovie

Whether or not you shot your video in high definition, you've shot scene after scene of amazing footage. (What could be more dramatic than Junior's first steps?) But remember Hitchcock's observation about getting rid of the dull bits? iMovie can help you do just that. First, though, you have to dump what you've captured into the computer. You can do this in several ways, depending on the type of camcorder, digital camera, or camera phone you're using. You can also import movies that already reside on your hard drive or solid-state drive (SSD), or capture scenes with the Mac's own iSight or FaceTime camera. And rest assured that importing video into iMovie doesn't erase any of the scenes from your camera.

Some of your video may just show up on your Mac automatically thanks to iCloud.

Whether you have an older tape-based camcorder, a digital camera, a DVD, a flash drive, a hard-drive-based camcorder, or a smartphone, connect it to your Mac through the proper cable. Then start the process by clicking the Import button in the toolbar.

Patience is a virtue in the moviemaking business, so be mindful that it may take some time for iMovie to grab all the video and generate thumbnail images of each clip.

Importing videos from other destinations

You may have existing video that you want to use in your final blockbuster — video that's already on your hard drive or SSD. Perhaps it's a project you previously created in iMovie (the old version), or video from a digital still or camera phone that resides in iPhoto or Photos. Or maybe you want to incorporate video on a CD, DVD, or memory card.

To import iMovie projects or other videos on your hard drive (or other disks) from Finder, select a file or ⌘+click to select multiple files and drag them from Finder to the Event in the Libraries list in iMovie. By the way, these files need not be just video files; as you'll discover, you can grab photos and audio files, too.

As an alternative, you can import media by clicking the Import button on the toolbar and selecting content in the Cameras section of the sidebar. You can also summon the Import window by choosing File ⇨ Import Media.

Using an iSight, FaceTime, or other camera to record directly to iMovie

Of absolutely no surprise to anyone, iMovie works fine with video captured by Apple's own iSight or FaceTime cameras: the stand-alone version that Apple stopped selling years ago or the kind built into most current Macs. Here's how to record to your Mac directly from your camera:

>> **Built-in camera:** Click the Import button and then click the iSight or FaceTime Camera that you want to use under the Cameras list on the side.

>> **Stand-alone camera:** Connect your web camera, camcorder, or iSight camera (if it's not built in), and select the appropriate camera from the list. If more than one camera is connected, you'll see each on the list. Choose the one you're calling into action.

Before clicking the red capture button to start recording your movie, make sure that you'll be importing the soon-to-be-recorded footage to the right destination in your iMovie Library — typically, an Event. You'll see your options in the drop-down Import to: field. The video can be directed into an existing event under your iMovie Library, of course. Or choose a New Event.

Mastering Postproduction

Your raw footage is in place — all in a single unified iMovie video library. In the following sections, you find out how moviemaking really gets accomplished: by arranging scenes and adding music, pictures, titles, transitions, and more. Get ready to unleash your creative juices. Assembling a movie is where the real joy begins.

Staging events

As you've already seen, the video you import into iMovie shows up in your iMovie library, organized into events. Think of events as folders containing clips tied to that occasion. I hope you provided reasonably descriptive names for these events: My Little Girl's Ballet Recital, Thanksgiving Pig-Out, whatever. If you didn't type a descriptor, iMovie substitutes one for you — something like 2-22-16 (in other words, the date that you created the event). Come on, folks; you can do better than that. And you always have the option to rename events later.

You may have created an event as noted earlier in this chapter as you went about importing your clips. You can just as easily start out fresh by choosing File ⇨ New Event.

Here are some of the options you have for putting your own stamp on events:

» **Merge them.** You can take video from multiple sources and place them in one event. Merge events by choosing File ⇨ Merge Events. Just remember to first highlight the events (in the Libraries list) that you want to merge.

» **Split them.** To split one event into two, create the new event(s) you need and then move the clips from the original event to the new one.

» **Drag them.** To move a clip from one event to another, drag the clip to the title of the designated event in the iMovie Libraries list. (Start dragging and then hold down Option while you continue to drag; you'll copy the clip rather than move it.)

Milking the skimming feature

Skimming is one of the coolest and most useful innovations in iMovie. By mousing over the dynamic clips or filmstrips representing your footage in the browser or timeline, you can skim through your entire video in a blink — faster than real time, anyway. Images move in both the filmstrips and the larger iMovie viewer. Click the arrows on the keyboard if you'd rather advance or retreat more methodically. You hear sound, too, as you skim through your video; the audio plays backward or forward, depending on which direction you skim.

TIP

You can unmute the sound while skimming by turning on Audio Skimming, because that feature is turned off by default. To turn it on, choose View ⇨ Audio Skimming or press Shift+S. You hear the sound when you skim by pressing the arrows on the keyboard, regardless of whether Audio Skimming is on or off.

REMEMBER

Turning off Audio Skimming doesn't affect the sound during normal playback.

Playing around with playback

You can play back your video from any starting point in several ways:

>> Place the pointer where you want to begin watching in the browser, and press the spacebar.

>> Select part of a clip and choose View⇨Play.

To stop playing a movie, press the spacebar or click anywhere in the iMovie window.

If you want to watch events from beginning to end, select any part of the clip and choose View⇨Play from Beginning or press the backslash (\) key on the keyboard. To play a given selection from the beginning, choose View⇨Play Selection or press the slash key (/). You'll know that you've selected a clip or portion of a clip by the yellow line that borders the clip or selection.

To admire your video full-screen, select the part of the video you want to watch and then choose View⇨Play Full Screen or press Shift+⌘+F. You can also click the full-screen icon, shown in Figure 15-2. Press Escape to leave full-screen mode or click the full-screen icon a second time.

FIGURE 15-2:
Controls to play video.

Previous clip | Next clip

Play

Play full screen

Working with video

As noted, the individual segments or video clips that make up an entire event look like filmstrips. A typical event has several clips.

The length of a clip has to do with when you (or whoever recorded the video) started and stopped the camera. Video clips are represented by a series of thumbnails, each a frame within a clip. The number of frames that make up a second of video varies, depending on the video format you chose when shooting. You can select *frame ranges* to determine the video you're working with; the range is designated by a thin yellow border. A range can span multiple clips within the timeline.

You can drag the yellow selection border to change the frame range as well.

Marking video

No matter how talented you are as a videographer, it will be evident as you skim that some of your footage stands out above the rest and other footage is amateurish at best. You can mark video gems as favorites while rejecting junk footage. Here's how.

>> **Mark favorites:** Select the frame range of the video portion you love, and choose Mark⟹Favorite or press the letter F on the keyboard. A green line appears over the ranges you've chosen as favorites.

>> **Reject footage:** You can just as easily put the kibosh on a clip that doesn't meet your lofty standards. Choose Mark⟹Reject or press the Delete key. Instead of a green line, you see a — don't all scream at once, please — red line.

>> **Filter to see only favorite or rejected footage:** By making choices from the small pop-up menu to the left of the iMovie search box, you can sort or filter the video shown in the browser. You can show all clips, favorites only, and all clips minus those you've rejected. If you choose to reveal only those clips that you've rejected, you may charitably give some of them a second chance. It's also necessary to display the doomed clips if you want to trash them.

>> **Remove ratings:** You can unrate clips that you've designated as favorites or duds. Select such clips and choose Mark⟹Unrate or press U on the keyboard.

Cropping video

Even under the best of circumstances — perfect lighting, subjects who actually flash a smile, terrific camera, terrific cameraperson (that would be you) — your video may need improvement. Here are a few tricks.

Just as you can crop a still image in the Photos app (see Chapter 14), you can highlight an area of a scene or focus on an otherwise-distant subject. Be aware that the crop applies to the entire clip. Follow the steps below to crop video:

1. **Select a clip to crop in the timeline and then click the Cropping icon, labeled in Figure 15-3.**

   As a reminder, the timeline is the area in iMovie where you can add and arrange clips and edit them as needed.

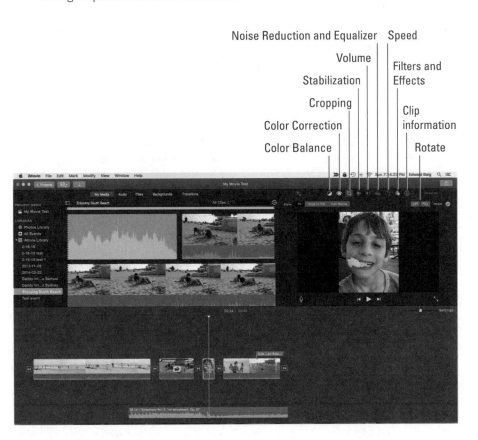

FIGURE 15-3:
Clicking Adjust lets you crop, change color and sound, and more.

2. **Click the Crop button.**
3. **Click the Crop to Fit button to summon an adjustable frame that appears on top of the clip in the viewer. Grab the rectangle's handles, resize it, and drag it over the crop-worthy portion of the image.**

4. **(Optional) Click one of the buttons with a small rectangle and arrows to rotate the image in either direction.**

5. **If you're satisfied, click the check mark to apply the crop adjustment.**

You can undo the crop by clicking the Reset button and then clicking the Apply button, which appears next to the cropping controls.

TIP

Click the Ken Burns button to apply the panning effects named after the famous documentary filmmaker.

Your cropped video may look grainy if you used a low-resolution camcorder, shot in low resolution, or crop to a small portion of the frame. Click Fit at any time to undo the cropping.

WARNING

Improving the sound

Bummer — the sound in one video clip is barely above a whisper, whereas in another, you must turn down the volume. Fortunately, you can tweak the audio in your video so that the sound remains consistent from one scene to the next. Adjusting the audio to give priority to the sound you want to be heard is known as *ducking audio*. Follow these steps:

1. **Start by selecting a clip in the timeline.**

2. **Click the Volume button (labeled in Figure 15-3), and choose Auto.**

   iMovie analyzes and automatically enhances the sound in the given clip.

3. **If you want to lower the volume of other clips at the same time, select the check box provided for that purpose.**

   You can drag a slider to set the levels relative to the volume of the clip you've selected. Why would you do this? Perhaps you've recorded a voiceover (a topic coming up) and want iMovie to lower the music playing in another clip while the voiceover plays.

4. **Repeat this exercise as needed in other clips.**

You can always restore the volume to its original level by clicking the Undo button (it has a small curved arrow on it) or by choosing Edit➪Undo Volume Adjustment. Still another option: Press ⌘+Z.

REMEMBER

Now suppose that you want to lower the background noise in a clip but not alter the overall volume of the clip. You know, a plane flies overhead, someone in another room sneezes, whatever. Here's what you do:

1. **Select your clip and click Adjust.**

2. **Select the Noise Reduction and Equalizer button on the toolbar.**

   It, too, is labeled in Figure 15-3, shown earlier in this chapter.

3. **Select the Reduce Background Noise check box.**

4. **Drag a slider to adjust how much the background distraction ought to be reduced.**

TIP

If you click the Equalizer, by the way, you can apply other audio settings. You can enhance voice or music, reduce humming, and boost or reduce treble or bass, for example.

Turning Your Clips into a Movie

The video looks good; the sound is right. And now that you've mucked with your video and chosen the right moments for your sure-fire Oscar winner, it's time to apply the tonic that turns raw footage into a multimedia marvel.

Choose File ⇨ New Movie, press ⌘+N, or click the + button in the toolbar and select Movie. From here, you can apply themes, music, voiceovers, transitions, and more. The following sections provide the details.

Pick a theme, any theme

iMovie generously provides for your — and your audience's — viewing pleasure so-called movie Themes that wrap the movie into a particular cinematic style. These can be a lot of fun. The current version of iMovie gives you a choice of 15 Themes: Comic Book, Neon, and Travel, to name just three. Peek at your other thematic options in Figure 15-4.

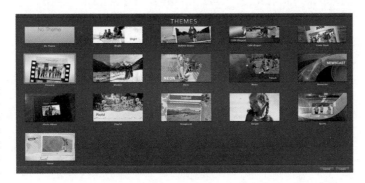

FIGURE 15-4:
The filmstrip selected here is one of the movie project themes you can choose.

Here's how to find and apply a theme:

1. **After you create your new movie, you can choose a theme.**

   Or choose no theme at all. Another route is to pick what are arguably the coolest themes in Movie Trailers, which I'll get to shortly.

2. **(Optional) To get a sense of what a chosen theme is like, and to examine how such a theme might play with your own video and video sensibilities, click the play button on a Theme thumbnail, and watch a demonstration.**

3. **When you've settled on a Theme, mark to select it, and click the Create button at the bottom-right corner of the screen. If you decide on a different theme, click Cancel instead.**

4. **Name your movie (mercifully changing the default from My Movie).**

5. **Choose the Event destination that houses your clips.**

   You can add or import more clips, if you want, and begin to add other elements: titles, transitions, music, special effects, and so on.

Movie trailers

If you go to the movies a lot, you know that the coming attractions are often as entertaining as the movie you're about to see (sometimes, more entertaining). The movie-trailer themes included in iMovie are an equal blast to watch and to create. Instead of choosing File ➪ New Movie, choose File ➪ New Trailer or, after clicking the +, click Trailer.

Apple provides 29 thematic trailer templates to choose among, ranging from film noir (a stylized ode to the films of the 1940s and 1950s) to the supernatural. Trailers have their own animated graphics, customizable titles, and credits, plus an original soundtrack recorded by no less impressive a collection of world-class musicians than the London Symphony Orchestra. You can preview these trailers by clicking the Play button when you mouse over a thumbnail. Just below the thumbnail, you can see how long the trailer will last, from 45 seconds to just over a minute and a half.

Each trailer also tells you how many cast members are needed. Depending on how many folks are in the clips you plan to include in your little movie, this number helps you determine which theme to go with. The romantic-comedy trailer calls for two cast members, for example, whereas the travel trailer can accommodate two to six.

WARNING

Think long and hard before committing to one trailer or another. Although you can always edit a trailer later, you can't change a trailer template. As Apple explains it, the required elements from one template won't fit another. If you want to go with a different template, you must create a new trailer from scratch.

Go ahead: Click a theme and type a name, or accept the one iMovie has chosen for you ("The Game" in the sports-theme trailer, "Forever is never long enough" in the spy trailer, and so on). Fill in the movie name, cast-member name(s), studio name, credits, and any other information in the Outline section of the tabbed interface that appears (see Figure 15-5). You simply type over the words that are in the various fields.

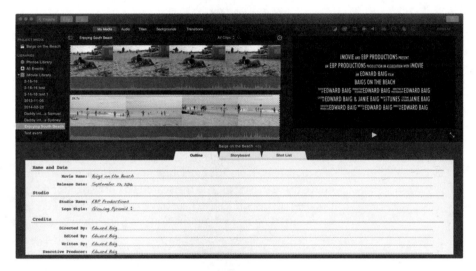

FIGURE 15-5:
Giving movie credits where credit is due.

Now tab to the Storyboard section. The storyboard includes text bars that represent editable onscreen text, along with placeholders for the video clips that will be included in the final project. Click the text to change the words on the various text bars.

To add video clips to the placeholders, click the video (or frame range) in the browser. Apple guides you by placing a time stamp on the left edge of the placeholder wells that lets you know how long the clip should be. After you add video to one well, the next placeholder becomes active so that you can add video there, too. Try to choose clips that match the style of the placeholder text. If you see a head shot, you want a clip with a tight close-up. If the image of a character is on the move, you want a similar scene, if you have one.

Before you're done, you'll head over to a shot list to take a look at the clips you've inserted into the trailer and to make any adjustments as needed.

You can delete a clip that you've inserted into the storyboard by selecting it and pressing Delete. Click Play or Play Full Screen to watch your trailer.

TIP

You can convert a trailer to a full-fledged movie. Start by choosing File ⇨ Convert Trailer to Movie, and go on to make your edits.

Adding music or sound effects

What would *West Side Story* be without Leonard Bernstein? Or *A Hard Day's Night* without The Beatles? Music is a vital part of most movies (even non-musicals). Here's how to add a background score or other sound effects:

1. **Click the Audio tab, and then click iTunes, Sound Effects, or GarageBand in the sidebar.**

2. **Choose the source of your music or sound effects from the browser's pop-up menu.**

   In Figure 15-6, I chose a Classical Music playlist in iTunes from the iMovie browser.

   Again, you have plenty of choices: ditties in your iTunes library, music you composed in GarageBand, other audio files on your computer or a server, dozens of canned sound effects (including booing crowds, crickets, thunder, and rain), and an electric typewriter. If you're looking for some specific sound effect, try searching for it in the search box provided for that purpose. Double-click a sound file to hear a preview, or click the Play button next to the sound-effect name to sample it. You see a line moving along the green waveform as the sound effect plays.

FIGURE 15-6:
Adding music and sound effects.

3. **Drag the music or sound effects file to the timeline.**

If you only want part of the sound effect or song, select a range in the waveform and then drag the range to the timeline.

The audio clip is attached to the video clip where you put it, in a so-called "background music well" below the timeline. A green background appears at the beginning of the first clip and lasts for the duration of the shorter song or video. If the music is longer than the video, the song still ends when the video stops. If the music is shorter than the clip, and you want to add to the soundtrack, drag more music to the project background. Drag background music to a music well located below the timeline.

4. **Trim the music clip, if you want.**

Follow these steps to trim:

a. *Choose Window⇨ Show Clip Trimmer (or press ⌘+\) to summon Clip Trimmer. Clip Trimmer brings up a magnified display that shows the waveform of the sound or music.*

b. *Drag the edges, and when you're satisfied with the trim, click the downward-pointing arrow.*

c. *Move your mouse pointer to either edge of the green waveform in the timeline, and drag it in either direction to choose the spots where the video starts and ends.*

d. *Click Play or press the spacebar to sample your trim.*

TIP

You can fade music in or out by dragging a handle at the beginning or end of a clip. You can summon such fade handles by positioning the pointer over the audio clip in the timeline. As you drag a fade handle in either direction, the number of seconds it will take for the audio clip to fade in or out is shown. A dot reveals the spot in which the fade in or fade out commences or ends.

Turn on Trim Background Music in project settings to automatically match the background music to the length of your movie. To get to project settings, click the Settings button on the middle right side of the iMovie display, just below the viewer.

To remove the background music, select the music in the background music well and press Delete. You can also choose Edit⇨Delete.

Recording a voiceover

What would your epic be without a James Earl Jones or Patrick Stewart voiceover? (You should be so lucky.) You can use your own pipes to narrate a movie and add your voice pretty much anywhere you want in your video.

Choose Window⇨Record Voiceover, and click the Start Recording button, which looks like a microphone. Click the adjacent Voiceover Options button to choose your actual microphone (or sound-input device). After you click Voiceover Options, you see an Input Source drop-down list from where you can make that selection. Drag the volume slider so that it jibes with the loudness of your voice. Remember that any sound in your video will be heard as you record your own voice unless you mute it.

When you click the microphone button to start your voiceover, the program prompts you with a 3-2-1 countdown. Click the microphone button again to cease recording. You see a green waveform with the letters *VO* wherever you've recorded a voiceover. Did you stutter (as Jones famously used to)? Choose Edit⇨Undo Add Voiceover to Timeline.

The cutting-room floor

From the get-go, some scenes are obvious candidates for the trash: the ones with blurry close-ups, pictures of your shoes (when you forget to turn off the camcorder), or Grandma hamming it up for the camera.

Fortunately, you can trim unwanted frames from your project clips. Select the frames you want to trim and choose Edit⇨Delete. Off they go.

If you have second thoughts, you can bring them back by choosing Edit⇨Undo Delete or pressing ⌘+Z.

REMEMBER

You don't need to worry about losing the video you've deleted. The video that you remove from a project isn't removed from the event it comes from.

Adding transitions between clips

Moving from scene to scene can be jarring unless you add a smooth bridge. In moviespeak, bridges are *transitions,* and iMovie gives you two dozen to choose among.

To add a transition manually, select Transitions in the Content Library. At your disposal are the various styles in the Transitions pane, which is shown in Figure 15-7.

When you choose the transition you want, drag it between two clips in your project, unless you're going with a lead-in or lead-out transition that only requires one clip. A small icon represents your transition. You can substitute one transition for another just by dragging another transition over the icon.

FIGURE 15-7:
Fade to Black is
one of several
iMovie scene
transitions.

To add transactions between clips automatically, click the Settings button, and select the Automatic Content check box. Had you chosen a theme, standard movie-style cross-dissolve transitions would have been added between clips automatically except where the theme dictates another transitional choice. iMovie adds a theme-style opening title that appears over the first clip and another at the end.

By default, iMovie makes all transitions the same length. Go to iMovie preferences to change the length by typing a new duration in the box provided.

You may not know the names of all these transitions, but you've undoubtedly seen ones such as Fade to Black and Cross Dissolve in movies and on television. You can preview others by dragging the mouse pointer over the various Transitions thumbnails.

Adding titles

Every good movie needs a decent title to hook an audience, even if the film is all about your recent vacation and the only people watching are the ones who took the trip with you. While you're at it, add closing credits. You're the person who put this darn thing together, and you want some recognition. Make the audience read every last name, too, before they get up to use the bathroom.

Anyway, selecting titles is easy. The assumption here is that you haven't selected a movie-trailer theme. To add titles, proceed as follows:

1. **Click the Titles tab.**

2. **Choose a title style from the ones that appear in the Title browser.**

   You might choose Formal for a wedding video or Scrolling Credits for the end of a movie.

3. **Drag the title to the clip where you want the title to appear.**

   If you drag the title to the center of the clip, it plays for the duration of the clip. If you insert the title into the first third or last third of a given clip, that's when the title appears in your movie. You can also drag the title above the clip where you want the title to appear without moving the playhead.

   Pay attention to the purple bubble that appears over the clip in the timeline. It lets you know whether the title will last for the entire clip or just the first or last third. After you've chosen a title, a blue icon appears above the clip.

4. **Click the bubble, and replace the placeholder text in the viewer with your own text.**

5. **Double-click the title in the timeline to change the font, size, color, or style of the text.**

   This step summons the adjustments bar above the viewer, which provides such options. You can preview your changes in the viewer.

TIP

You can lengthen or shorten the screen time of a title. Move the mouse pointer over either end of the title; when the pointer turns to a cross, drag to the left or right. You can also drag the title to a different part of the clip or have it straddle two clips. You can even add a title as a "clip" of its own, for example, over a black background.

Adding photos to a movie

Interspersing still photos inside your movie is a great way to show off your artistic prowess. And you can add a bit of pizzazz by adding motion effects to those pictures in the aforementioned Ken Burns effect. To do so, follow these steps:

1. **Select the Photos Library in the sidebar.**

   This step brings up the photo browser.

2. **Choose the photo(s) you want by browsing through albums, years, collections, moments, faces, or any other choices that appear.**

3. **Drag the selected picture to where you want it to appear: between two clips or between a clip and a transition on the timeline.**

   You can also drag a photo on top of a clip in the timeline to replace that clip with the photo.

Making further adjustments

You've got great music, sound, a title, and transitions. But you're still inspired to do so much more. That's where some of the other worthwhile tools provided on the adjustments bar come into play.

In the following list, I mention some of the things you can do here, but my best advice is to poke around, play around, and experiment with your video.

» **Correct shakiness:** You may want to start by clicking the Stabilization button, which helps compensate if you had the shakes while shooting. You can also select the Rolling Shutter button to correct for that type of distortion.

» **Correct color:** Now click the Color Correction button, and drag the sliders to change the hues of your scenes. (You can examine the changes in the viewer.) Or tinker with the Color Balance settings to try to match colors and tweak the white balance and skin-tone balance.

» **Change speeds:** Click the Speed button to alter how quickly or slowly your video hums along at varies intervals. When you can make a clip move faster, a rabbit icon appears on the clip in the timeline. And when you slow it down, you see a turtle icon instead. A slowed down clip becomes longer in the timeline; one that is sped up becomes shorter. You can also select a box here to play a clip backwards.

» **Add effects:** You may have the most fun toiling around with the clip filter video and audio effects, shown in Figure 15-8 (left and right). We've all seen movies with amazing special effects, and although iMovie doesn't provide anything close to what, say, George Lucas has available to him, you'll appreciate what's here just the same. As you roll over these clip filter effects (Aged Film, Film Grain, Cartoon, Black and White, and many more) you see the effect on your video. And as you roll over the audio effects (Cosmic, Echo Delay, Cathedral, and so on), you can hear how sound changes make an impactful difference as well.

FIGURE 15-8:
You can apply visual clip filter effects (left) and audio effects (right) to make your movie look and sound very different.

Sharing Your Blockbuster

What good would *The Godfather* be if nobody could watch it? So it goes for your classic. Take one last look at the movie you've produced so far. Watch it in full–screen mode on your Mac. If it's a wrap, it's time to distribute it to an audience — in a suitable format for the devices they'll use to view it.

I explore the options available when you click Share on the toolbar, noting that some of these avenues are preludes to sharing in another app or program or out in social media land:

» **iMovie Theater:** Add a finished gem to iMovie Theater to watch on another Mac, on an iOS device, or on the Apple TV set-top box. Sharing video across those other devices is tied to your iCloud account. Be aware that such movies can't exceed 15 minutes. Click the Theater button (in the center of the bar at the top) to watch your movie inside iMovie by clicking its thumbnail.

» **iTunes:** Here's another option if you plan on watching your finished project on an iOS device, an Apple TV, or a computer. You see various size choices based on the format that makes the most sense: standard-definition (480P), large (540P), and high-definition (720P or 1,080P). After making a selection, click the Share button. Keep in mind that rendering a movie can take a while, especially if you've chosen multiple formats. You can also add the movie to iMovie Theater by selecting the Add to Theater check box.

TECHNICAL STUFF

If you didn't shoot your original movie in high definition (HD), a large or HD movie isn't an option.

» **YouTube:** The wildly popular YouTube site (owned by Google) has come to practically define video sharing on the Internet. Add your YouTube account and password; choose a category for your movie (Comedy, Pets & Animals, and so on); and add the title (if it isn't already shown), description, and any tags. You can make the movie private by selecting the appropriate check box. Apple recommends using Medium size. After the movie is published on YouTube, click Tell a Friend to spread the word.

>> **Facebook:** Send your movie directly to Facebook. The movie can be viewed by you alone, by your Facebook friends, by your friends of friends as well, or by everyone.

>> **Vimeo:** Vimeo is another popular video destination on the web. You can share your work with your Vimeo contacts, anyone at all, or no one.

>> **Email:** Once again, you get to choose a size before sending your flick off — in this case, by email. You're advised to only email very short productions at small sizes lest you run into bandwidth or server bottlenecks.

>> **File:** Save the movie as a file and choose where on your Mac to put it. The Movies folder is the default and most likely destination.

QuickTime Marks the Spot

I've spent a lot of time in this chapter examining iMovie. But there's another app on your Mac that lets you not only watch video, but also capture audio and video, perhaps for a podcast or to explain to a friend how to do something on the Mac.

Making a quick QuickTime movie

To make a video recording, launch QuickTime Player, and choose File ⇨ New Movie Recording. Assuming that you're using the built-in iSight or FaceTime camera on your Mac, you see your own handsome face. This allows you to fuss with your makeup, adjust the lighting in the room, and so on. When you're all set, click the red Record button.

When you're finished, click Record again. It's that simple. Click the Play button to sample the clip. Save this clip wherever you like on your Mac.

Shortening the QuickTime movie

Now suppose that you want to edit your little gem. That's a breeze, too. Choose Edit ⇨ Trim (or ⌘+trim). The trimming bar you see in Figure 15-9 appears at the bottom of the screen. Drag the playhead (the red vertical line) to find the footage you can live without. Then use the yellow handles at the start and end of the trimming bar to select only that portion of the video that's worth preserving. Click Trim, and you're finished.

FIGURE 15-9:
Getting set
to trim your
movie.

Click the icon with the arrow trying to escape a rectangle for various sharing options: Send it off via an email, message, or AirDrop, or post it on Facebook, YouTube, Vimeo, or Flickr.

TIP

Forming a GarageBand

Do you fancy yourself a rock icon, with your face plastered on the covers of *Rolling Stone* and *Entertainment Weekly?* Groupies stalking you? Your band's very own tour bus? I know — it's all about the music. Whatever's driving you, GarageBand is Apple's digital recording studio for making your mark in the music biz.

If you're inclined to skip this section because you can't distinguish an F-sharp from a B-flat, take note: You need not read music, play an instrument, or possess a lick of musical talent to compose a ditty through GarageBand. You can even learn to play guitar or piano with GarageBand's assistance, as well as take lessons from artists such as John Legend, Sting, and Norah Jones.

Sure, having a good ear helps. And if you actually can belt out a tune, tickle the ivories, or jam with the best of them, all the better. Connect a microphone, piano keyboard, or electric guitar to the Mac, and exploit GarageBand to the max.

Although I'm only going to scratch the surface of all that GarageBand can help you accomplish, this section should provide more than enough impetus to send you on your way to becoming almost famous.

When you first launch GarageBand, you see the following ensemble of options: New Project, Learn to Play, and Lesson Store. (I get to the last two options later in the chapter.) You can also access any recent projects you've started.

Okay, maestros in waiting, here's how to start a new project:

1. Launch GarageBand.

Double-click the program icon (located in the Applications folder) or click the dock icon shaped like a guitar.

2. Select New Project, highlight the instrument or project you have in mind, and then click the Choose button at the bottom-right corner of the screen.

As shown in Figure 15-10, you can click templates for Keyboard Collection, Amp Collection, Ringtone, Hip Hop, Electronic and Songwriter, as well as Empty Project.

FIGURE 15-10:
Getting set
to play with
GarageBand.

I may be getting ahead of myself, but because you're peeking at Figure 15-10 now, you'll note the presence of a Details section. It's where you can change the tempo, change the key signature, and change the time signature of your nascent masterpiece.

3. For the purposes of this primer, choose Empty Project.

The dialog shown in Figure 15-11 appears.

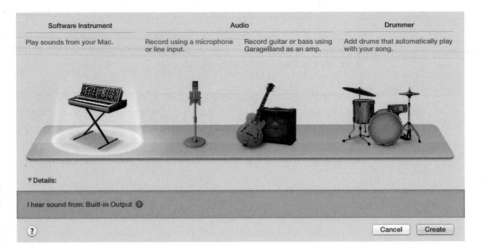

FIGURE 15-11:
Play sounds
from the Mac,
a microphone,
or drums.

4. **Choose Software Instrument.**

   Peek at your other options here: You could have chosen to record with a microphone (either the Mac's built-in mic or another). You might have connected a guitar or bass and used GarageBand as your amp. Or you might have added drums that automatically play along with you. Indeed, as part of GarageBand 10, Apple added a virtual session drummer option (discussed later in this chapter), which was created by session drummers and recording engineers.

5. **Click Create.**

6. **Select a software instrument.**

   Classic Electric Piano is the default (shown in Figure 15-12). Feel free to stick with this instrument to start. Be aware, though, that you can just as easily select an alternative virtual instrument from the library orchestra on the left.

   One other thing to consider: To match note sounds, you can type keys on the musical typing keyboard that correspond to the notes shown on the Mac QWERTY keyboard. Keys in the middle row play the white keys of a piano. Keys in the top row play the black keys. If you prefer, you can turn that onscreen keyboard into something that resembles a miniature piano keyboard instead. Either way, clicking the miniature piano keyboard or the musical typing keyboard sounds out the notes in the instrument you've selected.

7. **Click the Record button, and start playing on your chosen keyboard.**

   TIP

   You can set a *tempo*, or constant speed. To the left of the LCD display near the top of the GarageBand display, click the tempo icon and choose Beats & Project. Click and hold down on the tempo value (displayed as beats per minute, or *bpm)* in the LCD and drag up or down to change the tempo. Or double-click the tempo value and type a new value.

Add Instrument Track
Rewind
Software Library   Forward   Click to hear beat   Media Browser
Quick Help   Stop   Count In   Apple Loops
Smart Controls   Play   Track   Tuner   Notepad
Editors   Record   Cycle   Master Volume

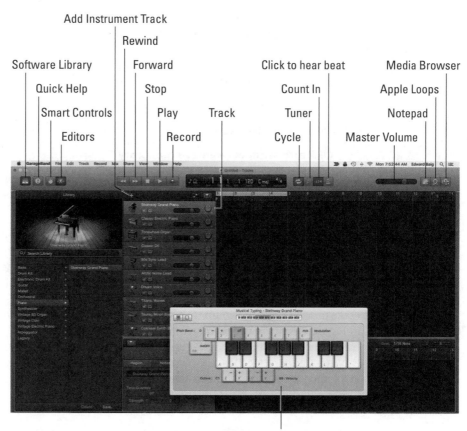

FIGURE 15-12:
The main
GarageBand
workspace.

Musical Typing Keyboard

Keeping on track(s)

Mastering GarageBand involves getting comfortable with tracks (discussed in this section) and loops (see the next section).

Most musical compositions consist of several *tracks,* or layers of individual parts recorded by different instruments. You can connect instruments to your Mac. Or, as you've already discovered, you can take advantage of numerous digitally sampled software instruments, heard as you play one of the aforementioned miniature onscreen keyboards. You can choose a wide variety of software instruments in all the major families (percussion, brass, and so on). You may have to download some instruments from the Internet. Besides the software instrument tracks, you can choose audio tracks (perhaps from imported audio files) or automatically generated drummer tracks.

Follow these steps to add a new track:

1. **Click the New Track (+) button in the upper-left corner of the program, choose Track⇨New Track, or press Alt/Option+⌘+N.**

   A window slides into view (refer to Figure 15-11).

2. **Select Software Instrument.**

3. **Click an instrument name in the library**

   You want to change the instrument so that when you click the faux piano keyboard or musical typing keyboard, the audio that emerges sounds just like the new instrument you've selected.

   A new track shows up in the Tracks list, accompanied in the header by its icon, name (again, Classic Electric Piano until you change it), and several tiny controls. Among other functions, these controls let you mute the track, make it a solo, and set volume levels.

You can add or change an instrument now, if you want. In the Library pane shown in Figure 15-13, choose an instrument category from the left column of the Track Info pane (Bass is shown in Figure 15-13) and a software instrument in the right column (Fingerstyle Bass). You also get to see an illustration of your chosen instrument. If you can't immediately find a new instrument to use, use the Search Library field to search for the music-maker you have in mind.

FIGURE 15-13: Changing a software instrument track.

If the name of an instrument appears dimmed, you don't have access to that instrument on your Mac.

TIP

Apple sells as an in-app purchase a complete GarageBand package with extra sounds, loops, drummer kits, and and basic piano and guitar lessons. Make sure you have sufficient storage on your computer to add to your virtual orchestra.

Connecting external instruments

Some of you, of course, are musicians who own real external instruments. If you'd rather not use the onscreen keyboard to control software instruments, you can connect a MIDI keyboard through a USB cable (on most newer gear) or a MIDI adapter (on older equipment). *MIDI* is geek shorthand for *Musical Instrument Digital Interface,* a standard that has been around for years. MIDI over Wi-Fi or MIDI over Bluetooth are also options on some newer devices.

TIP

You can connect electric guitars, woodwinds, and drums through MIDI or through an *audio interface* with the proper ports and cables you might need.

Click the red Record button when you're ready to rock. Move the playhead to just before where you want to start jamming.

If the high-quality instrument you have in mind is your own singing voice, connect a microphone (in lieu of the Mac's built-in microphone) to an *audio input* port on the computer. You'll have to let GarageBand know the input or source of the instrument.

Open System Preferences, click Sound, click Input, and then select Line In. Drag the Input volume slider to an appropriate level.

Back in GarageBand, choose Voice from the library and then choose the instrument that most closely matches your singing (or talking) style, such as Classic Vocal, Fuzz Vocal, and Telephone Vocal. I recommend sampling these styles before committing to one or the other.

If you choose to use GarageBand with a real guitar or bass (for example) and let GarageBand serve as an amp, click the Smart Controls button in the toolbar. Figure 15-14 shows some of the knobs, buttons, and sliders that you can play with to get your music just right with a virtual guitar (sorry I'm not a musician who owns the real deal).

FIGURE 15-14:
Controlling a
guitar.

Beating the GarageBand drums

Now you may be an outstanding guitar player but are useless as a percussionist. Or perhaps you're in a talented band that happens to lack a Ringo.

The drummer feature can supply just the percussionist beat you and your band mates need.

For a general overview on how to audition this drummer, and after choosing New Project, click Empty Project. As you may recall, a window slides into view, letting you select Software Instrument, Audio, or Drummer, which is the choice you should make here. (Refer to Figure 15-12.)

You get to select a genre for your drum set, a session drummer from that genre, and then a signature style preset available for that drummer. Rock is the genre by default, but you can opt for Alternative, Songwriter, or R&B instead. Each drummer choice in those genres has a character card and a description of the playing style, so you can get a feel for whether this virtual drummer fits your requirements.

Getting loopy

Don't let the heading scare you; I'm not advocating alcohol. I'm merely suggesting that you may become artistically intoxicated while experimenting with Garage-Band *loops,* the professionally prerecorded (and royalty-free) musical snippets at the foundation of your composition.

Loops supply drumbeats, rhythm parts, melody lines, bass sections, and so on. Apple includes a bevy of these loops gratis; you can get 1,500 more (as of this writing) if you purchase the optional GarageBand package from Apple, part of a $4.99 package. Click the Apple Loop button in the upper-right corner of the toolbar (refer to Figure 15-12). You can view Loop Browser by columns or musical buttons (as shown in Figure 15-15).

FIGURE 15-15: In the loops.

Search for loops in the browser by instrument (Bass, Guitars, and so on), genre (Rock/Blues, Urban, Country), mood (Relaxed, Intense, Dark), or combinations of these. Incompatible loop buttons appear dimmed.

The list of loop possibilities shows up on the right side of the browser. Click one of them to check it out, conveniently in the project's key and tempo. Most usefully, you can audition loops while the rest of your project is playing to hear how all the tracks blend. If the loop passes muster, drag it to your GarageBand workspace, where you can assemble and tinker with individual tracks and loops. To add a loop, click Reset in Loop Browser and make another selection.

The musical patterns in loops repeat. (Why do you suppose they're called loops, anyway?) You can tug on the right edge of a loop to lay down a track for the entire song. Loops don't have to start at the beginning of a track. And if you want to change the mood midstream, you can add a second loop to the same track. If you want more than one loop to play in a song (which is typical), create multiple tracks.

The *beat ruler* above the timeline serves as a guide; it displays beats and measures. The latter is how the units of musical time are . . . um, measured.

Building an arrangement

Adding loops or recording your own musical pearls (with real or software instruments) creates a *region* in a track. Regions are color-coded in the tracks area as follows:

>> **Purple:** Real guitar and bass audio regions you record

>> **Blue:** Real instrument regions created by loops

>> **Orange:** Real instrument regions from imported audio files

>> **Green:** Software instrument regions from recordings, loops, or imported MIDI files

>> **Yellow:** Drummer regions

Regions can be cut, copied and pasted, or resized to play as long as you need them to. They can also be moved to another track or another area of the workspace.

GarageBand lets you add *arrangement markers* to help you organize the structure of your composition. You can define sections (intro, verse, chorus, bridge, and more) and resize, copy, and drag them around in any order that makes sense. When you move a section, all associated tracks for that region move, too. Choose Track⇨Show Arrangement Track to get started.

Multitake recording

If you're a perfectionist, you can keep recording part of a composition until you feel that your performance is just right. Choose the section of the song you want to work on by clicking the Cycle button (labeled in Figure 15-12). A yellow cycle region appears in the upper part of the beat ruler. Drag and resize it so that its left side aligns with the area where you want to start recording and the right side aligns with where you want the region to end.

Click Record to start recording the appropriate track. The playhead moves across the region and then starts over again and again. Click Play when you want to stop recording.

When you're finished, a number appears in the upper-left corner of the cycle region, indicating the number of active takes or the last take you recorded. So if you recorded five takes, the number is 5. Click Play to hear that take, or click the number (5, in this example) and choose another take from the Take pop-up menu. After auditioning all your takes, you can delete the ones you have no use for.

TIP

You can take the best performance from one take and combine it with another. To do so, select the cycle region and move the playhead to the point where you want to seamlessly transition from one take to another. Choose Edit⇨Split Regions at Playhead and then assign each take as before.

TIP

You may want to display your composition in *notation view,* with standard notes, clef signs, and so on. Select a software instrument region, and click the Editors button in the upper-left corner of the toolbar. Click the Score View button (it's labeled Score and is adjacent to the Piano Roll button), and start composing. You can print professional-looking sheet music of your composition by choosing File⇨Print in GarageBand.

Staying in the groove

Although Apple makes it easy to lay down tracks and add loops, you won't become Quincy Jones overnight. Even when you match tempos and such, some music just doesn't sound good together. In the past, I haven't had much success blending a Classic Rock Piano with a New Nashville guitar, for example. Mixing or balancing all the parts so that one track doesn't drown out another is a challenge as well.

That's where the groove-matching feature comes in, which Apple compares to a spell checker for bad rhythm. Groove matching works across different instrument tracks. To exploit the feature, Control-click the track header, and from the menu that appears, choose Track Header Components⇨Show Groove Track. Now mouse over the left edge of the track that you've decided should function as the *groove track* — the drum major, as it were, for your little marching band. Click the star that appears. Select the check boxes next to each track you want to match to the groove track so that everything sounds swell together.

Apple helps you get your timing down too. A *Flex Time* feature can help you change the timing of audio recorders so that the entire work sounds more professional. You double-click a song region to open an audio waveform editor and select the Enable Flex check box. You can also click a Show/Hide Flex button (bow tie icon). Then you can click and drag along the waveform to change the timing of notes and beats without influencing other recordings.

Learning to Play

Have you been itching to learn to play an instrument since you were a kid? GarageBand sends you on your way to your first gig by teaching you guitar or piano. Start by clicking Learn to Play from GarageBand's opening screen (refer to

Figure 15-11) and choose Guitar Lessons or Piano Lessons. You also find an Artist Lessons option, but skip that for the moment.

REMEMBER

You have to visit the Lesson Store to download the Basic Lessons that you get for free.

Connect a USB or MIDI-compatible keyboard or guitar, depending on your choice of lessons.

In each full-screen lesson an instructor demonstrates his or her craft. Lessons, which start simple and become more challenging as you progress, include a video glossary and a mixer (to change how you hear the teacher, instruments in GarageBand, or your own instrument). You'll also find a setup button that leads to options that differ depending on the instrument you're using. If you're learning guitar, you also see a separate tuner button.

TIP

A How Did I Play? feature answers that very question with gentle visual feedback. You can check a progress bar that gives you a numeric score; GarageBand keeps a history of your progress. It's like having a music teacher inside your Mac.

If you want your music teacher to be a real headliner, go to the Lessons Store and click Artist Lessons. Sting teaches you to play "Roxanne," and Norah Jones explains techniques in "Thinking About You." Each artist lesson costs $4.99. You can sample an excerpt from these lessons and other artist lessons before purchasing them.

Sharing Music Projects

It's great that you're so creative. But what good does it do you if no one notices? Fortunately, you can share your GarageBand jewels with your soon-to-be adoring public in several ways. You can email the song off (using the Mail Drop feature discussed in Chapter 10) or exploit AirDrop. You can send a song or an iPhone ringtone you created in GarageBand directly to a playlist in your personal iTunes library.

Choose Share➪Song to iTunes, and choose the compression (typically, AAC Encoder) and audio settings (Low Quality, Medium Quality, High Quality, Highest Quality, or Uncompressed) you want. Then click Share. You can also export the song to a disk or burn it to a CD (assuming that you have access to a CD burner). And you can whisk it off to SoundCloud, a popular third-party online destination for audio files, found at https://soundcloud.com. (You'll have to sign into your SoundCloud account.)

In the case of a ringtone, choose Share⇨Ringtone to iTunes.

TIP

You can send a single track (or a group of tracks) instead of a complete song to iTunes. Just mute all the tracks you don't want to send before sending the ones you do want.

You don't have to export your ditty to iTunes. You can send it as an audio file by choosing Share⇨Export Song to Disk. Still another option for your composition is burning the song to a recordable CD. Just place a blank disc in your Mac's optical drive (if it has one), choose Share⇨Burn Song to CD, choose the settings you want, and click Burn. You can burn only one song to a CD this way. To burn multiple songs, create or add them to an iTunes playlist first and then burn the playlist to a CD via iTunes.

Whichever way you go, remember — the show must go on. Whether you're creating music, making movies, or both. Your fans are waiting.

The Creepy
Geeky Section

IN THIS PART . . .

Unravel the mysteries of home networking.

Find out how you can make your way in a Windows world from the comfort of your Mac.

Learn how to deal with the unexpected (or what to do when your Mac smile turns into a frown).

Chapter 16

Networking Madness

I n some ways, a treasured Mac is like a baby. The machine is loved, pampered, even spoiled. But the reality for most of us is that our chosen computer is but one among many. It may very well have siblings . . . um, other computers in the house. Or your Mac may reside in a company or dormitory, where it almost certainly has to get along with other computers. If you've bitten into one Apple, you've perhaps bitten into others. For that matter, chances are quite good that the Mac must share quarters with a Windows machine. It's such a brave new world that your Mac may even sit next to a computer that runs the operating system known as Linux.

In the ideal computing environment, the various machines can share files, data, music, printers, an Internet connection, and other resources. That's what *networking,* or the practice of connecting multiple computers, is all about. Although networking topics are as geeky as any you'll come across, Apple, in customary fashion, simplifies them as much as possible.

Networking Done Right

You have many right ways and a few wrong ways to network computers. In this day and age, you can set up a wired or a wireless network — or, more than likely, a combination of the two.

I'll start with the traditional tethered approach to putting together a network. You'll be that much happier when you're liberated from wires later.

The wired way

If the Macs you intend to network are almost always going to stay put in one location, the wired approach is arguably the best way to proceed. Wired networks are zippier, more secure, not as prone to interference, typically less expensive, and arguably the easiest to set up unless dealing with a mess of wires becomes . . . well, a real mess.

TECHNICAL STUFF

In Chapter 2, I introduce you to Ethernet, the data cable whose end looks like an oversize phone plug. Such cables also go by the names *CAT-5*, *CAT-5e*, and *CAT 6*. You may also see terms such as *10BaseT*, *100BaseT*, and *1000BaseT*, which denote networks that use the aforementioned cables. And Intel-era Macs employ blistering-fast *Gigabit Ethernet* connections.

To get started with a wired network, plug one end of the cable into the Ethernet port included in any modern Mac that has the connector. (Otherwise, you must rely on an optional USB Ethernet dongle accessory.) The other end typically plugs into an inexpensive network *hub, switch,* or *router,* which in turn is connected to the box feeding your Internet connection — usually a broadband cable modem or DSL (digital subscriber line) or increasingly a fiber network.

Although technical distinctions exist among hubs, switches, and routers (and routers usually contain built-in hubs), I use the terms interchangeably here. In any case, routers contain multiple jacks, or *ports,* for connecting each Mac (or other computer) or printer that becomes part of your network.

Cutting the cord

Certain benefits of technology are so obvious that they practically explain themselves. Wireless is one of those liberating technologies. By eliminating cables, you can

>> Wander around with a laptop and still hold onto a connection.

>> Drastically reduce the tangle of cables and cords so the area behind your desk won't be nearly as untidy.

>> Add to the network later without worrying about connecting cables.

>> Access other wireless networks outside your home or office, through public or private *hotspots* (available in numerous coffeehouses, airports, libraries, parks, and elsewhere). Accessing these hotspots may or may not be free.

Landing safely at the AirPort

All the Macs introduced during the past several years are capable of exploiting wireless networking through radio technology that Apple brands as *AirPort*. Most of the computing world, including Apple, refers to the core technology as *Wi-Fi*.

Macs with built-in wireless communicate over the air — even through walls and at times over considerable distances — with a compatible router or *base station*.

As of this writing, Apple sells a $199 AirPort Extreme Base Station with Gigabit Ethernet and the latest flavor of Wi-Fi, as well as a $99 AirPort Express Base Station. Apple also sells two versions of what it calls Time Capsule, which weds an 802.11ac AirPort Extreme base station with a wireless Time Machine–capable hard drive for networked backups. (See Chapter 12 for more on Time Machine.) A Time Capsule with 2TB of storage commands $299; a 3TB version, $399.

TIP

Although Apple would love to sell you an AirPort base station, wireless-capable Macs can also tap into routers produced by the likes of Belkin, D-Link, Linksys, and Netgear, among others, even if you previously set them up to work with a Windows network. Windows machines can also take advantage of an AirPort base station.

TECHNICAL STUFF

The range and speed of any wireless network are affected by all sorts of factors, including interference from other devices, concrete, and metal walls.

You can set up a network with AirPort Extreme in several ways. Here's the most common method:

1. **Connect the Ethernet cable hooked up to your cable, Verizon's FIOS, or DSL modem to the WAN port on the base station.**

   See, not *all* cords are eliminated in a wireless scenario. You'll find no power switch (though you do find a Reset button, which you may have to push on occasion); status lights are your only immediate clue that your AirPort has taken off.

2. **Connect any additional Ethernet devices to the LAN ports.**

3. **If you want to network a USB printer, connect it to the USB port on the AirPort.**

   You may not have to; your printer may work wirelessly. Moreover, you can also connect a USB external hard drive to store or share files across the network.

4. **Plug the AirPort Extreme into a power outlet.**

   AirPort Extreme doesn't have an on–off switch. It comes alive when you plug it in; the only way to shut it down is to pull the plug.

5. **To go wireless, run the AirPort Utility setup-assistant software, located in the Utilities folder inside the Applications folder.**

This step involves responding to a series of questions on what to call your network, passwords, and so on. You may have to enter specific settings from your Internet provider, along the lines of a static IP address or DHCP client ID. Through the AirPort Utility software, you can manually apply various advanced security and other settings.

If you live in an apartment building or are right on top of your neighbors, their routers may show up on your Mac's list. In some instances, the signals are strong enough that you can piggyback on their setups, not that I'm advocating doing so. Let this be a lesson that your neighbors should have implemented their security settings (requiring robust passwords) and that you should do the same when setting up your own Wi-Fi network.

You can determine the signal strength of your wireless connection by examining the radiating-lines icon on the menu bar pictured here.

Boarding the AirPort Express

It looks kind of like the power adapter that might come with an older Apple laptop, right down to its built-in plug. But the rectangular, near-7-ounce AirPort Express device is a versatile little gadget. This portable hub has just four ports on its underbelly: two Ethernets (WAN and LAN), USB, and an analog/optical audio minijack.

If you plan on using AirPort Express as a router, plug the device into an AC outlet; then, using an Ethernet cable, connect the AirPort Express to your cable modem or DSL. You'll use the same AirPort software as you do for the AirPort Extreme base station (see the preceding section).

TIP

You'll find no on–off button; status lights clue you in on how things are going. A steady green status light tells you that you've connected with no problem. Flashing amber means that the device is having trouble making a connection, and you may have to resort to other means, including (as a final resort) taking the end of a straightened paper clip and holding down the Reset button for 10 seconds.

AirPlay

Another clever feature is available, and it involves the aforementioned audio minijack. If you connect AirPort Express to your home stereo receiver or powered speakers, you can pump the music from your Mac (or Windows) iTunes library through your stereo system. You can use either a ministereo-to-RCA cable or a minidigital, fiber-optic TOSLINK cable, if your stereo can accommodate that kind of connector.

Either way, iTunes detects the remote connection. From a small pop-up menu, choose Computer to listen to music through your Mac (or whatever speakers it's connected to), or choose Express to listen through Express and whichever speakers or stereo it is hooked up to. Apple used to refer to this wireless symphony as *AirTunes* when it was an audio-only hookup. The name was changed to *AirPlay* as the technology became more versatile.

Apple has built an online ecosystem around AirPlay. These days, you can wirelessly stream music — and, for that matter other content — to third-party AirPlay-compatible speakers, A/V receiver systems, and stereos.

AirPlay Mirroring

If you have a Mac running Mountain Lion, Mavericks, Yosemite, or El Capitan and an Apple TV set-top box, you can display whatever's showing on your Mac screen on a high-definition television connected to the Apple TV. It's all done through technology called *AirPlay Mirroring.* You can even stream up to the 1080p high-definition video standard.

To take advantage of AirPlay Mirroring, the Mac and Apple TV (second generation or later) must be on the same wired (Ethernet) or wireless network. And you'll need a MacBook Pro dating from early 2011 or later, or another Mac model from mid-2011 or later.

Click the AirPlay toolbar icon (shown in Figure 16-1) and click Apple TV on the menu that appears. The icon turns blue. (If you don't connect to Apple TV, the icon remains black.) Note your mirroring options. You can scale the desktop resolution to best suit either the Apple TV or your Mac screen. You can also click Use as Separate Display so that what you see on your computer differs from what is on the TV screen.

If you don't see such options, visit System Preferences, select Displays, and make sure that the Show Mirroring Options in the Menu Bar When Available check box is selected.

If you're playing a movie or TV show through iTunes when you exploit AirPlay Mirroring, you enjoy a full-screen AirPlay Mirroring experience on the television.

WARNING

Having a robust wireless network makes a difference. In my experience, under less-than-ideal networking scenarios, any video that's playing may pause or stutter on the TV.

FIGURE 16-1:
Show off
what's on your
Mac on your
TV via AirPlay
Mirroring.

Testing your network

With all your equipment in place, it's time to make sure that everything works as it should. Fortunately, testing your network is as easy as opening Safari and seeing whether you can browse.

If you run into problems, click the Signal Strength icon on the menu bar and make sure that an AirPort network or other router is in range. If you're still having trouble, open System Preferences, choose Network, click the Assist Me button, and then click Diagnostics in the dialog that appears. You can check the status of AirPort and network settings, your Internet service provider (ISP), and so on.

Let's Share

Responsible parents teach kids how to share toys. When the youngsters grow up and their toy of choice is a Macintosh, with any luck, they'll still be in that sharing frame of mind.

Anyway, with your networking gear in place, do the following to share some or all of the contents from one computer with another:

1. **Choose ⇨ System Preferences.**

2. **Click Sharing.**

   The pane shown in Figure 16-2 opens.

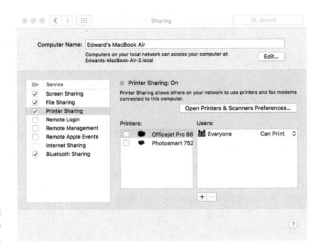

3. **Change your computer's name at this point, if you want to.**

   Calling it *Edward 's MacBook Air,* as I do in Figure 16-2, makes it sound like you're saying "It's my computer, and you can't play with it." Naming it *Basement Air,* for example, would help you distinguish the computer from, say, *Bedroom MacBook Pro.*

4. **Select the various sharing preferences you feel comfortable with.**

   If you select File Sharing, for example, users of other machines can access any Public folders on the Mac. If you change your mind about sharing — you may feel uneasy about having just anyone on the Net read those publicly available files — deselect that check box.

Other Mac users can access your machine by choosing Go ⇨ Network in Finder.

If you're an iCloud member who plans on taking advantage of the Back to My Mac feature, make sure to select the Screen Sharing check box.

AirDrop

If two or more Macs are running Mountain Lion, Mavericks, Yosemite, or El Capitan and are connected to Wi-Fi, and are reasonably close to one another, you can share files among the machines, even if they're not on the same Wi-Fi network. No special setups or passwords are required, either, though all the machines must have the *AirDrop* feature — the feature that makes all this possible — turned on. And AirDrop works with iOS devices that have the feature turned on as well.

There are two simple ways to share a file via AirDrop:

» In Finder, Control+click the file you want to send, and then choose Share⇨AirDrop.

» From an app such as Safari or Maps, click the Share button and choose AirDrop from the ensuing menu.

In both instances, click the name of the other Mac or iOS device that you want to send the file to. Click Don't See Who You're Looking For? if that indeed is the case. Note that in opening AirDrop, you can choose to have your computer visible by everyone, contacts only, or no one.

In Figure 16-3, I'm about to send a picture from an iMac to a MacBook Air. You can also share text documents, entire folders, snippets of highlighted text, URLs, audio files, and more.

FIGURE 16-3:
Sharing a photo via AirDrop from one Mac to another.

Handoff

Sometimes the person you want to share something with is yourself, as in when you start something on one device (be it a Mac, an iPhone, an iPad, or even an Apple Watch) and want to resume on another device. The Handoff feature enables you to do just that, as long as every device is on iCloud, signed in with an identical Apple ID, and on the same Wi-Fi network.

Handoff works across numerous apps — Apple's own Calendars, Contacts, Keynote, Maps, Mail, Messages, Notes, Numbers, Pages, Reminders, and Safari apps — as well as some third-party apps.

On your Mac, start by making sure that the feature is enabled. Go to System Preferences⇨General and make sure the Allow Handoff between this Mac and your iCloud devices box is selected.

Then when you come to the Mac on which you're resuming work, note the icon at the left end of the dock (assuming that the dock is in its default place). The icon is shown here in the margin. Click that icon and you're good to go.

And if you started work on the Mac and now want to resume on an iOS device, you'll see the Handoff icon on the Lock screen of that device. Swipe up or double-click the Home button to get going, and from the multitasking screen swipe right until you see the Handoff icon. On the bottom of the iOS device, tap the Handoff strip that appears with a message informing you which app and computer you were previously working on, such as *Notes from Edward's MacBook Air*.

Brushing Up on Bluetooth

Of all the peculiar terms you come across in the tech world, *Bluetooth* is probably my favorite. The name is derived from the 10th-century Danish monarch Harald Blåtand, evidently the wireless networking champ of his time. Blåtand was considered a peacemaker in warring Scandinavia, and after all, isn't networking about bringing people — or things — together? In any case, *Blåtand* apparently translates to *Bluetooth* in English.

Fascinating history, Ed, but I thought I bought Macs For Dummies, *not* European History For Dummies. *What gives?* Fair point. Here's the drill: Bluetooth (the technology, not the Viking king) is a short-range wireless scheme that lets your Mac make nice with a gaggle of compatible gadgets from up to 30 feet away.

Among the tricks made possible by Bluetooth are these:

>> Connect the Mac to a Bluetooth cellphone. If you don't have access to a Wi-Fi hotspot, you may be able to use the phone as a modem to connect wirelessly to cyberspace.

>> Print wirelessly on a Bluetooth printer.

>> Use Bluetooth File Exchange to swap files with another Bluetooth-ready Mac or another computer or gadget.

>> Schmooze via Messages through a Bluetooth headphone.

>> Synchronize data with a mobile device.

>> Control a wireless Bluetooth keyboard or mouse.

Getting discovered

The path to a meaningful Bluetooth experience starts in System Preferences. Click Bluetooth, and you're taken to the pane shown in Figure 16-4.

FIGURE 16-4:
Control everything through Bluetooth preferences.

Before the Mac can communicate with a Bluetooth device, or vice versa, the machine's Bluetooth feature must be powered on, or *discoverable:* visible to other Bluetooth devices in the area.

WARNING

Obviously, you want your other Bluetooth devices to be placed in discoverable mode too so that your Mac can communicate with them. But be wary. If you're out in public, you may want to be wary of having Bluetooth turned on for security or privacy reasons.

Click Advanced for more control of your Bluetooth behavior. When you do, you can

>> Open the Bluetooth Setup Assistant at startup when your Bluetooth keyboard isn't recognized.

>> Open the Bluetooth Setup Assistant at startup if no mouse or trackpad is detected.

>> Allow a Bluetooth keyboard or mouse to wake up a sleeping computer.

My best advice is to keep these options selected.

You can also control how various devices share files with your Mac. Head back to the main System Preferences screen, and click Sharing. Make sure that the Bluetooth Sharing check box is selected. Then you get to make other choices, including whether to Accept and Open or Accept and Save items sent from other Bluetooth computers and devices.

You can also determine the Public or other folders that Bluetooth devices are permitted to browse on your computer. As one other key measure of security, select the Require Pairing for Security option (described next), which means that a password is required before files can be transferred.

Pairing off

To *pair*, or set up, Bluetooth devices to work with your Mac, follow these steps:

1. **Choose Bluetooth in System Preferences to make sure Bluetooth is turned on.**

   You can also open Bluetooth preferences by clicking the Bluetooth icon on the menu bar. A message appears in System Preferences, indicting that the machine is discoverable.

2. **Click Pair next to the names of any Bluetooth devices in the vicinity that your Mac finds.**

   Alternatively, if the Bluetooth status icon appears on OS X's menu bar, you can turn Bluetooth on from there. Either way, you again see the Bluetooth preferences pane (refer to Figure 16-4), displaying a list of the available Bluetooth devices with which you can pair your Mac.

3. **Confirm that the passkey shown in Figure 16-5 matches the passkey on the Bluetooth device that you're pairing, such as a smartphone, tablet, wireless speaker, or printer.**

   Waiting for "iPhone " to accept pairing.
   Make sure code shown on "iPhone " matches the one below.

   920092

   Cancel

   FIGURE 16-5:
   Pairing an iPhone and a Mac.

4. **Click or tap Pair on the device that you're connecting to the Mac, assuming you're satisfied that the passkeys match.**

   And that's it. The gizmo and your Mac can share a Bluetooth connection.

Back to My Mac

Suppose that you're using a Mac laptop from your hotel room to prepare a presentation and want to retrieve a picture from the hard drive or solid-state drive (SSD) on your machine at home. Through iCloud, you can exploit Back to My Mac, a feature that lets you remotely connect to your computer from another Mac running OS X. The feature was introduced in Leopard.

Some prep work is involved. Choose iCloud in System Preferences and then select the Back to My Mac check box to ensure that the feature is enabled. You also have to turn on screen sharing in the Share pane in System Preferences. Repeat this procedure on all the machines you want to access; they must use the same iCloud account. You may have to open ports in your firewall for Back to My Mac to work in all its remote computing glory.

Then, to locate the file you want to lift off the home computer, select that home machine in the Shared section of the Finder sidebar, and browse its drive for the file you need. Drag the file to the desktop of the computer you're using for remote access.

You can also share and control your home screen remotely by selecting the Share Screen button on the physical Mac in your possession. In Figure 16-6, I'm accessing an iMac from a MacBook Air.

FIGURE 16-6:
You're never too far away from your home computer.

After you select the Mac that you're hoping to access remotely in the Finder sidebar on the Mac you have with you, you'll see the aforementioned Share Screen button in the upper-right corner of the Finder window. It's adjacent to the Connect As button, which you can select separately if you want to peek at files on the remote computer. (Before you leave on your trip, remember to select the Screen Sharing option, located on the Sharing pane of System Preferences. It sure beats lugging a desktop computer on your travels.)

Chapter 17

Handling Trouble in Paradise

'm reluctant to morph into Mr. Doom-and-Gloom all of a sudden, but after talking about all the wonderful things Macs can do, it's my unpleasant duty to point out that bad @#$& happens. Even on a Mac.

Fortunately, most issues are minor. A stubborn mouse. Tired hardware. Disobedient software. Under the direst circumstances, your computer (or a key component within) may be on its last legs. After all, a Mac, like any computer, is a machine. Still, rarely is a problem beyond fixing. So stay calm and scan this chapter; with luck, you'll come across a troubleshooting tip to solve your issue. If not, I provide recommendations on where to seek help.

A Cranky Computer

Your Mac was once a world-class sprinter but now can barely jog. Here are possible explanations and a fix to go with each one:

>> **Your Mac needs more memory.** The programs you're running may demand more RAM than you have on hand. I always recommend getting as much memory as your computer (and wallet) permit. Adding RAM to a certain class of Mac machines isn't difficult (check your computer's documentation for specifics), though it does involve cracking open the case and making sure that you're buying the right type of memory. In some instances — certain models of MacBook Air, for example, MacBook Pros from late 2012 on — the memory you have onboard is all your particular model can handle.

>> **Your Mac is running out of storage space.** This problem is an easy one to solve: Remove programs or files that you no longer use. You must be able to live without something. But if every last bit is indispensable, purchase an additional drive and move large data collections to it (such as your iTunes library, Photo libraries, or iMovie data).

>> **Your Mac's processor is overtaxed.** If you suspect that this might be the case, open Activity Monitor, which is shown in Figure 17-1, by choosing Applications➪Utilities. Activity Monitor reveals a lot about the programs and processes currently running on your machine. Click the CPU header to display the applications exacting the heaviest workload on your CPU (central processing unit). The most demanding are at the top. Quit those that you don't need at the moment.

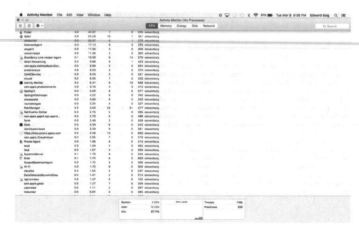

FIGURE 17-1: Monitoring your activities.

A Frozen Computer or Program

Mentioning beach balls to anyone but a Mac maven usually conjures up pleasant images of the surf, sand, and a glorious summer afternoon. Now, Mac people love a day at the beach as much as anybody else. But the sight of a colorful spinning beach ball is less welcome on your Apple, at least when that ball never seems to leave the screen. A beach ball that spins — and spins and spins some more — is a sign that a cranky Mac has turned into a frozen Mac — or that at least one of the programs on the machine is throwing a high-tech temper tantrum. (In some cases, you may see a spinning gear cursor instead.) Those of you who are familiar with Windows can think of this beach ball as the Mac equivalent of the hourglass that lingers onscreen or in more recent versions, the rolling blue circle or doughnut.

It isn't often that a frozen program crashes the entire system, but it does happen. Your first instinct is to stick a pin inside this virtual spinning beach ball of death, if only you knew how. If you're a model of patience, you can attempt to wait the problem out and hope that the spinning eventually stops. If it doesn't, consider the options described in the following sections.

Force Quit

Force Quit is the Mac's common way of telling an iced application, "I'm as mad as hell, and I'm not going to take it anymore." (If you're too young, that's a reference to the 1976 movie *Network*, as in *television* network.)

FIGURE 17-2:
Bailing out through the Force Quit command.

Choose ⇨ Force Quit or press ⌘+Option+Esc. A window like the one shown in Figure 17-2 appears. Click the name of the deviant application (*not responding* probably appears next to its name). With Force Quit, you typically don't have to reboot your computer.

WARNING

Because you lose any unsaved changes, Apple throws up a little admonition before allowing you to Force Quit. Alas, you may have no choice.

TIP

Control-clicking a dock icon brings up a pop-up menu whose bottom item is Quit. If you hold down the Option key, Quit becomes Force Quit.

When a program quits on you

Sometimes, for reasons known to no one, a program keels over. Just like that. You could reopen the app and hope the problem was a one-time aberration caused by mischievous space aliens en route to the planet Vista. Or you might have a chronic ailment on your hands.

When programs suddenly drop dead, you may see dialogs with the words `quit unexpectedly`. Sometimes, the dialog lets you click Reopen to relaunch the fussy program; sometimes, the option is Try Again. OS X restores the application's default settings (thus setting aside newer preferences settings) in case something you did (imagine that?) caused the snafu.

Assuming that everything went swell from there, you'll be given the option of keeping the new settings upon quitting the program. Your old preferences are saved in a file with a `.saved` extension, in case you ever want to go back. If that's the case, move the current preferences file from its present location and remove the saved extension from the older file.

If the problem continues, it may be time to visit the library. No, not that kind of library. A Preferences folder lives inside your Library folder, which in turn resides in your Home folder. Whew! Got it?

Actually, it's no longer even that simple, because starting in Lion, Apple decided to hide the Library folder, presumably because it doesn't want you routinely messing with the place (for good reason, I might add). The Mac library is kind of like the registry in Windows. Mountain Lion, Mavericks, and El Capitan keep the library at bay. So though it's not exactly off limits, you do have to run through a couple of hoops to get in the door.

To access the library, hold down the Option key while clicking the Go menu in Finder. The Library option appears. You can also choose Go ⇨ Home. Now (while still in Finder), choose View ⇨ Show View Options, and select the Show Library Folder check box in the resulting dialog.

TIP

You can make the library crawl out of its hiding space on a more-or-less permanent basis, too, but this process involves going through Terminal, which feels a lot scarier than the rest of Mac-land. Launch Terminal from the Utilities folder (inside the Applications folder). Then enter the following command: **chflags nohidden ~/Library**. The library now resides in Finder, the way it used to before Lion concealed its presence. If you want the library to go back into hiding, return to Terminal, and enter **chflags hidden ~/Library**.

Now that the library has reappeared, go into its Preferences folder. Preferences filenames have the .plist suffix, and the filenames typically begin with com.

followed by the names of the developer and program, as in com.microsoft.Word.plist. Try dragging a .plist file with the name of the troubled application out to the desktop. If the program runs smoothly, trash the corrupted preferences file. You'll have to reset any preferences you want to maintain.

Forcing a restart

Force Quit usually rescues you from minor problems, but it's not effective all the time. If that's the situation you're in now, you'll likely have to reboot. The assumption is that your frozen computer won't permit you to start over in a conventional way by choosing ⌘⇪Restart. Instead, try holding down the power button for several seconds, or press Control+⌘ and then the power button. If all else fails, pull the plug (or, if you have an old-enough Mac, remove the battery from a laptop), though only as a last resort.

Safe boot

TECHNICAL STUFF

Starting OS X in Safe mode activates a series of measures designed to return your computer to good health. It runs a check of your hard drive (see the next section), loads only essential *kernel extensions* (system files) while ignoring others, trashes what are called *font cache* files, and disables startup and login items.

To start in Safe mode, press the power button to turn on your computer, and press and hold the Shift key the instant you hear the familiar welcome chime. Release Shift when the Apple logo appears. You'll know you've done it correctly because you see a status bar as the computer boots up, after which the words Safe Boot appear in red in the upper-right corner of the login screen.

WARNING

Because of the under-the-hood machinations, it takes considerably longer to boot in Safe mode. This is perfectly normal. So is the fact that you can't use AirPort, a USB modem, or your DVD player, if you have one. You can't capture footage in iMovie, either, and you can't use certain other applications or features.

If the Safe-mode boot resolved your issue, restart the Mac normally next time, without pressing Shift. If your problem didn't get solved, it may be time to check your warranty or call in an expert, as noted later in this chapter.

Disk Utility

Just about every championship baseball team has a valuable utility player to fill nearly every position. The versatile Disk Utility tool on your Mac serves this purpose for all things hard drive–related and many things optical drive–related.

Prior to El Capitan, you could repair damaged disks and fix bungled *permissions,* the file settings that affect the capability to read, write, or open or run the file.

With El Capitan, your Mac automatically protects file permissions and updates them as required during software updates.

You might choose, however, to run First Aid, shown in Figure 17-3, by clicking the First Aid tab after selecting a disk or volume in the Disk Utility sidebar. Running this tool will check your disk for errors and repair them if necessary. If Disk Utility reports back that your disk is about to fail, back up your disk and then come to grips with the fact that you'll need to replace it.

FIGURE 17-3:
First Aid can repair your hard drive.

Get S.M.A.R.T

After booting from the installation disc, you may want to get really S.M.A.R.T. — as in *Self-Monitoring Analysis and Reporting Technology.* When you select a hard drive in Disk Utility, the S.M.A.R.T. status appears at the bottom of the window. If the status shows Verified, your disk is in okay shape.

WARNING

If About to Fail appears in red, you have a ticking time bomb on your hands. Immediately back up your disk and critical files, and replace the disk pronto. Be aware that you can't check the S.M.A.R.T. status of all external drives.

Take note of your other options in Disk Utility. You can partition or resize selected disks. (Choose the Partition tab.) You can erase or mount a disk (choose the appropriate tabs). And you can get other information about the state of the disks on your Mac by clicking the Info tab.

Startup Problems

I've just discussed a few ways to get you out of a pickle. But what if you can't even start the Mac? This circumstance is very unusual. You probably have no power because the plug came loose (blame it on the dog), the switch on the power strip is off, your battery ran out of juice, or your neighborhood is having a blackout. (Did you even notice that the lights went out?)

On some older laptops, you can tell whether a battery needs recharging by pressing a small button on the battery. Lights on the battery let you know how much strength the battery has.

TIP

Here's another thing to try: Press the power button, hold down the ⌘, Option, P, and R keys at the same time, and wait until you hear the startup chime a second time.

If you've added memory, installed an AirPort card (something you'd do only on an older Mac), or installed another component, and the machine fails to start, make sure that the installation is correct, and try again. If your computer still can't be revived, try removing the memory or card that you just installed and then giving a restart another shot.

After that, if you still can't restart, you may have to seek warranty service, as discussed later in this chapter.

Reinstalling OS X

If a problem has truly brought your computer to its knees, it may be time to reinstall your favorite operating system. It's bad enough that you have to suffer through the hassle. You're understandably panicked about retaining files and user settings.

Remain calm. Then do the following, if you have an installation disc and optical drive (which, frankly, is going to cover an older version of the operating system):

1. **Insert the OS X installation disc into your CD or DVD drive.**

2. **Double-click the Install Mac OS X icon, and go through the usual installation drill.**

3. **When you're asked to do so, choose your current OS X disk as your destination disk (which in all likelihood is your only option anyway).**

4. **Click Options.**

   You've arrived at an important point in the process.

5. **Do one of the following:**

   - If you want to salvage existing files and settings, select Archive and Install, and then select Preserve Users and Networks Settings.

   - If you prefer starting anew, select Erase and Install, keeping in mind that you can't undo this action, so existing files and settings may as well be toast.

6. **Click Continue.**

7. **To install certain parts of OS X, click Customize; to perform Apple's recommended basic installation, click Install.**

8. **Because the OS X disc you have may not have all the latest tweaks, pay a visit post installation to Software Update (choose it from the menu) to bring Snow Leopard, Lion, or whichever version of OS X you're using up to date.**

   Remember that on newer versions of OS X, all software updates are handled inside the Mac App Store.

WARNING

Don't reinstall an earlier version of OS X over a later one. If for some reason you feel compelled to do so, however, first erase your hard drive completely or select the Erase option in the OS X installer. You'll have to reinstall any software updates.

But what if you don't have an installation disc, which is more common nowadays? That's been the scenario since Mavericks in fact. Apple has a built-in OS X Recovery feature that not only lets you reinstall the operating system, but also enables you to do so while keeping other files and settings intact. Here's what to do:

1. Press the power button.

2. **Press ⌘+R when the computer restarts to summon OS X Utilities and release the keys when you see the Apple logo.**

3. **Connect to the Internet via Wi-Fi or Ethernet.**

4. **Select Reinstall OS X in the list of options that appears onscreen.**

   Note your other options in the OS X Utilities section. You can restore from a Time Machine backup, get help online, or visit the Disk Utility toolshed mentioned earlier in this chapter.

5. **Click Continue, and follow the onscreen instructions.**

TECHNICAL
STUFF

If you're running Mavericks, Yosemite, or El Capitan, you can create a bootable installer for OS X with a USB flash drive or other removable media. But this procedure is meant for system administrators comfortable with navigating the Terminal app — in other words, probably not most readers of this book. But if you want to take this route, start with the createinstallmedia command. You'll find examples of how to proceed at `https://support.apple.com/en-us/HT201372`.

Common Fixes for Other Problems

Sometimes all your Mac needs is a little tender love and care rather than major surgery. In this section, I consider some minor snags.

A jumpy mouse

Real mice live for dust and grime. For a long time, so did computer rodents. But the optical-style mice included with the most recent Macs don't get stuck like their ancestors, because this kind of critter doesn't use the little dust-collecting rolling ball on its underbelly.

Optical mice deserve some care and feeding too, however. Be aware that the species doesn't like glass or reflective surfaces, so if you find your mouse on one, place a mouse pad or piece of paper underneath.

If your old, wired mouse doesn't respond at all, unplug it from the USB port and then plug it in again, just to make sure that the connection is snug. If you have a wireless mouse, make sure that it's turned on and that the batteries are fresh or, in the case of the Magic Mouse 2, fully charged. You can check the battery status of a Bluetooth device on the Mac's menu bar.

Meantime, if you find that your wireless mouse hiccups from time to time, click the mouse and wait momentarily for it reconnect with your Mac.

Why does this happen? Sometimes a nearby microwave oven or cordless phone may wreak havoc if it operates on the same 2.4GHz as a wireless mouse. If you suspect that is the cause of the interference, keep such devices as far away from your Mac as possible.

If your mouse is unresponsive, try moving it over a different surface.

Another piece of advice: Turn the mouse over, inspect the sensor, and use compressed air to gently remove dust or debris.

Meanwhile, if you want to change the speed of your onscreen mouse pointer or want to change clicking speeds, visit Mouse Preferences in System Preferences, as described in Chapter 4.

A clueless keyboard

If you press a keyboard on your keyboard and it doesn't respond, try this: Head to System Preferences ⇨ Keyboard ⇨ Input Sources and select the Show Input Menu in Menu Bar check box. (You can get there also by clicking Language & Region in System Preferences, choosing Keyboard Preferences ⇨ Input Sources.)

Now click the keyboard icon in the menu bar, and choose Show Keyboard Viewer from the ensuing menu. When you type keys on your physical keyboard, the corresponding keys on the keyboard viewer should be highlighted in tandem. If a key does not get highlighted, you've got a problem that needs fixing.

A stuck CD

It's cool, the way most Macs with optical drives practically suck up a CD or DVD. Here's what's not cool: When the drive, particularly the slot-loading kind, won't spit out the disc. (Such drives are no longer standard on modern Macs.)

Take a stab at one of these fixes:

>> Quit the program that's using the disc and then press Eject on the keyboard.

>> Open a Finder window, and click the little Eject icon in the sidebar. Or try dragging the disk icon from the Mac desktop to the Trash.

>> Log out of your user account (on the menu) and then press Eject on the keyboard.

>> Restart the computer while holding down the mouse button.

If all else fails, you may have to take the computer in for repair (if possible) or replacement. I know of at least one episode in which a toddler (mine) stuck an SD memory card into the slot, thereby preventing the DVD that was already inside from escaping. Apple had to replace the drive. In fact, the slot-loading drives once included on modern Macs can't handle anything but full-size CDs and DVDs.

My Mac can no longer tell time

If your computer can no longer keep track of the time and date, its internal backup battery may have bitten the dust. On some models, you can't replace this battery yourself; you have to contact an Apple Store or an authorized service provider.

Kernel clink

Out of the blue, you're asked to restart your computer. In numerous languages, no less. Your machine has been hit by a *kernel panic.* The probable cause is corrupted or incompatible software, though damaged hardware or a problem with RAM can also unleash this unpleasant situation.

The good news is that a system restart usually takes care of the problem with no further harm. If it doesn't, try removing any memory or hardware you've recently added. Or if you think that some new software you installed may be the culprit, head to the software publisher's website to see whether it has issued a download-able fix or upgrade.

SOS for DNS

If you're surfing the web and get a message about a DNS entry not being found, you typed the wrong web address or URL, the site in question no longer exists (or never did), or the site (or your own Internet provider) is having temporary prob-lems. *DNS* is computer jargon for *Domain Name System* or *Server*. Similar messages may be presented as *404 not found on this server* errors.

Curing the trash-can blues

In the physical world, you may try to throw something out of your trash can but can't because the rubbish got stuck to the bottom of the can. The virtual trashcan on your Mac sometimes suffers a similar fate: A file refuses to budge when you choose Finder ⇨ Empty Trash.

TIP

Try junking the files by holding down the Option key when you choose Empty Trash.

A file may refuse to go quietly for several reasons. For starters, you can't delete an item that is open somewhere else on your computer, so make sure that the item is indeed closed. Moreover, you may be trying to ditch a file to which you don't have sufficient permission. Perhaps a file has been opened and temporarily locked by some running application. The other most likely explanation is that a locked file is in the Trash. You can unlock it by choosing File ⇨ Get Info and making sure that the Locked check box isn't selected.

TIP

After a program unexpectedly crashes, one or more Recovered Files folders may appear in your Trash after a restart. Temporary files are often used and disposed of by your applications, but during a crash, the files may not get disposed of. If any file is valuable, drag it out of the Trash. More often than not, however, it's safe to discard these files with the rest of the garbage.

Useful Routine Maintenance

Your computer can use some TLC every so often. The following sections have a few tips for helping it out.

Purge unnecessary files and programs

If you've had your Mac for a while, you've probably piled on programs and files that no longer serve a purpose. Maybe drivers are associated with a printer you replaced a couple of years ago. Maybe you have software you fell out of love with. Even if these files aren't slowing the system, they're hogging disk space. These programs may even be agitating in the background. Activity Monitor, which I mention earlier in this chapter may clue you in.

Bottom line: It's time to send these files and programs off to retirement for good (with generous severance packages, of course). You already know how to trash files, but it's not always obvious *which* files to dispose of. Some programs leave shrapnel all over your storage drive.

Type the name of the application you're getting rid of inside a Finder search box, and do your best to determine whether files shown in the results are associated with the application you want to blow off.

WARNING

Don't delete files that you know little or nothing about. The consequences aren't pretty if you accidentally trash a crucial system file; you'll need administrative access to get rid of some key files. If you do throw unfamiliar files in the Trash, wait a day or so until you're satisfied that you don't need them before you trash them permanently.

Backing up your treasures

I know that I've beaten you over the head with this topic throughout the book. Consider this the final nag. Back up. Back up. Back up. Whether you use Time Machine, an online backup service, third-party software, or another method, JUST DO IT. SOONER RATHER THAN LATER. There. I've finished shouting.

Updating software

Software upgrades are usually made available for good reasons. In System Preferences, click App Store. I certainly recommend selecting the Automatically Check for Updates option and the option to Download Newly Available Updates in the Background. (Don't worry; you receive notifications when this happens.) You can also select the check boxes titled Install App Updates and Install System Data Files and Security Updates. I certainly opt for these options on my own Macs, but the choice is up to you. I also leave it to you whether to select the Automatically Download Apps Purchased on Other Macs check box. If you have enough disk space and think that you'll want all the programs on all your Macs, by all means, go for that. But if your secondary Mac — a notebook, say — is fairly tight on disk space, you may want to refrain from selecting this check box and just download the apps individually as you see fit.

To see all the applications on your Mac, use System Report. Choose ⟳ About This Mac, select System Report, and scroll down to Applications in the Software list. Then head over to the support areas of the websites of the publishers of other software on your computer to see whether they've updated their programs. Downloads typically are free. You'll often be notified by a software publisher when an update for its app is available, and you may also be made aware of such an update in the Mac App Store.

Summoning Outside Help

Pretty much everything I've described in this chapter up to now, you ought to be able to handle on your own. But eventually, you'll run into situations beyond your expertise, especially serious hardware issues. Or perhaps you merely lack time, patience, inclination, or confidence. I understand your reluctance. Fortunately, you can find help in plenty of places, though the help isn't always free.

Third-party software

For all the fine troubleshooting tools included on a Mac, you may at times want to look to outside software. Here are some programs that may bail you out of a jam or help with routine maintenance (prices and version numbers subject to change):

>> **Alsoft DiskWarrior 5** (www.alsoft.com)**:** A $120 repair utility that warns you of impending drive failure and helps you repair damaged directories (some of which Disk Utility says it can't fix). Check to make sure that DiskWarrior is compatible with your model and OS release.

>> **Cocktail** (www.maintain.se/cocktail)**:** A general-purpose utility from Maintain that offers a mix of maintenance and interface tweaks. A license for a single computer costs $19, though I've seen it discounted as low as $14. You can try it before buying.

>> **OnyX for Mac OS X** (www.onyxmac.com)**:** A free downloadable program from that can run a variety of maintenance tasks.

>> **Prosoft Engineering's Data Rescue 4.2** (www.prosofteng.com)**:** A program designed to help you recover files from a corrupt hard drive. A personal license costs $99.

>> **TechtoolPro 8 (**`www.micromat.com`**):** A $100 problem solver from Micromat. Apple must be fond of Techtool Pro, because it made some versions available as part of AppleCare (see the next section).

AppleCare

Your Mac comes with 90 days of free telephone support and a year of free support at an authorized Apple retailer. The extended-warranty program called AppleCare lengthens the time you can get phone support to three years (from the date of purchase).

AppleCare covers the computer itself, plus AirPort Express and Extreme base stations, Time Capsule, USB SuperDrives when purchased with your Mac, and Apple RAM (used with the Mac, of course). With certain models, including the Mac mini, you can also cover one Apple display purchased at the same time.

Fees depend on the gear you're covering. AppleCare for an Apple display is $99; Mac mini, $149; iMac, $169; MacBook, MacBook Air and 13-inch MacBook Pro, $249; Mac Pro, $249; and 15-inch MacBook Pro and MacBook Pro with Retina Display, $349. Extended warranties are like any form of insurance — a crapshoot, but a crapshoot worth taking for some folks.

TIP

If you purchased your Mac with certain credit cards, you may have a longer warranty than you realized. Check with your card issuer to see whether an extended warranty is among your membership benefits.

Consulting Einstein

One of the features of the Apple Store is the Genius Bar, where Apple's in-store experts can answer questions about your Mac and, if need be, install memory and handle repairs (sometimes for a fee). My own experience leads me to believe that these (mostly) young men and women are quite knowledgeable about the subjects you're likely to hit them with. Judging by blog posts, however, not all of them are ready for Mensa. Now, the bad news: You can't exactly mosey up to the Genius Bar. Which leads me to . . .

Making a reservation

Meeting with an Apple-branded Genius requires an appointment. Go to `www.apple.com/retail`, click Genius Bar, click Make a Genius Bar Reservation, and choose the Apple Store near you (if one exists). When you make the reservation, you can choose Genius Bar or Workshops. (For the purposes of this example, choose Genius Bar and then choose Mac as the product requiring help; you could have otherwise chosen Apple Watch, Apple TV, iPod, iPhone, or iPad.)

Available appointments are shown in 15-minute intervals; stake a claim on the next opening. Sign in with your Apple ID, or list your first and last names, email, and (if you're cool with providing it) your phone number.

TIP

If you're already in an Apple Store that isn't crowded, make a reservation on the spot, using one of the Macs in the store.

If you choose Workshops instead, you can sign up for a general workshop on, say, iMovie, or attend a class that gives you an overview on the machine. Such workshops are an hour long and free. Apple also offers free workshops for kids 6 to 13. (Never mind that the youngsters often know more about computers than their parents do.)

Other handholding

I recommend taking a look at the support options at Apple.com. Click your product type (Mac, Accessories, and so on), click the product area you need help with (such as an unexpected shutdown or restart), and let Apple know how you want to receive help. You can supply your phone number and have an Apple rep call you; the website will tell you how long the wait time is before you can expect a callback. You can also schedule a call. Or you can provide your contact information and call Apple support later. Apple will ask for the serial number of your product, presumably to make sure that you're eligible for coverage. You can also check your hardware through Apple Diagnostics. If a problem is found, Apple will help you reach out to support personnel for assistance.

Help, I need somebody

It sounds like a cliché, but free (or low-cost) help is all around you. Check out these samples:

» Politely request help from the geeky next-door neighbor, your cubicle-mate, or the friends you didn't know you had on the web.

» At a social networking site such as Meetup.com, you can search for and perhaps find a Macintosh user-group meeting in your neck of the woods.

» Get referrals from Apple at www.apple.com/usergroups. You'll find an events calendar; enter your zip code to find a group close by.

>> For free online answers, poke around the newsgroups and computer bulletin boards.

>> Check out the troubleshooting articles at www.apple.com/support/downloads.

Before leaving a chapter on troubleshooting and the geek part of this book, I'd be remiss if I didn't mention one other avenue for help. It's the Help menu, available in almost every program you use. In some cases, you see a question mark indicating that help topics are at the ready.

To be sure, not every one of your questions will be answered satisfactorily, and you have to be careful how you phrase your question. But before heading on a wild goose chase in search of an enlightening response, give the Help menus a try. Apple often delivers helpful tutorial videos that just might guide you to a solution. They've been right there all along.

Chapter 18

Surviving in a Windows World

I f it weren't for the fact that their darling computers are so darn special, you might expect loyal Macintosh users to have an inferiority complex. But nothing is inferior about the Mac operating system, and even a market share that has been teeny-tiny is climbing.

Apple has been able to persuade more and more people to switch sides. The runaway successes of the iPod, iPhone, and iPad have helped Apple lure more Windows defectors. So did the clever and funny TV ads Apple ran for a while, pitting a hip Mac guy against a nerdy PC counterpart.

The bottom line is that this is, for better or worse, still a Windows-dominated planet, at least when it comes to personal computers. Over the years, and more times than not, the Apple user has had to adapt to the Windows environment rather than the other way around. Even now, the Mac user encounters programs and websites that get along only with the Windows platform, though that's far less often the case nowadays. Still, the remarkable Apple–Intel alliance that by now has been in place for a while demonstrates that in this topsy-turvy world, anything is possible.

What's more, as you see in this chapter, you can actually transform the newest Macs into fully functioning Windows PCs, even ones that run the latest Windows 10 operating system. That bears repeating: *You can actually transform the newest Macs into fully functioning Windows PCs.*

What the Mac and Windows Have in Common

For all their differences, the Mac and Windows are more alike than you may initially grasp. And common ground is a good thing, because

>> Macs and Windows PCs can share printers, scanners, digital cameras, mice, keyboards, and other peripherals.

>> Both systems are fluent in common file types, including PDFs, JPEGs, and text.

>> Microsoft produces versions of Office for both platforms, so you can work in programs such as Word, Excel, and PowerPoint with little difficulty. The Mac and Windows versions of Office have used the same files since Office 97 for Windows came onto the scene.

>> The Mac can read most Windows PC–formatted CDs and DVDs.

>> Both sides can easily communicate by email or by instant-messaging services.

>> You can access an iCloud account from a Windows PC.

>> iTunes works on both systems. So do versions of QuickTime Player and other software.

>> The two systems can be on the same wired or wireless network and share files.

>> And for several years now, Intel processors have been inside both computers.

Making the Switch

Okay, so you've read enough of this book to satisfy your curiosity about the Mac, and you're ready to defect.

But frankly, you've invested time and energy over the years in getting your Windows files and preferences just as you like them. The following sections describe ways to replicate your Windows environment (within certain limits) on a new Mac.

Help from Apple

When you buy a new Mac at the Apple Store, and opt for the $99 One to One service, you can get a certified Mac technician, not so modestly known as a Genius (see Chapter 17), to transfer all your data.

Of course, you may be better off doing it yourself via the Migration Assistant by following the instructions found here: `https://support.apple.com/en-ca/HT204087`.

Burning a disc

Because your Mac can read CDs or DVDs formatted for Windows (assuming that the machine has a built-in or connected optical drive), you can burn your important files to a disc and copy them to your Mac. You may not have to burn all your files to a disc, but a good place to start is the My Documents (XP) or Documents (Vista, Windows 7, Windows 8, Windows 10) folder on the Windows machine. This folder may very well include photos and videos.

External hard drives

You can exchange files on external USB or FireWire-based hard drives and USB thumb drives.

TIP

You can even use an iPod as an external drive by setting it up for disk use. Temporarily dump songs off the iPod to create more room (and add the music back later). Visit `http://support.apple.com/kb/HT1478` for a detailed explanation.

WARNING

Not all Windows PCs recognize external hard drives that have been formatted for a Mac.

Using an existing network

Another way to get files from Windows to a Mac is to use a network. Make sure that file sharing is turned on in Windows. Head to the HomeGroup (inside Control Panel) on an older Windows PC or Networking and Sharing Center on a Windows 10 machine.

Add your Mac to your wired or wireless network (if it's not already part of it), and exchange files as outlined in Chapter 16.

The KVM switch

If you just bought a Mac mini but are holding on to your Windows computer for a while, consider a *KVM* (keyboard–video–mouse) switch. This device uses USB to let the two machines share the monitor and various peripherals. I've seen a two-port Belkin KVM switch with all the necessary cables priced between $20 and $30.

Enlisting in Boot Camp

In the preceding section, I touch on various strategies for allowing *separate* Mac and Windows machines to coexist. But if you own Intel-based Macs, you can run OS X *and* Windows on one machine.

It may seem like divine intervention. In fact, it's been possible to run Windows on a Mac for some time — with agonizing limitations. Near-extinct Mac models that go back nearly a decade or more and were loaded with Virtual PC emulation software could do Windows, too, but the program was painfully slow. Even if you find an old copy of the software, it won't work with any current Macs.

Boot Camp software from Apple shook up the computing public upon its apocalyptic arrival in April 2006. Boot Camp graduated from beta, or near-finished, status with the arrival of Leopard. Boot Camp Assistant software is stored in the Utilities folder inside the Applications folder.

REMEMBER

Boot Camp itself is free. You have to supply your own single-disc or downloadable full-install version or ISO file of Windows; an upgrade disc won't cut it.

TECHNICAL
STUFF

It's also important to note that you can use a 64-bit version of Windows, Windows 7 (Home Premium, Professional, or Ultimate), Windows 8, Windows 8.1, or Windows 10. Consult http://support.apple.com/kb/ht5634 to see which Mac models are compatible with which versions of Windows. Boot Camp isn't compatible with 32-bit versions of Windows.

Other requirements follow:

>> An Intel Mac with OS X version 10.6 or later.

>> At least 2GB of RAM and 30GB of available space on the Mac's storage drive that you want to donate to Windows

>> A USB storage device (at least 16GB) that you'll use for Windows software drivers

If you don't run into snags, the entire installation (including Windows) should take about an hour.

Windows 8, Windows 8.1, and Windows 10 are optimized for a touchscreen environment, though you can use it with a standard mouse and keyboard. For now, Macs don't support touchscreen computing. That's not to say that Macs aren't welcoming to touch, as anyone who employs scrolling, pinching, or other gestures via a trackpad has come to appreciate.

To install Windows 8 or Window 10 via Boot Camp, you still must have a legitimate Windows 8 license from Microsoft and a Win8 installation disc, assuming that you have an optical drive. If you don't have an optical drive, you may be able to create a Windows installer from an ISO file downloaded from Microsoft on a USB flash drive that's 8GB or larger. (An *ISO file* is a disk-image file that effectively serves as a stand-in for an entire disk.)

Because snags *are* possible, back up all your important information on the Mac's startup disk.

Basic training

Following are the basic steps to get through Boot Camp (assuming that you haven't already installed Windows through Boot Camp):

1. **Run Boot Camp Assistant (in the Utilities folder inside the Applications folder) to make sure that you have the latest firmware on your computer and to install any support software from Apple that you might need.**

You'll find any updates at www.apple.com/support/downloads. Follow any onscreen instructions if you're updating the firmware. If you're using a portable computer, make sure to connect the power adapter. You will also be given the option to create a Windows 7 (or later version) install disk for which you'll need a USB flash drive and an ISO image downloaded from Apple.

2. **Follow the prompts in Boot Camp Assistant to create a partition for Windows.**

You're essentially carving out an area of your hard drive for the Windows operating system, as shown in Figure 18-1. This partition must be at least 30GB and can swell to the total free disk space on hand minus 30GB. If you don't plan on doing much in Windows, keep the partition small. If you plan on running graphics-heavy games and a lot of Windows programs, you might devote a more generous chunk to Windows. Drag the divider to set the partitions for both OS X and Windows, or click Divide Equally to make equal partitions. You can't resize a Windows partition after creating it, though you can replace it with a larger Windows partition.

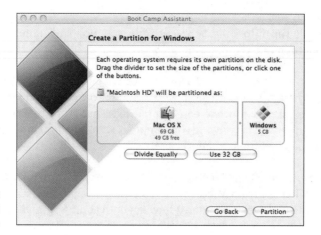

FIGURE 18-1:
Making space
for Windows.

If you have a Mac Pro with more than one internal hard drive, you can select which drive to partition. If any of this makes you nervous, know that you can remove the Windows partition later and go back to a single-partition Mac.

3. **Insert the Windows CD or a USB flash drive with the Windows ISO file and then click Start Installation.**

   If you exited Boot Camp Assistant before installing Windows, open it again, choose Start the Windows Installer, and click Continue.

4. **When you're asked to choose the Windows partition, select the partition that says BOOTCAMP.**

   You may have to scroll down to see it.

   Don't erase any partitions that you see or create a new partition here. Failure to heed this warning could wipe out your entire Mac OS X startup disk.

WARNING

5. **If you see a listing for Drive Options, click it; otherwise, proceed to Step 6.**

6. **Reformat the partition by using the Windows installer (the software that is actually installing Microsoft's operating system): Click Format.**

WARNING

   You're using the reliable and secure NTFS file system, but you won't be able to save files to Windows from Mac OS X, at least not without a techie workaround.

7. **Follow the onscreen instructions to finish installing Windows.**

   Boot Camp 5.1 (the current version as of this writing) includes several Mac drivers so that Windows will recognize your trackpad, Thunderbolt, USB 3.0, the iSight (or FaceTime) camera, the Eject key on the Mac keyboard, networking, audio, graphics, and so on.

   A Boot Camp Control Panel for Windows and an Apple Boot Camp system-tray item will be added.

As with any new Windows computer, Microsoft requires that you activate your Windows software within 30 days.

It's great that you can use Windows on the Mac, but by now, you may be longing to return to the OS X environment. The next section tells you how.

Switching operating systems

You can go back and forth between OS X and Windows on your Mac, but you can't run both operating systems simultaneously under Boot Camp. Instead, you have to boot one operating system or the other — thus, the name *Boot Camp.*

Restart your Mac, and hold down the Option key until icons for each operating system appear onscreen. Highlight Windows or Macintosh HD, and click the arrow to launch the operating system of choice for this session.

If you want OS X or Windows to boot every time, choose ⌘ ➪ System Preferences, click Startup Disk, and choose the OS you want to launch by default.

TIP

You can perform the same function in Windows by clicking the Boot Camp system-tray icon and selecting the Boot Camp Control Panel. Click either the Macintosh HD or Windows icon, depending on your startup preference.

A Parallels (and Fusion) Universe

Boot Camp's biggest drawback is its requirement that you reboot your computer every time you want to leave one operating system for a parallel universe. Can anyone spell *hassle?*

Remedies are readily available. Try Parallels Desktop (about $80 from Parallels, Inc., based in Renton, Virginia) or VMware Fusion (about $80 from VMware of Palo Alto, California). Each software program takes the form of a *virtual machine,* simulating a Windows computer inside its own screen within OS X. Or, if you feel like it, go full-screen with Windows. The faux machine behaves just like the real deal. You can add software, surf the web, listen to music, and play Windows games on a Mac.

You can even apply this virtualization stuff in versions of Windows dating back to Windows 3.1, as well as Linux, Solaris, OS/2, MS-DOS, and other operating systems. Be aware though that your computer may be noticeably be slower when running two operating systems.

TECHNICAL
STUFF

Parallels and Fusion differ from Boot Camp because they let you run any operating system *while* you run OS X, without having to restart. What's more, you can share files and folders between OS X and Windows, and cut and paste between the two. The Coherence feature of Parallels lets you run Windows programs as though they were Mac apps.

Check out Parallels at www.parallels.com and VMware Fusion at www.vmware.com/products/fusion. The latest versions support Windows 10.

TIP

Virtually or not, you're running Windows on or inside your Mac. So take all the usual precautions by loading antivirus and other security software.

It's also worth noting that although most consumers will do just fine with the virtualized versions of Windows through these programs, you may see some degradation in performance, particularly in 3D-type gaming environments, compared with running Windows on a Windows PC or even in Boot Camp.

Comforting, isn't it, to know that Macs do well in a Windows world?

6

The Part of Tens

IN THIS PART . . .

Check out ten indispensable Mac websites.

Explore ten more things your Mac can do, such as file transfer and compression, making a phone call, and sharing stuff with the family.

Chapter 19

Ten Indispensable Mac Websites

In my line of work, I often get the "How come you didn't" email or phone call, as in "How come you didn't write about my company or product?" So I won't be shocked to hear folks asking about this chapter, "How come you didn't choose my favorite Macintosh website?" Limiting any list to ten is exceedingly difficult — especially when it comes to websites about your trusted computer. Heck, one of my editors wanted me to shoehorn in a mention of www.mactech.com because it's an incredible compendium of Mac-related technology discussions and articles. And how could I possibly leave out www.macdailynews.com? Jeez, I guess I managed to squeeze these in just now — don't you think I'm cheatin' — and they don't even count against my ten.

AppleInsider

www.appleinsider.com

As on many other comprehensive sites devoted to the Cupertino crowd (including some in this list), you'll find lots of news, forums, and reviews concerning all things Apple. But AppleInsider also wants to solicit your help. You're invited to submit rumors and information to the site — and may even do so anonymously.

Cult of Mac

www.cultofmac.com

This well-regarded daily news site is also on top of the latest out of Apple-land, with forums on the Mac that cover vintage computers to the latest models. Cult of Mac will also happily accept a news tip from you.

MacFixIt (CNET)

http://reviews.cnet.com/macfixit

When something has gone wrong, and you're still seeking answers despite my best efforts in Chapter 17, check out MacFixIt, now part of CNET. This troubleshooting site tackles a gaggle of issues, with help from your Mac brethren. And because of the CNET acquisition, you no longer have to fork over $24.95 a year for a Pro version with tutorials, full access to more than a decade of content, and more. Among the many topics I've came across through the years are making banking sites work with Safari, fixing a stalled Safe-mode boot in OS X, taming annoying alert sounds, and iTunes authentication problems. When you get to the site, search for MacFixIt.

MacRumors

www.macrumors.com

Apple is one of the most secretive outfits on the planet. Seldom does the company spill the beans on new products in advance; the notable exception is features for the next iteration of OS X. That doesn't prevent numerous Apple watchers from speculating on what might be coming out of Cupertino. Besides, who doesn't love a juicy rumor now and then? Is Apple merging with Nintendo? (Don't count on it.) Is Apple going to add a subscription music plan to iTunes? (Okay. That happened through Apple Music.) Head to MacRumors for the latest dirt, some of which may even turn out to be true.

MacSurfer's Headline News

www.macsurfer.com

MacSurfer's Headline News is a wonderful resource for the Apple news junkie. The site sports links to articles on all things Apple, including traditional media, websites, Apple itself, and bloggers. Links are organized by category: Apple, OS X, General Interest, Hardware/Software, How-To/Reviews, Op/Ed, Press Releases, Computer Industry, and Finances.

Macworld

www.macworld.com

It's all here at Macworld: news, how-tos, product reviews, discussion forums, and past articles from *Macworld* magazine, which no longer publishes a print version. One of the sites that used to make this top-ten list as a stand-alone site — Mac OS X Hints — is now part of Macworld too.

9to5Mac

9to5mac.com

Mac news and rumors are listed at 9to5mac. I have to hand it to the crew there because they pick up on Apple rumors often and early — and more times than not, they get it right, as if they have a mole inside the company. (Maybe they do!) The site will happily welcome your tips too.

Other World Computing

www.macsales.com

Need more RAM for your computer? An extra hard drive, perhaps? Maybe even an add-on that lets you watch TV on your Mac? Other World Computing (OWC) has been specializing in sales of Mac accessories since the first Bush administration. The online retailer has earned a stellar reputation for prompt delivery and reliability. (Hey, I know I'm supposed to mention only ten sites, but if my editors aren't looking, other online retailers worth checking out include MacMall and Small Dog Electronics.)

VersionTracker

http://download.cnet.com/mac

VersionTracker is a repository for downloadable shareware, freeware, and updates to Mac software. Click a name to discover more about what a program does and to eyeball ratings and feedback. VersionTracker, too, is now part of the CNET empire — specifically, the Mac Software area of Download.com.

Last but Not Least, Apple.com

www.apple.com

Apple may seem to be an obvious place to go. Heck, you probably already landed there just by opening Safari the first time. You may not love the full blitz of Mac, iPhone, Apple Watch, and iPad advertising and promotions, even if you already drink Apple's Kool-Aid. But presumably, most of you already have sweet feelings about the company's products.

As I hint in Chapter 17, this website is full of helpful resources, especially for, but not limited to, newbies. You can download software updates and manuals, view video tutorials, post questions in discussion forums, read press releases, and consult the Knowledge Base. Mostly, I think, you'll walk away with a renewed sense of good will toward the company that's responsible for the computer that most of you fancy so much.

Chapter 20

Ten Things to Leave You With

So here we are, hundreds of pages into this book, and there's still more to tell. Truth is, I could probably go on for hundreds more pages and still not do justice to everything your Mac can accomplish (with more than a little help from you, of course). So even though the programs, functions, or capabilities covered in this chapter didn't quite make it into the book elsewhere, don't consider them to be unloved or afterthoughts.

At the risk of tossing another well-worn cliché your way, last is most definitely not least.

Remote Software Installation

At various points in this book, I mention that the most recent Macs have ditched the optical drives that were once staple features. If you've been employing such drives for years to install software, you're probably left wondering how to complete the task given their absence.

You can connect an optional USB accessory to replace the missing drive, of course. In many instances, you can download new programs directly from the Internet. And the Mac App Store makes it a breeze to fetch programs that you buy there.

Still, you may have come upon installation discs that are required to load older programs (and possibly new ones as well). Even without a built-in disk drive, you figure that there must be a way to install the software.

You figure right, at least if you have an available DVD or CD drive on another computer, whether that computer is a Mac or even a Windows PC. That other machine must be connected to the same network as the Mac on which you want to load software. Also, your Mac must support the Remote Disc feature, but the good news is that all the recent models do.

Proceed as follows: If the optical drive you're sharing is on a Mac (and if it's not, see the end of this section), open System Preferences, choose Sharing, and select the check box for DVD or CD Sharing. At your discretion, also select the Ask Me Before Allowing Others to Use My DVD Drive check box. Place the DVD in the drive you're sharing from and then go to the Mac that doesn't have an optical drive.

On that computer, open a Finder window, and select Remote Disc on the Sidebar. You should see an icon for the computer that has the optical drive. Double-click the icon, and click Connect. Click Ask to Use if the other computer chose the aforementioned Ask Me option. The other computer must then accept your request. Assuming that this happens, you can install the program as though the optical drive were local to the computer that's gaining the new software.

TIP

If the optical drive you're sharing from is on a Windows PC, you must download DVD or CD Sharing Update 1.0 for Windows, available at http://support.apple.com/kb/DL112. Then enable DVD or CD Sharing in the Hardware and Sound section of Control Panel. Back on your Mac, open a Finder window, and proceed as before.

If Math Moves You

I don't pretend to know a conchoid (see Figure 20-1) from a Lorenz attractor; frankly, the mathematics are lost on me. But the Grapher bundled with OS X and accessed through the Utilities folder (inside the Applications folder) lets you graph 2D and 3D mathematical equations. Moreover, the program's animations are pretty darn cool. If you're curious about what the aforementioned conchoid, Lorenz attractor, and other 2D and 3D formulas and equations look like, choose their names from the Grapher Examples menu.

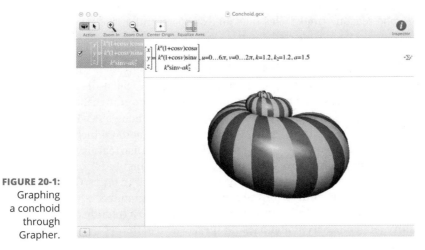

FIGURE 20-1:
Graphing a conchoid through Grapher.

Make or Receive a Call

iPhone owners with Macs can make or receive a call from or on the computer. And your Mac, with its bigger speakers, can substitute as a fine speakerphone. Incoming calls appear as notifications.

I'm speaking not of the FaceTime calls described in Chapter 11 but rather regular calls made over cellular to ordinary phone numbers. Ringtones come through the Mac the same as they do on the phone. The same is true for call waiting calls, which you can accept or reject on the fly.

To dial from the Mac, hover your cursor over a phone number wherever you see it (in Contacts, Calendar, Mail, Messages, or Spotlight), and then click the phone icon that appears adjacent to that number. You can also highlight a number you come across on the web in Safari to initiate a call. Or dial conference calls with a single click from the Calendar (passcode included).

The only requirements are that your iPhone and your Mac must be signed into the same Wi-Fi network and iCloud account. And because calls are routed through the iPhone, the phone has to be fairly close to but not necessarily in the same room as the Mac. Oh, and go into FaceTime preferences and make sure the Calls from iPhone check box is selected.

Zip It in the Bud

Files that you download from the Internet are often compressed or zipped — and for good reason. Zipped files take up less space and arrive much faster than files that haven't been squeezed down.

Compressed files are easily identified by their extensions, such as .zip (a common standard used in OS X and Windows) and .sit. Such files must be unzipped before you can read them. Apple used to include a program called StuffIt Expander for this purpose. OS X lets you decompress .zip files — but not .sit files — sans StuffIt.

StuffIt, from SmithMicro Software, still comes in handy for opening those other types of compressed files — notably, the .sit and .sitx types. Go to www.stuffit-expander.com to splurge for the Deluxe version (around $50, though I've seen it discounted for less). In addition to shrinking files to a fraction of their size, StuffIt Deluxe lets you encrypt and back up files.

TIP

Meanwhile, you can archive or create your own .zip files through OS X, which is useful if you're emailing several meaty files to a friend. Right-click (or Control-click) files that you want to compress inside Finder, and choose Compress *Filename* from the contextual menu. The newly compressed files carry the .zip extension. The archive is created in the same location as the original file and is named *originalfilename*.zip. You can also choose File⇨Compress. If you compress a lot of files at the same time, the archive takes the name Archive.zip.

By default, compressed files are opened with Archive Utility. It appears on the dock while the files are being unsqueezed unless you choose to open them with StuffIt Expander or some other program.

Family Sharing

The Mac may be your very own. Or you may share it with multiple members of your clan, including your spouse and kids.

Through Family Sharing, you can share your Mac with up to six people in your household. What exactly are you sharing? A family calendar, family photo album, and oh yes, purchases made via iTunes, the iBooks Store, and the App Store. Purchases are made with a single credit card from a single iCloud account with the sole designated family organizer (usually mom or dad) picking up the tab. He or she gets to approve purchase requests from the youngsters. Moreover, if each family member also carries an iOS device such as an iPhone, you can see its location in the Messages app on the Mac.

Set up Family Sharing in System Preferences under iCloud. That's where the designated family organizer goes to manage the family account too.

Screen Capture (Stills and Video)

Unless you're planning to write a book similar to this one, you're probably wondering why the heck you'd ever want to take a picture of your computer screen. Let me suggest a few possibilities. Maybe you want to take a picture of the screen for a presentation at work. Or perhaps you want to show precisely what a funky error looks like to the person who just might help you correct the problem. Whatever your motivation, if you want to grab a picture of the Mac screen (or any of its windows), it may be time to open the Grab utility. Choose Applications⇨Utilities, and click Grab. Through Grab's Capture menu, you can take a picture of a full screen, window, or menu, as follows:

>> Select Window (or press Shift+⌘+W), click Choose Window, and then click the window to grab its picture.

>> Select Screen (or press ⌘+Z). Then, to capture the full screen, click anywhere outside the window that appears.

>> Choose Capture⇨Timed Screen (or press Shift+⌘+Z) and then click Start Timer in the window that appears. Grab captures the full screen 10 seconds later. This time delay gives you a chance to prepare the screen to your liking (perhaps by activating a menu) before the image is captured.

>> Select Selection (or Shift+⌘+A). Then use the mouse to drag over the portion of the screen you want to grab.

TIP

Still other universal system shortcuts follow. These shortcuts don't require you to open the Grab utility.

>> Press ⌘+Shift+3 to take a picture of the whole screen.

>> Press ⌘+Shift+4 and drag the mouse to select the part of the screen you want to grab.

>> Press ⌘+Shift+4, press the spacebar, move the pointer to highlight the area you want in the picture, and then click. This shortcut is useful for taking a picture of, say, the menu bar. If you press the spacebar again, you can select the area by dragging the mouse instead. Press Escape to cancel.

TIP

Screen shots captured in this matter are saved as files on the desktop. If you'd rather paste the captured image into a document, press the Control key when you press the other keyboard combinations, which places the picture on the Clipboard. From there, you can paste the image into your chosen document.

Meanwhile, with any luck, my descriptions throughout this book are helping you accomplish the very things you need to do on your Mac. But despite an author's best efforts, it's sometimes better to see than to be told. Through QuickTime Player, you can record everything that appears on the computer screen, backed up, if you want, by your narration.

With QuickTime open, choose File⇨New Screen Recording. If you want to be heard while the person watching the video sees the goings-on of the screen, click the arrow button and select an audio input from the pop-up menu. You can also decide whether to show mouse clicks in your recording.

When you're ready to record the screen, click the Record button. To record only a portion of the screen, drag the pointer to choose that portion and then click Start Recording. To capture the entire screen, click anywhere on the screen. All screen actions from then on are captured until you direct QuickTime to stop the recording. To do that, click the Stop button on the menu bar or press ⌘+Control+Escape.

TIP

Because I'm on the topic of QuickTime, let me also mention here that you can also use QuickTime to make an audio or movie recording. Choose File⇨New Audio Recording or File⇨New Movie Recording.

Get Transit Directions

The Maps app is useful, of course, for helping you determine where you are, what is around you, and how to get to the next place, even accounting for traffic. But you're not always going to want to (or be able to) drive to that next destination, even if it is too far from your current location to walk.

Apple's solution, at least for select cities, is public transit directions. Maps can display bus, subway, rail, and even ferry routes, along with schedules based on when you want to leave.

To get going, make sure the Transit tab is highlighted (as opposed to the Map or Satellite tab), click Transit in the Directions sidebar, and choose your starting and ending points. Next, from the drop-down menu, indicate when you want to leave (soon, 30 minutes, 60 minutes, 2 hours, or a custom time).

Click a step in the itinerary you've chosen from the options presented (assuming you have more than one choice) to have Maps zoom in on that area. That itinerary will also direct you to the appropriate exit if, say, the subway station where you're getting off has more than one. Place cards for certain stations will also show you the other transit lines you can pick up at that station as well as their schedules.

If your route has service changes or disruptions, you'll receive indications of them as well, as shown in Figure 20-2.

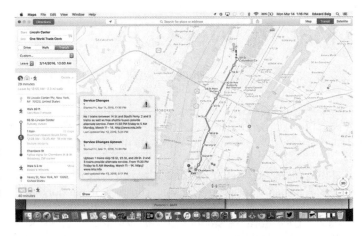

FIGURE 20-2:
You can receive detailed transit directions in some cities.

What's more, because it is typically impractical to schlep the Mac with you (especially a desktop), you can send the directions to an iPhone or Apple Watch. You can print directions otherwise.

As this book went to press, the Maps app included transit directions for the following global cities: Baltimore, Berlin, Boston, Chicago, London, Mexico City, New York, Philadelphia, San Francisco Bay Area, Toronto, Sydney, and Washington DC — plus more than 300 cities in China.

Would You Like to Play a Game of Chess?

Ah, the question posed by the (ultimately) defiant HAL 9000 computer in the classic film *2001: A Space Odyssey*. It turns out that your Mac can play a mean game of chess too, without, as HAL did, turning on its human masters. The Mac's Chess program, located in the Applications folder, lets you compete against the computer or a human partner. You can open Chess and compete within the Game Center environment.

What's more, by choosing Chess ⇨ Preferences, you can change the board style and pieces, from the wooden board to grass, marble, or metal. You can also drag a slider inside Chess Preferences to make the computer play faster or stronger.

Just like HAL, your Mac can speak as it makes its moves — in about two dozen voices, no less, from Deranged (probably appropriate for HAL) to Hysterical. Then again, you can speak back, so long as Allow Player to Speak Moves is selected in Chess Preferences. Try it out for size by saying something like "Pawn e2 to e4 to move the white king's pawn." (See "Speech Recognition" later in this chapter.)

Using the Mac for Work

Now that you've finished playing chess, it's time to get down to serious work.

Obviously, the Mac works with a lot of great software, but I'd be remiss if I didn't pay a nod to Microsoft's splendid Office: Mac productivity suite and Apple's own productivity software, under the umbrella of iWork.

For all the poking between Apple and Microsoft, the companies have been longtime partners. Microsoft has produced Mac-compatible versions of Office for years.

Microsoft Office Home & Student for Mac 2016 costs about $150 for a single version license that includes Word, PowerPoint, Excel, and OneNote. Or you can pay about $70 a year for an Office 365 subscription that lets you run Office on a single Windows PC or Macs. It includes the aforementioned programs plus Outlook and some other software and works on select mobile devices, too. You also get 1TB of cloud storage and 60 monthly minutes on Skype.

For $100 a year, you can extend the subscription to up to five PCs or Macs or a combination, and give up to five people 1TB of cloud storage each, plus an hour each of Skype.

Apple's alternative to Office is built around three of the friendly programs that have come to define iWork: — Pages (word processing), Numbers (spreadsheets), and Keynote (presentations) — each now free, at least if you buy a new Mac. You're looking at $19.99 each to add the apps to older computers.

Such programs easily fit into a world dominated by . . . well, Office. You can open Microsoft Word, Excel, and PowerPoint files, in Pages, Numbers, and Keynote, and save documents as Word, Excel, or PowerPoint files. The apps are all seamlessly integrated with iCloud Drive.

It's easy to embrace iWork. Pages, Numbers, and Keynote all include friendly templates and themes to get you going. In Pages, you can start with a variety of templates for letters, résumés, brochures, and more. In Numbers, templates include spreadsheets for your budget or invoices. And Keynote themes are built around a gaggle of handsome designs. Via iCloud Drive, you can share your work across all your other computers and devices, including Windows PCs, other Macs, and iOS devices.

You have other ways to use your Mac for work. *FTP* (*File Transfer Protocol*) sites are usually set up by companies or individuals to make it easy to exchange sizable files over the Internet, typically (but not exclusively) video or picture files. The Mac has a built-in file server for giving other folks access to your machine.

To grant such access, choose ⇨ System Preferences, and click Sharing. Select the File Sharing box, and click Options. Then select Share Files and Share Files and Folders Using AFP. (*AFP* is shorthand for *Apple Filing Protocol.*) People on other Macs can now share and copy files to and from your machine. You may have to open ports in your router's software to allow access. If you select Share Files and Folders Using SMB, you can share stuff with your Windows and Linux friends. (*SMB* stands for *Server Message Block* protocol.) If you choose this option, you must enter the password for the account from which you're sharing.

Now suppose that you want to access someone else's FTP site. In a Finder window, choose Go ⇨ Connect to Server, enter the server address in the dialog that appears, and click Connect. Depending on the server you're attempting to connect to, you'll likely have to enter a username and a password.

You may be able to drag and drop files from your machine to that FTP server, but often you need help from outside software. I've relied on FileZilla, which is free (`https://filezilla-project.org`), as well as a $29 shareware program called Fetch (available at `www.fetchsoftworks.com` or the Mac App Store) to dump files to an FTP server. Other fine FTP choices include Transmit 4 ($34; `www.panic.com` or the Mac App Store), Cyberduck (free; `http://cyberduck.en.softonic.com/mac`), and RBrowser (free unlicensed version and a $29 licensed version; `www.rbrowser.com`).

Speech Recognition

Are you the bossy type who likes to bark orders? For people who are physically unable to type or handle a mouse, speech recognition and dictation (spoken commands) may be the only way to get things done on a computer.

First, choose System Preferences⇨ Dictation & Speech, and then click the Dictation option to turn the capability on or off (see Figure 20-3). Note your options here. You can choose a different language (other than English), select an Enhanced Dictation feature that lets you dictate without an Internet connection, and perform tasks on your Mac (you'll need to devote some free space on your storage drive).

FIGURE 20-3:
The Mac is all about free speech.

And you can choose a shortcut to start or stop dictation: pressing the Fn (function key) twice does this by the default.

You'll know that you can dictate text or bark commands when you see a small microphone in a rectangle

You can also choose a word or phrase to enable Dictation. In System Preferences, go to Accessibility⇨Dictation and select the Enable the Dictation Keyword Phrase option. Then type the word or phrase you'd like to use for that purpose, unless you want to stick with Computer, the default word Apple chose on your behalf.

To check out a list of the commands your computer can understand, click the Dictation Commands button. The list includes such commands as Select Paragraph, Capitalize That, and Redo That. Select Enable Advanced Commands for more listings, including commands in apps (Switch to *application name*).

The Mac can also read aloud descriptions of items on the screen, useful for people who have poor eyesight or are blind. Back in Dictation & Speech preferences, select the Text to Speech tab. You can choose a male or female speaking voice and drag a slider to determine the rate at which that voice speaks. In Accessibility preferences, you can turn on or off the VoiceOver feature and receive VoiceOver training.

While you're here, I recommend that Mac owners who have a disability of any sort explore the many Accessibility options available. These tools may help people with poor eyesight or hearing loss, as well as those with physical motor difficulties, using controls for your keyboard, mouse, trackpad, and special switches.

Indeed, as I hope is evident by now, Apple has designed the Mac to be for everyone.

Index

devices, unmounting, 30

diagnostics data, sharing, 17

dialog, 18

dialup modems, 146

Dictation feature, 125, 381–382

Dictionary, 58

digital cameras, connecting, 268–269

dimming screen, 70

disabling

  fonts, 120

  plug-ins, 155

discoverable, 340–341

discs, burning, 361

Disk Utility, 347–348

Display preferences, 96–97

displaying

  events from Facebook, 54

  maps, 52–53

  sidebar, 275

  users on login window, 84

disruptive technology, 267

DNS, 353

Do Not Track option, 164

dock

  about, 34–35, 43–44

  components of, 44–46

  docking, 47

  exiting apps, 50–51

  loading, 46–47

  re-opening minimized windows, 48

  resizing icons, 47

  stacks, 48–50

docking dock, 47

documents

  creating, 110–113

  formatting, 121–125

  renaming, 128–129

  revising, 128–129

  saving, 125–127

  selecting text in, 113–115

dot-matrix printer, 134

double-clicking, 21, 274, 278

drafts, email, 174

dragging

  about, 22

events in iMovie, 300

  windows, 37

dragging and dropping, 115–116

drums, in GarageBand, 322

DSL, 147

ducking audio, 304–305

dye sublimation, 134

E

editing photos in Photos app, 284–288

effects, adding to movies, 313

Eject button, 24–25

El Capitan

  about, 99

  Dashboard widgets, 108

  Spotlight, 100–107

  upgrading to, 99–100

email

  about, 167–168

  account setup, 168–170

  addressing messages, 170–172

  alternatives to Mail, 169

  attaching files, 174–176

  building Smart Mailboxes, 184–185

  choosing stationery, 173–174

  choosing VIPs, 180–181

  composing messages, 172–173

  junk mail, 182–183

  managing, 173–189

  marking up attachments, 186–187

  opening attachments, 186

  opening mail from strangers, 181–182

  organizing by conversation, 180

  replying to messages, 179–180

  saving drafts, 174

  searching, 185–186

  setting rules, 183–184

  sharing movies via, 315

  signatures, 177

  spam, 183

  spell checking, 177

  what to read, 179

emoticons, adding in Messages app, 198

emptying Trash, 129–130

About the Author

Edward C. Baig writes the Personal Technology column in USA TODAY and makes regular appearances on USA TODAY videos and TV. He is also the coauthor of *iPhone For Dummies, iPad For Dummies, iPad mini For Dummies* (all published by John Wiley & Sons, Inc.).

Before joining USA TODAY as a columnist and reporter in 1999, Ed spent six years at *Business Week,* where he wrote and edited stories about consumer tech, personal finance, collectibles, travel, and wine tasting. He received the Medill School of Journalism 1999 Financial Writers and Editors Award for his contributions to the "Business Week Investor Guide to Online Investing." That came after a stint on staff at *U.S. News & World Report,* where Ed was the lead tech writer in the News You Can Use section.

Ed began his journalistic career at Fortune, gaining the best training imaginable during his early years as a fact checker. Through the years, Ed covered leisure-time industries, penned features on the lucrative dating market and the effect of religion on corporate managers, and was heavily involved in the magazine's Most Admired Companies project.

Ed has been passionate about tech since buying his first reel-to-reel tape recorder and shortwave radio as a boy. He has a B.A. in political science from York College and an M.B.A. from Adelphi University. Follow him on Twitter (@edbaig), and watch him bang away on a computer (at warped speeds) in this TV commercial: www.youtube.com/watch?v=hb1fg0GF5PY.

Dedication

This book is dedicated to my remarkable and gorgeous children: daughter Sydney, who at a very early age became fascinated with the iTunes Visualizer, and son Samuel, who as a small boy couldn't resist pounding (quite literally) on the keyboard. They are already teaching me. This book is also dedicated to my beautiful wife, Janie, who takes on more than any other human being I know, with grace, passion, and love, and to my canine "daughter" and constant companion Sadie, who believes that everyone who rings the doorbell must be visiting her. It is also dedicated to my late dog Eddie, who always reminded me through his barks that it was I who lived and worked in his house, not the other way around. Finally, it is dedicated to the memory of my late parents — Sam, my dad, and Lucy, my mom — for the values they both instilled in me. I love you all.

Author's Acknowledgments

No book like this is written in isolation, and I've received wonderful support from lots of people. Let me start by again thanking my agent, Matt Wagner, for turning me into a *For Dummies* author. It has been a pleasure.

At Wiley, I'd like to thank acquisitions editor Steve Hayes, and especially copy and project editor Susan Pink. Thanks also go out to tech reviewer Matthew Fecher, who did a bang-up job following in the footsteps of the late Dennis Cohen.

I couldn't pull off a book like this without considerable help from many people at Apple, through this and other editions. Not everyone works at Apple anymore, but special thanks go to Katie Cotton, Steve Dowling, Natalie Kerris, Bill Evans, Keri Walker, Teresa Brewer, Greg (Joz) Joswiak, Trudy Muller, Tom Neumayr, Colin Smith, Ryan James, Amy Bessette, Amy Barney, Christine Monaghan, Kirk Paulsen, David Moody, Monica Sarker, Janette Barios, and Jennifer Hakes. Apologies if I've left your name off.

Thanks, too, to Dave Callaway, Jon Swartz. Nancy Blair, Jefferson Graham, Laura Petrecca, Laura Mandaro and other work colleagues and friends for your backing and for supplying USA TODAY's stamp of approval.

Last but certainly not least, to all my friends and family members who not only encouraged me to write this book, but also forgave my disappearing acts when deadlines loomed. I've run out of excuses.

Publisher's Acknowledgments

Acquisitions Editor: Steve Hayes
Project and Copy Editor: Susan Pink
Technical Editor: Matthew Fecher
Editorial Assistant: Matthew Lowe
Sr. Editorial Assistant: Cherie Case

Production Editor: Shaik Siddique
Cover Image: ©Charts and BG/shutterstock.com